ACA Simplified

Strategic Business Management Exam Room

Recognised as an ICAEW Partner in Learning, working with ICAEW in the professional development of students

ICAEW takes no responsibility for the content of any supplemental training materials supplied by the Partner in Learning.

The ICAEW Partner in Learning Logo, ACA and ICAEW CFAB are all registered trademarks of ICAEW and are used under licence by ACA Simplified.

A Reminder About Copyright

Please do not photocopy or otherwise distribute this book. Copyright theft is a clear breach of professional ethics and may therefore be reported to ICAEW. We have put a considerable amount of time and effort into developing innovative materials which we genuinely feel will give you an edge in the exams. We would be grateful if you would respect these efforts by not copying this text.

Copyright © 2018 ACA Simplified. All rights reserved.

No part of this publication may be reproduced, stored in a retrieval system or transmitted in any form or by any means without the prior written permission of ACA Simplified.

Disclaimer

The text in this book does not amount to professional advice on any particular technical matter and should not be taken as such. No reliance should be placed on the content as the basis for any investment or other decision or in connection with any advice given to third parties.

ACA Simplified expressly disclaims all liability for any losses or other claims, whether direct, indirect, incidental, consequential or otherwise arising in relation to the use of these materials.

We have made every effort to ensure that the materials are accurate and free from error. Please inform us immediately if you believe that you have discovered any problems with the text.

Whilst we strongly believe that our learning materials are an effective method of preparing for your examinations, ACA Simplified does not accept any liability whatsoever for your ultimate performance in the examination as a result of using this text.

Contents – Complete Alphabetical Listing

Contents – Complete Alphabetical Listing	3
Contents – Listed By Topic Area	7
List of Formulae	12
How To Use This Book	13
General Advice on SBM Answer Style	21
Acquisitions – Benefits & Risks	22
Acquisitions – Debt-Funded	25
Acquisitions – Due Diligence	26
Acquisitions – Financing	29
Acquisitions – Impact on Financial Statements	32
Acquisitions – Post-Acquisition Integration	34
Acquisitions – Struggling Company	35
Acquisitions – Synergies and Challenges	37
Agreed Upon Procedures	39
Assurance – General Points (ISAE 3000)	42
Assurance Engagements on Greenhouse Gas Statements	44
Assurance Reports on Controls at a Service Organisation	46
Balanced Scorecard	48
Bank Loans	49
Big Data – audit and data analytics	50
Big Data – ethics	51
Big Data – general	52
Big Data – impact on business models	55
Bonuses – Audit Procedures	59
Bonds (Loan Notes) v Bank Loans – Comparisons	60
Branding and Rebranding (IFRS 13)	62
Brexit	65
Business Plans	67
CAPM	69
Cash Flow Forecasts – Evaluation	72
Change – Definition & Models	73
Change – Management & Implementation	75
Cloud computing	76
Compilation Engagements	79
Convertible Bonds	81
Corporate Governance – Definition and Concepts	83
Corporate Governance – Past Paper Points	86
Corporate Governance – The Board and NEDs	87
Corporate Social Responsibility (CSR)	90

© ACA Simplified 2018. No copying or reproduction permitted.

Contents – Complete Alphabetical Listing

Costs of Quality	91
Critical Success Factors	92
Currency Risks	93
Customer Relationship Management (CRM)	94
Cyber security	95
Debt Factoring	98
Derivatives Calculations – Currency Forward	99
Derivatives Calculations – Currency Futures	101
Derivatives Calculations – Currency Options	103
Derivatives Calculations – Summary of Currency Hedging Methods	105
Derivatives Calculations – Forward Rate Agreements (FRAs)	106
Derivatives Calculations – FTSE Hedging	108
Derivatives Calculations – Interest Rate Futures	110
Derivatives Calculations – Interest Rate Options	112
Derivatives Calculations – Interest Rate Parity Concept	114
Derivatives Calculations – Interest Rate Swaps	115
Derivatives Calculations – Money Market Hedging	118
Digital Strategies	120
Digital Transformation	123
Disposals and Assets Held for Sale (IFRS 5)	125
Ethics – Independence	126
Ethics – Frameworks and Problems	127
Finance – Sources for SMEs	131
Financial Performance Review in SBM – Some Advice	132
Financial Performance Review in SBM – Audit Procedures	134
Financial Reconstruction	135
Forensic Audits	140
Franchising	142
FRC Risk Guidance	143
Globalisation	145
Hedging – Audit and Financial Reporting Points	146
Hedging – Choices, Methods and Risks	148
IFRS 9 – classification and measurement	153
IFRS 9 – embedded derivatives	156
IFRS 9 – hedge accounting	157
IFRS 9 – impairment	159
IFRS 13 and Valuation of Intangibles	160
IFRS 16	161
Impairment (IAS 36)	163
Insurance	164
Integrated Reporting	165

Contents – Complete Alphabetical Listing

Interest Rate Calculations	169
Internal Audit – Objectives, Contribution and Comparison to Statutory Audit	171
Internal Audit – Types of Assignment	173
Internal Audit – Process and Reporting	175
Internal Controls	177
Investment Appraisal Methods	178
Investment Appraisal Methods – APV	180
Investment Appraisal Methods – Free Cash Flow Model	181
ISAE 3402 – example answer points	184
IT Due Diligence	186
IT – Strategic Information Systems	187
Joint Arrangements – Assurance	189
Joint Arrangements – Strategy and Financial Reporting	191
Key Performance Indicators	194
Lease or buy?	196
Liquidation	198
Loan Decision by a Bank	202
Marketing Strategies	203
Modified Internal Rate of Return (MIRR)	204
Online Sales Strategies	206
Option Valuation	207
Organic Growth	209
Outsourcing	211
Overseas Operations – Exporting	214
Overseas Operations – Financing	215
Overseas Operations – Operational Aspects	216
Overseas Operations – Risks	218
Overseas Operations – Strategic Considerations	220
Pensions – Strategic Impact, Accounting and Auditing	222
Pricing Strategies	223
Professional Scepticism	224
Project Management	225
Prospective Information (ISAE 3400)	226
Provisions and Reorganisations	230
Q1 – Technique Reminders	231
Ratios – Calculations	233
Real Options	236
Recommendations – Keeping It Practical	237
Remuneration Strategies	238
Reporting on Information Contained in a Prospectus	239
Revenue accounting (IFRIC 13, IAS 11, IFRS 15)	241

Contents – Complete Alphabetical Listing

Review Engagements (ISRE 2400)	**243**
Risks – Governance	**247**
Risks – Horizontal Acquisition	**248**
Risks – Types and Examples	**249**
Risks – Risk Reviews	**253**
Sale and Operating Leaseback	**254**
Segmental Reporting (IFRS 8)	**255**
Sensitivity Analysis	**256**
Share Options – Strategic Impact, Accounting and Auditing	**257**
Shareholding Percentages – Narrative Comments	**259**
Stakeholders and Stakeholder Management	**261**
Strategic Analysis Tools & Models	**262**
Strategic Case Study – Tips from the Study Manual	**266**
Supply Chain Improvements	**267**
Sustainability Reporting and Social Reporting	**269**
Treasury Operations	**274**
United Nations Sustainable Development Goals	**275**
Valuations – Standard Points	**278**
Valuations – Asset-Based Model	**281**
Valuations – Administration Scenario	**283**
Valuations – Dividend Valuation Model (DVM)	**285**
Valuations – Earnings-Based	**287**
Valuations – EBITDA Model	**289**
Valuations – Economic Value Added (EVA®)	**291**
Valuations – Free Cash Flow Model	**293**
Valuations – High Growth Startup	**294**
Valuations – PE Model	**296**
Valuations – Shareholder Value Analysis (SVA)	**298**
Value-Based Management	**299**
Withdrawal from a Business	**300**
Withdrawal from a Business – Director Considerations	**303**
Working Capital	**305**

© ACA Simplified 2018. No copying or reproduction permitted.

Contents – Listed by Topic Area

Acquisitions

MBO - 1130 SM

Acquisitions – Benefits & Risks	22
Acquisitions – Debt-Funded	25
Acquisitions – Due Diligence	26
Acquisitions – Financing	29
Acquisitions – Impact on Financial Statements	32
Acquisitions – Post-Acquisition Integration	34
Acquisitions – Struggling Company	35
Acquisitions – Synergies and Challenges	37
IT Due Diligence	186
Shareholding Percentages – Narrative Comments	259
Stakeholders and Stakeholder Management	261

Assurance (Specialist Audit & Assurance topics)

Acquisitions – Due Diligence	26
Agreed Upon Procedures	39
Assurance – General Points (ISAE 3000)	42
Assurance Engagements on Greenhouse Gas Statements	44
Assurance Reports on Controls at a Service Organisation	46
Compilation Engagements	79
Corporate Governance – Definition and Concepts	83
Corporate Governance – Past Paper Points	86
Corporate Governance – The Board and NEDs	87
Forensic Audits	140
Integrated Reporting	165
Internal Audit – Objectives, Contribution and Comparison to Statutory Audit	171
Internal Audit – Types of Assignment	173
Internal Audit – Process and Reporting	175
Internal Controls	177
ISAE 3402 – example answer points	184
Joint Arrangements – Assurance	189
Prospective Information (ISAE 3400)	226
Reporting on Information Contained in a Prospectus	239
Review Engagements (ISRE 2400)	243
Sustainability Reporting and Social Reporting	269

Change and Change Management

Brexit	65

© ACA Simplified 2018. No copying or reproduction permitted.

Contents – Listed by Topic Area

Change – Definition & Models	73
Change – Management & Implementation	75
Cloud computing	76
Cyber security	95
Digital Strategies	120
Digital Transformation	123
Globalisation	145
Liquidation	198
Strategic Analysis Tools & Models	262

Ethics

Corporate Social Responsibility (CSR)	90
Ethics – Independence	126
Ethics – Frameworks and Problems	127
Sustainability Reporting and Social Reporting	269

Finance

Bank Loans	49
Bonds (Loan Notes) v Bank Loans – Comparisons	60
CAPM	69
Convertible Bonds	81
Debt Factoring	98
Finance – Sources for SMEs	131
Financial Reconstruction	135
Lease or buy?	196
Loan Decision by a Bank	202
Modified Internal Rate of Return (MIRR)	204

Financial Reporting Issues

Branding and Rebranding (IFRS 13)	62
Disposals and Assets Held for Sale (IFRS 5)	125
Hedging – Audit and Financial Reporting Points	146
Hedging – Choices, Methods and Risks	148
IFRS 9 – classification and measurement	153
IFRS 9 – embedded derivatives	156
IFRS 9 – hedge accounting	157
IFRS 9 – impairment	159
IFRS 13 and Valuation of Intangibles	160
IFRS 16	161
Impairment (IAS 36)	163

Contents – Listed by Topic Area

Joint Arrangements – Assurance	189
Joint Arrangements – Strategy and Financial Reporting	191
Pensions – Strategic Impact, Accounting and Auditing	222
Provisions and Reorganisations	230
Revenue accounting (IFRIC 13, IAS 11, IFRS 15)	241
Sale and Operating Leaseback	254
Segmental Reporting (IFRS 8)	255
Share Options – Strategic Impact, Accounting and Auditing	257

Growth and Business Development

Big Data topics	
Bonuses – Audit Procedures	59
Business Plans	67
Cash Flow Forecasts – Evaluation	72
Cloud computing	76
Customer Relationship Management (CRM)	94
Cyber security	95
Digital Strategies	120
Digital Transformation	123
Financial Performance Review in SBM – Some Advice	132
Financial Performance Review in SBM – Audit Procedures	134
Franchising	142
Globalisation	145
Marketing Strategies	203
Online Sales Strategies	206
Organic Growth	209
Outsourcing	211
Project Management	225
Remuneration Strategies	238
Value-Based Management	299
Withdrawal from a Business	300
Withdrawal from a Business – Director Considerations	303

Investment Appraisal

Investment Appraisal Methods	178
Investment Appraisal Methods – APV	180
Investment Appraisal Methods – Free Cash Flow Model	181
Real Options	236
Sensitivity Analysis	256

© ACA Simplified 2018. No copying or reproduction permitted.

Contents – Listed by Topic Area

Performance Management

Balanced Scorecard	48
Big Data topics	
Cloud computing	76
Costs of Quality	91
Critical Success Factors	92
Digital Strategies	120
Digital Transformation	123
IT – Strategic Information Systems	187
Key Performance Indicators	194
United Nations Sustainable Development Goals	275

Risk and Risk Management

Cyber security	95
Derivatives Calculations topics	
FRC Risk Guidance	143
Insurance	164
Interest Rate Calculations	169
Option Valuation	207
Risks – Governance	247
Risks – Horizontal Acquisition	248
Risks – Types and Examples	249
Risks – Risk Reviews	253

Overseas Business Activities

Currency Risks	93
Globalisation	145
Overseas Operations – Exporting	214
Overseas Operations – Financing	215
Overseas Operations – Operational Aspects	216
Overseas Operations – Risks	218
Overseas Operations – Strategic Considerations	220

Valuations

Shareholding Percentages – Narrative Comments	259
Stakeholders and Stakeholder Management	261
Valuations – Standard Points	278
Valuations – Asset-Based Model	281
Valuations – Administration Scenario	283
Valuations – Dividend Valuation Model (DVM)	285

© ACA Simplified 2018. No copying or reproduction permitted.

Valuations – Earnings-Based	287
Valuations – EBITDA Model	289
Valuations – Economic Value Added (EVA®)	291
Valuations – Free Cash Flow Model	293
Valuations – High Growth Startup	294
Valuations – PE Model	296
Valuations – Shareholder Value Analysis (SVA)	298

Working Capital and Treasury Management

Supply Chain Improvements	267
Treasury Operations	274
Working Capital	305

SBM Technique Issues

Professional Scepticism	224
Q1 – Technique Reminders	231
Ratios – Calculations	233
Recommendations – Keeping It Practical	237
Strategic Case Study – Tips from the Study Manual	266

List of Formulae

Please also see our Ratios – Calculations section on page 233.

Exam tip – remember to take in your own set of annuity tables – these will not be provided!

CAPM

$k_e = r_f + \beta_e (r_m - r_f)$

Degearing and Regearing for CAPM

$\beta_e = \beta_a [(E + D(1 - T)) / E]$

Perpetuity with no growth

$$\frac{earnings\ or\ cash\ flow}{discount\ rate}$$

Perpetuity with positive growth

$$\frac{earnings\ or\ cash\ flow \times (1 + g)}{(discount\ rate - g)}$$

Perpetuity with negative growth

$$\frac{earnings\ or\ cash\ flow \times (1 - g)}{(discount\ rate + g)}$$

WACC

$WACC = k_e \times (E / E + D) + k_d \times (D / E + D)$

Use market value, not book value, if possible.

© ACA Simplified 2018. No copying or reproduction permitted.

How To Use This Book

Thank you for purchasing this set of *Strategic Business Management Exam Room Notes 2018*. This book provides you with notes on over 100 key SBM scenario areas, all summarised into condensed sections for super-quick usage under time pressure.

The Strategic Business Management examination is a very open assessment: this is indicated by the extremely long Study Manual and the fact that "strategic management" can include a wide range of topics. You will have to generate your business ideas very quickly under time pressure but with so many potential areas to know, we thought it would be helpful to produce a simple, clear and quick reference set of reminders of what to write about to ensure that you are **sticking closely enough to the kinds of points that are going to score marks**, rather than just writing good general business ideas.

The Expected Mark Allocation in SBM

The examiners have confirmed that the standard weightings in a typical SBM examination will always be as follows:

Topic	Standard weighting
Strategy	35-45%
Finance, valuations & investment appraisal	30-40%
Financial reporting[1]	15-20%
Assurance	10%
Ethics	5-10%

From the above we can see that the areas covered in this set of *Exam Room Notes* (all elements except financial reporting, although we do include **some** financial reporting notes: see below) should generally account for **80-85%** of the marks in SBM. It is thus absolutely vital that you get accustomed to how these *Exam Room Notes* work and where to find the information under time pressure.

At the SBM Workshop at the 2016 and 2017 ICAEW Tutor Conferences, the examiners stated that SBM draws heavily on prior knowledge of Business Strategy and Financial Management for the strategy and finance elements above (65-85% of the marks) but reminded tutors that the following topics are new at the SBM level:

- Strategic marketing and brand management

- Supply chain management

---

[1] The examiners generally use the term "corporate reporting" to refer to this angle or perspective but because we think this may lead to confusion with the separate Corporate Reporting ACA paper, we have adopted the term "financial reporting" to refer to this perspective. By "financial reporting" we do **not** just mean the lessons that you learned in the Financial Accounting & Reporting paper but also the new IFRS corporate reporting rules that you learn at the Advanced Level.

How To Use This Book

- Operations management

- Corporate Governance (meaning the appropriate governance structure for a business rather than testing the detailed rules of the UK Corporate Governance Code or similar codes)

- Human Resources Management

- Information strategy

- Performance management

- Treasury and working capital management

We would expect the examiner team to have the above list in front of them when designing an SBM examination so please do check any SBM syllabus content on the above areas very carefully.

Please note that for the purposes of these *Exam Room Notes*, we have not necessarily created sections which are named in a way which matches the above headings as this may not necessarily be the best way of organising and splitting out our notes – instead, we have in some cases included relevant points from within the above list of headings under other topic areas, based on how we would like to organise the information. In other cases (such as Corporate Governance, Treasury Operations and Working Capital), the section names for our notes in these *Exam Room Notes* do map closely to the above list of new topic areas as we feel that this does represent an appropriate way of organising or notes but we have not done this in all cases.

Memory Joggers and See Also Reminders

Under examination pressure, it is quite normal to find it harder to think of ideas than when you are more relaxed … but unfortunately in an examination you only have a limited time to generate those ideas (and much less time than you would have in a real-world assignment).

Examination nerves can also lead to the ultimate examination nightmare of a **mind blank**, something that is highly unlikely ever to happen to you outside the examination hall.

We have produced our *Exam Room Notes* to help you avoid these problems and thus improve the quality of your answers. Our *Notes* are designed to stimulate ideas and remind you of areas that you may not have otherwise considered: we hope that this will give you the required range and breadth of points, preventing you from overdeveloping just a few basic ideas (something that can happen when you only have 1 or 2 useful points to say). As set out in our sister book *Smashing SBM™ – How to Pass the ACA Strategic Business Management Examination*, the SBM examiners want to see a broad **range** of ideas and therefore lots of **different** ideas, rather than just 1 or 2 very detailed points. By providing you with many different options in any given scenario or topic, our *Exam Room Notes* will help you to develop the **range** that you need.

For this reason, please do make use of the "See also" reminders provided at the end of many sections of this book – we have taken quite a bit of time to carefully cross-reference certain topics so that you can spot the next logical link in the chain if you need more ideas. Our "See also" references also serve a very important purpose of reminding you of connected topic areas – sometimes the examination question will not specifically ask you to look at some of these areas: instead, you are just supposed to know that they are connected. So, again, do make use of these cross-references.

Methodology to Develop the Book

To ensure that you stick to points that will be rewarded, we have reviewed the following materials to develop this book:

1. **All available Strategic Business Management past papers, ICAEW mock examinations and the Strategic Business Management Electronic Question Bank**
2. **TI Business Change Question Bank 2014-15**
3. **Sections from the Corporate Reporting Study Manual 2018**
4. **Sections from the SBM Study Manual 2018**

We have used the Corporate Reporting Study Manual 2018 to create notes on what we call "Specialist Audit & Assurance" areas such as Internal Audit, auditing social and environmental statements and Agreed Upon Procedures: in other words, assurance types other than statutory audit. We know that non-statutory assurance is **very likely** to be tested in Strategic Business Management.

We have reviewed the TI Business Change Question Bank 2014-15 (old ACA syllabus) because the syllabus is very similar indeed to Strategic Business Management and Business Change was examined by the same examiner team that now writes the Strategic Business Management examinations. Also, business strategy ideas do not "date" in the same way as, for example, tax rules so it is entirely valid to use all these materials as part of the development of this book.

In developing these materials, we have also used the philosophy and methodology set out in our student-focused textbook *Smashing SBM™ – How to Pass the ACA Strategic Business Management Examination*. *Smashing SBM™* is really intended to be a "sister" publication to these *Exam Room Notes*: you will find many explanations as to how to use these *Exam Room Notes* within Smashing SBM™ and the book also explains how to plan and achieve points that will be on the markscheme.

Organisation of the Notes

Our *Exam Room Notes* are organised alphabetically so that you can very quickly access the correct topic areas. We provide 2 listings of topics:

1. Complete Alphabetical Listing

This listing provides all topics in alphabetical order, regardless of what topic area or discipline (strategy, financial management, assurance, ethics etc) the notes relate to. Use this method if you know which specific topic you are looking for.

2. Listed By Topic Area

This listing provides all topics grouped into several key thematic areas, based on typical scenarios examined in SBM:

Acquisitions

Assurance (Specialist Audit & Assurance topics)

Change and Change Management

Ethics

How To Use This Book

Finance

Financial Reporting Issues

Growth and Business Development

Investment Appraisal

Performance Management

Risk and Risk Management

Overseas Business Activities

Valuations

Working Capital and Treasury Management

SBM Technique Issues

Use this listing if you know the basic general area that the question is driving at but you are not quite sure which specific topics to look for. In other words, this second listing also serves as a kind of "memory jogger" or "idea generator".

2018 Syllabus Update Process

We have carefully reviewed the model answers to the 2 past papers set in 2017 to add further relevant points to these *Exam Room Notes*. Unfortunately, most of the questions in the ICAEW 2017 SBM Mocks were repeats of ICAEW Mock questions set in earlier years so we were not able to add much from this source.

Although there have been relatively few updates to the SBM Study Manual in 2018, we would draw your attention to the following points.

Chapter 2 adds a new detailed section on the impact of Big data on business models (Section 4.4) and also a section on Digital Strategies (Section 6).

Chapter 3 adds a new Learning objective on data security and Digital Strategy.

The Study Manual no longer contains references to the "Turnbull Guidance" on Corporate Governance as the relevant references have been replaced with references to the "2014 FRC Guidance". However, the underlying syllabus content is relatively unchanged because the FRC Guidance largely implements the findings of the Turnbull process.

Chapter 9 makes a number of additions in relation to cybersecurity and cloud computing. See, for example, pages 659, 662, 663, 710 and 713 from the 2018 edition of the Study Manual. Many of these additions constitute full sections or sub-sections, indicating that these areas are considered important by the examiners. Increased emphasis on cloud computing (provision of IT services by a third-party) could also mean that ISAE 3402 is now more likely to be examined than in the past: this standard deals with assurance over controls at a third-party organisation which provides services to the client of the assurance provider. We have accordingly increased our coverage of ISAE 3402 in this edition of our Exam Room Notes, drawing on a recent SBM Mock model answer on ISAE 3402.

Chapter 13 adds some major new sections on IFRS 9 (p1039 to p1048) and IFRS 16 (p1057 to p1064). Pages 1062 to 1064 add content and questions on Debt factoring: please note that page 1128 of the 2018 Study Manual drops a statement that Debt factoring was covered in the Financial Management syllabus. It therefore appears that this topic has been moved to the Advanced Level only and may therefore have become more examinable in SBM than in the past.

Chapter 15 adds a new Worked Example on Interest Rate Swaps (p1173), Section 3.3.1 on Option forward contracts (p1182), Section 3.4.3 on Choosing the hedging method (p1186) and a table which compares different hedging methods (p1193). Section 4.6 on Hedge accounting under IFRS 9 (p1210) has been substantially rewritten.

As in the case of the updates to the 2017 ICAEW learning materials, we would emphasise that the areas of **cyber-security, Big Data and cloud computing** account for most of the changes. Please therefore prepare well for the testing of these areas which are currently a "trendy" topic with the accountancy world in general.

Finally, we would note that the 2018 Corporate Reporting Study Manual has a large number of statements which indicate that new financial reporting standards such as IFRS 9 and IFRS 16 may now be "examined" in the context of considering how future accounting periods could be affected: in previous years, the Corporate Reporting Study Manual stated that candidates should have an "awareness" of the forthcoming new standards but did not specifically state that the new standards would be "examined". The 2018 SBM Study Manual is consistent with the updates to the 2018 Corporate Reporting Study Manual, indicating that forthcoming financial reporting standards are now more likely to be tested in the examination. For example, see page 1057 of the 2018 SBM Study Manual which explains that "candidates need to be aware IFRS 16 as a current issue and when considering how future accounting periods may be affected. It may be examined in this context."

Please Practise Some Exam Papers Using the Book!

Our *Exam Room Notes* are not something that you need to study in detail before the examination: this is because you can always refer quickly to the book if needed. However, **this does not mean that you should just take our *Exam Room Notes* into the examination with you without doing any prior practice using the book**: if you did so, you would not know which topics were contained in the book and you would not know your own best personal method of using the notes. We have tried to place our notes under the most appropriate heading and where possible we have **duplicated** key points so that you do not miss these depending on which heading you refer to – however, we do not know what the examination will test and therefore we do not know what combination of topics from this book will be relevant so it is important that you invest some time looking through the book so that you know where to find particular sections or points. Please do feel free to add your own annotations and cross-referencing if you feel this is useful to you individually, in order to find sections quickly under time pressure.

We **strongly recommend** that you use the book in a few mock examination attempts: this is the only way to get to know how to make best use of our notes. You are obviously welcome to make use of our SBM Mock Exam Packs (our own original mock exams written to full ICAEW standards) as part of your practice attempts!

How Not to Use the Book

Please do not treat these *Exam Room Notes* as **points that you just copy out in the examination**: you must firstly ensure that you only pick **relevant** points and, secondly, you must take the general reminder included here and connect it to the examination scenario **data** in order to gain the credit. You can make this connection quite simply by quoting specific figures or people or products from within the examination data but just ensure that you are not simply copying out the reminders that we have included here with no additional added value points. As a general rule, we would want you to be **starting most SBM sentences** with a point taken from the **exam paper Exhibits** rather than from this book – this will ensure you are not just copying out our notes.

Our aim is really to provide you with a list of "**reminders**" or "**memory joggers**" to help you make the connections and comments that the examiner wants to see – our aim is not to provide you with fully formed "ready-made" answers and **you will simply not be given the marks if you just copy out this book**.

Smashing SBM™ – How to Pass the ACA Strategic Business Management Examination 2018

This set of *Exam Room Notes* is designed to pair up well with its sister publication, *Smashing SBM™*. *Smashing SBM™* contains over 300 pages of practical planning and revision tips, including our MAP planning strategy which is designed to ensure that you can correctly estimate the mark allocation of the different Tasks that you need to complete for each of the 2 questions, given that the examination will not break these down for you. *Smashing SBM™* also explains the correct writing style to succeed in SBM and revises some key technical areas and calculations.

We strongly recommend that you study the principles and methods of *Smashing SBM™* very well as part of your preparations but this set of *Exam Room Notes* does not assume that you have purchased *Smashing SBM™*.

Specialist Audit & Assurance Areas

This set of *Exam Room Notes* includes detailed notes on the following specialist areas which are generally newly introduced at the Advanced Level[2]:

- Agreed Upon Procedures
- Assurance Engagements on Greenhouse Gas Statements
- Assurance Reports on Controls at a Service Organisation (ISAE 3402)
- Compilation Engagements
- Corporate Governance
- Forensic Audits
- Integrated Reporting
- Internal Audit

---

[2] The topic of Prospective Information (ISAE 3400) is included in the Professional Level Audit and Assurance learning materials but as this standard does not tend to be examined very often at the Professional Level, we are aware that most SBM candidates do not really know ISAE 3400 very well. As ISAE 3400 is one of the most frequently tested standards in SBM, please ensure you fix this knowledge gap as part of your preparations for SBM.

How To Use This Book

- Prospective Information (ISAE 3400)
- Reporting on Information Contained in a Prospectus
- Review Engagements (ISRE 2400)
- Sustainability Reporting and Social Reporting (Social and Environmental Audit)

We give emphasis to these areas because we know that around 10% of the marks will be for assurance areas and looking at the existing past papers and mock exams it seems that it is assurance, rather than statutory audit, which is likely to be tested in SBM.

Whilst the emphasis is likely to be on these "specialist" assurance areas rather than statutory audit, the examiners can do as they wish and **could** include statutory audit testing or assurance areas that use similar tests to statutory audit. Such tests and procedures are reasonable elements of brought forward knowledge. We therefore recommend that you consider purchasing our *Advanced Level Audit & Assurance Exam Room Notes 2018* book: this book applies the same approach that we have used in these SBM *Exam Room Notes* but also covers the area of statutory audit (and therefore is also very useful in Corporate Reporting). (Please note that the non-statutory assurance content of this set of Exam Room Notes and our *Advanced Level Audit & Assurance Exam Room Notes 2018* is identical: this is because non-statutory assurance is more likely to be tested in SBM so we want to ensure that SBM-only students who only purchase this set of *Strategic Business Management Exam Room Notes* have access to the relevant content. We must then also allow for CR-only candidates who will only be purchasing our *Advanced Level Audit & Assurance Exam Room Notes 2018*.)

Financial Reporting Notes

Unfortunately, given that all financial reporting rules examined in the Financial Accounting and Reporting Professional Level paper and the Corporate Reporting Advanced Level paper are examinable in SBM, it is not possible to provide notes on all such issues in this book as the book would then become too long and unusable. However, these *Exam Room Notes* **do** provide notes on key financial reporting topics for SBM. To determine whether the topic is "key", we have looked at what has been tested in SBM past papers and mocks as certain financial reporting rules are obviously more likely to be tested in scenarios relating to substantial business change (the focus of SBM).

If you require a more detailed set of quick reference notes for financial reporting concepts (whether to be safer in SBM or because you are sitting the Corporate Reporting paper), please consider our *Advanced Level Financial Reporting Exam Room Notes 2018*. This publication contains alphabetically-organised, quick reference notes for all key financial reporting topics (including brought forward topics from the Professional Level paper in Financial Accounting and Reporting).

The Accountant in Business Concept

The SBM examiners have been keen to emphasise that SBM is designed to be a strategic examination which only an accountant (not a "pure" strategist) can pass. This is termed the "Accountant in Business" concept. In all your answers (and not just answers which specifically ask for it), you must consider the **financial reporting implications** of strategy: you will be rewarded whenever you provide appropriate advice that only a qualified Chartered Accountant could give.

How To Use This Book

Please see our book *Smashing SBM™ – How to Pass the ACA SBM Examination* for more information on how to apply this concept. Our MAP planning sheets contained in *Smashing SBM™* also contained reminders of the Accountant in Business concept.

Disclaimer – We Cannot Cover Everything!

We have tried our best to produce a thorough yet useable summary of as many potentially examinable areas as possible. Unfortunately, SBM is a very wide-ranging examination and therefore it is impossible to cover all potential scenarios, particularly given the huge size of the Study Manual. We therefore cannot be sure that everything within your examination will be covered by these notes. We strongly recommend that you add to our notes based on your own studies if something important arises which we have not been able to cover. We would be grateful if you could let us know at **getqualified@acasimplified.com** if you believe that there is a notable omission so that we can look at including this in future (but again repeating that it is never possible to include everything for an examination of this nature).

Despite these limitations, we strongly believe that this set of *SBM Exam Room Notes* will benefit your studies and we wish you the very best for your examination!

On-Demand Video Tuition – Special Offer!

Our popular on-demand video courses provide a convenient way to obtain expert tutor guidance for CR and SBM. Our courses can be viewed at any time and as often as you wish – perfect for revising the tricky technical areas of the syllabus!

Our courses contain advice on examination technique, planning methods and time management. We also provide a large number of Tutor Talkthroughs of past paper, Question Bank and ICAEW Mock questions. We also review the mark allocation in past paper answers so that you can understand how to allocate your time effectively.

As a thank you for purchasing this book, we are delighted to offer you a **10% discount on the 2018 edition of our CR or SBM on-demand courses (or both!)**. Simply email us with your proof of purchase for this book and we will send you a discount code to obtain your 10% discount. This offer is only available if you contact us **before** purchasing your on-demand course(s): retrospective discounts will not be provided. Your discount request must be received no later than 30 June 2018 (in respect of the July 2018 sitting) and no later than 15 October 2018 (in respect of the November 2018 sitting). This offer is limited to one discount per course per original purchaser of this book: no discount will be provided on any second-hand purchase of the book. No cash alternative will be provided. This offer is not available to students on our classroom CR or SBM tuition courses and not to any students whose access to our on-demand courses is paid for by their employer. Please allow 5 working days for your unique access code to be sent by email. All other aspects of the discount are subject to our reasonable discretion and the offer may be withdrawn at any time without notice.

For further information on our on-demand courses, including a free video explanation of how the courses work, please see our website at **www.acasimplified.com**.

General Advice on SBM Answer Style

The mark allocation for Tasks and sub-Tasks within a question **will not be equal** – find a reasonable method to estimate the differences

Apply an MS^2 approach – **M**ake **S**cenario-**S**pecific points – avoid generic points

> Avoid copying out standards or lists of points: connect the point to the SBM business

> Define financial reporting points quickly and more briefly than in Corporate Reporting, using "inline definition"*

Adopt the perspective of the "**Accountant in Business**" – explain both the practical business impact and the financial reporting impact

Apply professional scepticism

Offer conclusions and recommendations (even if not specifically stated to do so in the question)

The SBM examination is created based on the Case Study skills areas so follow these:

> **Assimilating & Using Information** – identifying the key information

> **Structuring Problems & Solutions** – processing the information to produce results

> **Applying Judgement** – deeper points including scepticism

> **Conclusions & Recommendations** – summarising main points and offering practical advice

Keep everything **as practical as possible** – the client needs advice on what to **do**, not just what to **report**

Short, succinct writing – "almost bullet point" and clinical style – avoid introductions, long section headings, linking between paragraphs, phrases like "Following on from the above discussion" or even just "Furthermore" or "Additionally"

Use lots of headings – easier for the marker and keeps you focused on the different things you need to do

*See our book *Smashing SBM™ – How to Pass the ACA Strategic Business Management Examination* for further explanation of "inline definition".

Acquisitions – Benefits & Risks

Reasons to acquire

- Synergies
- Marketing advantages
- Enhanced image
- Diversification
- Opportunity to share certain functions and rationalise
- Increase profits and RoCE
- Economies of scale
- Gain access to expertise
- Gain access to technology

Alternative could be **organic growth**

Risks

Strategic risks

- May not be close enough relationship to competences of target
- May result in overlap or duplication of resources/functions
- May require change in direction
- Management of acquiring company is reliant on information, honesty and ability of target management
- Will customer relationships continue?
- Earnings volatility
- Higher level of business risk
- Pricing – amount and/or form of consideration may be wrong
- Synergies may not occur
- Reputation risk if working with a company with the wrong image
- Reporting risk – impact on corporate reporting and group as a whole
- Strategic differences between the 2 entities – problems at Board level and waste of resources
- Becoming involved in an unfamiliar market
- Overpaying for an acquisition
- Failing to understand demand and supply
- Reliance on others for knowledge and skills
- Lack of strategic fit or direction
- Reputational damage
- Consider the size of issue – is it material to the whole business? If so, then a strategic issue
- Lack of managerial skills and experience
- Moving out of a core area
- Few common marketing activities
- Minimal level of integration
- Lack of gaining a competitive advantage over competitors
- Lack of strategic fit and brand confusion
- Lack of anything distinctive
- Few barriers to entry to prevent others entering the market (contestable market)

Acquisitions – Benefits & Risks

Operating risks

- Synergies failing to emerge
- Delays
- Cost overruns – who pays?
- Service quality could change
- Integration problems – culture, IT, pricing, support processes
- Management skills and time availability – unsuitable for new group?
- Hidden contractual or other legal obligations
- Hidden financial liabilities
- Debt financing → gearing
- Debt financing → security must be offered – possible loss of asset/control
- Dependent on individual(s) or individual product(s)?
- Operating gearing – share of fixed costs in total operating costs
- Exit costs high – specialist machinery or intangibles which cannot be sold on
- Target may have existing commitments which are expensive
- Overcapacity in the short term?
- Post-integration problems in an acquisition
- Administrative integration
- Problems in integrating cultures, accounting, HRM, IT, internal controls, supply chain management, deliveries and marketing
- Hidden contractual and other legal obligations (assuming that there are no indemnities)
- Hidden financial liabilities (assuming that there are no indemnities)
- Financing methods such as debt
- Dependence on key suppliers or individuals
- Limited amount of assets against which to raise future debts
- Uncertain sales of surplus assets
- Forecasts not achieved
- Sales uncertainty
- Cost overruns
- High level of fixed costs in cost structure → significant operational gearing and operating risk
- Significant up front sunk costs
- High exit costs
- Initial cash deficit
- Going concern issues
- Hidden liabilities

Financing risks

- Re-financing risk – problem if term of financing is short term or medium but the project cash inflows are long-term
- Interest rate risk – variable rates and costs of insurance/hedging
- Fair value risk – FV could change – FV and interest rates are inversely related
- Gearing – increased volatility and bankruptcy risks
- Cash flow and liquidity
- Covenant risk – risk of breaching covenants, resulting in lost of control
- Availability risk – poor takeup of shares/loans – cost of underwriting to insure against this

Acquisitions – Benefits & Risks

Governance risks

- Control environment
- Culture – entrepreneur v corporate
- Management style
- UK Corporate Governance Code applies? (exemptions for AIM and more limited exemptions for non-FTSE 350)
- Board size, balance and control – role and powers, rotation, changes after an acquisition
- Director pay and performance
- Non-Executive Directors – are there any NEDs? Independent? Quality?
- Committees (e.g. audit, remuneration or nomination)? Independent? Quality?

Other risks

- Overpaying
- Use consideration which is risky (e.g. shares, derivatives, performance target-based)
- Acquiring too much capacity
- Legal costs and problems
- Conflicts in interests of parties/control issues
- Financing considerations – cost, control, tax
- Cultural differences
- Staffing problems including redundancy costs
- Poor change management
- Poor integration plans
- High integration costs
- Unquoted target with uncertain value – normally a discount for lack of liquidity

Risk Mitigation

- Undertake thorough due diligence on feasibility
- Negotiate correct clauses into contract e.g. responsibility for cost overruns or delays or integration problems
- Ensure information fully disclosed – good quality due diligence procedures

See also

Other Acquisitions topics
Bank loans	49
Change – Definition & Models	73
Change – Management & Implementation	75
IT Due Diligence	186
Marketing Strategies	203

Overseas Operations topics
Prospective Information (ISAE 3400)	226
Segmental Reporting (IFRS 8)	255
Strategic Analysis Tools & Models	262

Valuations topics

Acquisitions – Debt-Funded

Consider the **current debt to equity (gearing) ratio** of the company and how this may be altered

Consider whether there are **fixed assets such as PPE to provide security** over the debt

Consider **interest cover** and how this may be affected by the acquisition

Consider the **potential earnings** of the target – adding these into the consolidated earnings will affect ratios such as interest cover and even gearing through increases in retained earnings over time

Consider the **impact on finance costs** if funding is hard to obtain or gearing changes to such an extent that providers of debt require a higher interest rate

Consider the **debt of the target** – how will this affect the consolidated SFP? How will any extra interest payments affect the consolidated IS and related ratios?

Cash may be used up in the acquisition, affecting the ability to meet obligations when due

The **growth prospects** of the target are particularly important if a risky strategy is being followed

Debt capacity

An advantage of degearing now is that if profitable investment opportunities were to present themselves in future, the entity would find it easier to raise debt in order to take advantage of the opportunity – reducing gearing preserves the entity's "debt capacity"

See also	Other Acquisitions topics	
	Bank loans	49
	Change – Definition & Models	73
	Change – Management & Implementation	75
	Marketing Strategies	203
	Overseas Operations topics	
	Prospective Information (ISAE 3400)	226
	Segmental Reporting (IFRS 8)	255
	Strategic Analysis Tools & Models	262
	Valuations topics	

Acquisitions – Due Diligence

Mention that does not involve the level of detailed testing that would be carried out in a statutory audit – advisable to wait for a statutory audit to be completed if possible before doing the deal

Provides only limited assurance

Types of Acquisition Due Diligence

Financial	financial position, risks and projections, likely returns on investment
Commercial	markets and external economic environment; renewal of contracts?
Technical	new technologies
IT	nature and reliability and risks of IT systems and IT skills
Legal	legal rights and obligations on contracts, employment law
Human Resources	skills, contracts, redundancies
Tax	liabilities, losses available for relief, structuring

Note – certain types of DD will be more relevant depending on the type of company involved:

Services company	HR DD more important
Tech company	Technical and IT DD more important

Due Diligence Procedures for an Acquisition

identify legal title

confirm accuracy and assumptions of financial data and projections

commercial review – order book, contracts, realism of growth rates assumed and projected

identify and quantify areas of commercial and financial risk

identify possible areas of synergy

identify key personnel

give assurance to providers of finance if required

Acquisitions – Due Diligence

Due Diligence and Valuation Models

Clearly, some valuation models are very sensitive to changes in variables so these should always be part of the financial and commercial due diligence process

Ensure you make some points explaining or querying specific model variables

You may wish to note that the acquisition will change the risk profile of the combined company so previous cost of capital/discount rate figures may be out of date

Financial due diligence – some procedures

- Test forecasts against industry trends and recent sales patterns
- Test assumptions on production process and costs
- Verify projections of expenditure to suitable evidence e.g. independent evidence
- Assess costs and prices against plans
- Review marketing plans
- Determine capacity for further borrowing
- Test projected capital expenditure
- Discussions with management – reasons, alternatives, contingencies and Plan B

Income Statement Due Diligence

Note – these are simply examples taken from the SBM QB – you must ensure that they are applicable to your exam scenario

Issue	DD Procedures
Revenue	Verify price and volume changes including timing of the price change Confirm that policy is consistent with IAS 18
Cost of sales	Procedures to verify volume changes Verify reasons for changes
Depreciation	Confirm treatment fits with IAS 16 Confirm useful economic lives Confirm that depreciation policy reasonable Determine if assets incorrectly grouped
Impairment	Determine if impairment needed If impairment already proposed, determine if there are other assets that need writing off Confirm value in use and impairment methods used
Provisions	Professional scepticism if provision being reversed – why? Can relate to aggressive earnings management Consider causes and consequences Review the measurement of the original provision and the necessity of the reversal – has there been an intentional effort to distort profit?
Financing costs	Determine if changes are in line with other business changes such as loans and capital expenditure

Issue	DD Procedures
PBT	Check for unusual movements such as increased PBT but falling GP or margins

SFP Due Diligence (Asset-based valuations)

Note – these are simply examples taken from the SBM QB – you must ensure that they are applicable to your exam scenario

Issue	DD Procedures
PPE	Inspect any relevant valuer's reports Check whether depreciation rates are low Check FV of assets
Inventory	Physical inventory count at the acquisition date with attention to cut off Determine if any impairment is needed, especially if a technology company with high risk of obsolescence Determine inventory turnover rates
Receivables	Investigate returns and impairment Verify title to receivables
Cash	Probably low risk as an objective item but confirm whether cash is included as part of the deal
Loans	Determine carrying amount in accordance with IAS 38/IFRS 9 Review terms of the loan agreement
Pension obligation	Could be either over or understated Determine competence of actuary if used Assess discount rate – rate should be rate on AA corporate bonds Confirm that entries appear in IS, especially if errors made
Tax liability	Consider under and over provisions from last year and any tax payments needed Confirm whether a deferred tax balance is included and whether needed
Trade payables	Assess cut off issues Review whether trade payables days appear reasonable

See also

Other Acquisitions topics
Bank loans   49
Change – Definition & Models   73
Change – Management & Implementation   75
IT Due Diligence   186
Marketing Strategies   203
Overseas Operations topics
Prospective Information (ISAE 3400)   226
Segmental Reporting (IFRS 8)   255
Strategic Analysis Tools & Models   262
Valuations topics

Acquisitions – Financing

Useful mnemonic: CSL – **c**ash, **s**hares, **l**oans

Impact on cost of capital

Cost of equity should rise if the company increases its gearing by borrowing and should fall if you raises new capital with the share issue

This will affect the valuation of the company by affecting the WACC and therefore discounted value of future earnings/cash

Therefore the financing method is important

Cash financing – advantages

Shareholders of target company receive a certain amount (compared to contingent consideration)

Could be good use of surplus cash

No dilution of control

No issue costs

Cash financing – disadvantages

Acquiring company may need to find additional cash

May be tax issues for shareholders of target company

Shareholders of the target may not be happy to lose their interest in the business

Director-shareholders in the target are given cash but no shareholding – incentives for good performance reduced or removed?

Summary comparison of loans versus shares

Issue	Loan	Shares
Liquidity	Uncertain Capital repayable and interest payable	Certain No repayment Dividends optional
Gearing	Increased **!Calculate where possible**	Reduced **!Calculate where possible**
Transaction costs	Low	High
Draw down	When needed	All received up front
Tax	Interest tax deductible	Dividends not deductible

Acquisitions – Financing

Share issue (including share for share exchange) – advantages

Preserves cash and liquidity – dividends only need to be paid at the discretion of the directors

Shareholders of the target company retain an equity interest

No immediate tax issues

Group has control over dividend policy – not obliged to pay every year

Reduces gearing as additional equity is issued with no extra debt – consider **recalculating** your gearing ratios to show the impact (if using the debt/equity equation then only the bottom half of the fraction will change)

If a substantial amount is issued to a particular entity, that entity will have a strong motivation to promote and demand improvements in the company's performance to improve the share price

Share issue (including share for share exchange) – disadvantages

Issue costs can be high – up to 15% of finance issued

Shareholders of the target receive an uncertain amount

Shareholders of the acquiring company have their shareholdings diluted

May not be possible to maintain a similar dividend per share to the previous year if the number of shares has increased substantially

Could impact on the market price of shares, affecting shareholder wealth

Share for share exchange – considerations for directors

- Are shares received quoted? If not, may be hard to dispose of and illiquid
- If shares received are quoted, can these be disposed of without overloading the market?
- What % is retained? What profit flow and control does this yield?
- What are the growth prospects of the new group?
- Has a subsidiary now become only an associate with a lower control premium/value?

Debt/Loan financing – advantages

Shareholders of the acquiring company can keep control

Shareholders of target company get a certain return so may accept a lower price for the acquisition

Acquisitions – Financing

Tax deductible and value of the tax debt shield

Minimal issue costs

Debt/Loan financing – disadvantages

Obligation to pay interest – cash implications

Shareholders of target company may want equity

Increased gearing* and risk

Refinancing risk – look at the term involved

Adds to financial risk
Loan covenants may exist

(*Could be an advantage if the increased gearing brings the company nearer to its optimum level)

Why are retained earnings not a source of financing?

Retained earnings are the cumulative profit since the company started training

Profits are not the same thing as cash so there may not be cash available for acquisitions purposes

Retained earnings are represented by an increase in net assets (not just cash)

Debt capacity

An advantage of degearing now is that if profitable investment opportunities were to present themselves in future, the entity would find it easier to raise debt in order to take advantage of the opportunity – reducing gearing preserves the entity's "debt capacity"

See also	Other Acquisitions topics	
	Bank loans	49
	Change – Definition & Models	73
	Change – Management & Implementation	75
	Loan Decision by a Bank	202
	Marketing Strategies	203
	Overseas Operations topics	
	Prospective Information (ISAE 3400)	226
	Segmental Reporting (IFRS 8)	255
	Strategic Analysis Tools & Models	262
	Valuations topics	

Acquisitions – Impact on Financial Statements

Areas to Consider

Earnings per Share – a key ratio considered by the financial markets

Gearing – a key indicator of risks of bankruptcy and could affect ability to secure more financing but also leads to tax savings compared to issue of equity – impact on covenants?

Non-current asset turnover – revenue earned per investment into fixed assets (ideally a high figure)

Interest cover – impact on covenants?

Note – compare the size of the changes in the above to the investment amount – is it worth it?

Types of structure

Subsidiary, Associate, Joint venture, Investment

Intangible assets (IAS 38)

For many companies (particularly services companies), the value of the company exceeds the book value of its net tangible assets

On acquisition, there may be recognition of assets such as customer lists, software, Internet domains, databases and so on at fair value. The remaining balance of the purchase price over the fair value of all net assets is treated as goodwill.

It must be possible to establish the fair value of the intangible assets reliably – the assets must be identifiable and under the control of the acquirer and there must be probable future economic benefits from the assets

Once recognised, intangible assets should be amortised on a systematic basis over their expected useful lives

Goodwill is not amortised but is subject instead to annual impairment reviews – any impairments in value are written off to profit or loss

The acquisition of substantial amounts of intangible assets could lead to high charges to profit or loss for amortisation costs, potentially reducing earnings – this would be increased further if there is impairment of an intangible, including goodwill – there would be a substantial increase in intangible assets on the consolidated SFP, affecting ratios based on assets

Acquiring a 50%+ Subsidiary – Specific Considerations

Provides full control

Acquisitions – Impact on Financial Statements

Must follow the requirements of IFRS 3 *Business Combinations*

Consolidate in all revenue and expenses (and allow for NCI share) – could boost EPS but depends on whether profitable **and whether shares issued as part of the acquisition** (likely in SBM)

Eliminates intra-group trading and unrealised profits

Various items must be measured at fair value

Consolidate in all assets and liabilities – impact on gearing and SFP ratios?

If applicable, assets/liabilities should be initially translated at the historic/acquisition date exchange rate

Goodwill may arise an acquisition and is recognised as an intangible asset in the group financial statements – this could affect certain ratios – as this is treated as an asset of the subsidiary, if the subsidiary uses a different currency the goodwill is retranslated at the year-end using the closing rate

Controls company so has full access to information and ability to dictate changes based on that information

Can replace management team – no one else to depend on (or blame!) for performance outcomes

Acquiring a <50% Associate or Investment – Specific Considerations

Does not provide control – unknown control aspect – does not provide access to all information and shareholding of less than 25% lacks power

Share of profit from associate may boost EPS

No consolidating in of assets and liabilities – just an asset line for Investment in associate – less impact on gearing than a full subsidiary?

Subject to quality of management team and does not have full influence over this

See also	Other Acquisitions topics	
	Bank loans	49
	Change – Definition & Models	73
	Change – Management & Implementation	75
	Marketing Strategies	203
	Overseas Operations topics	
	Prospective Information (ISAE 3400)	226
	Segmental Reporting (IFRS 8)	255
	Strategic Analysis Tools & Models	262
	Valuations topics	

Acquisitions – Post-Acquisition Integration

Possible problems/differences

Scale and size

Marketing positioning – top end quality versus lower end price considerations

Location of operations – different locations but alternatively may be too close and "cannibalise" each other's sales, resulting in little net improvement

Product range

Customer perception and brand awareness

Change in brand style and nature of merging low and high quality

Ensuring synergies

Management challenges if continue to be operated separately

See also	Other Acquisitions topics	
	Bank loans	49
	Change – Definition & Models	73
	Change – Management & Implementation	75
	Marketing Strategies	203
	Overseas Operations topics	
	Prospective Information (ISAE 3400)	226
	Segmental Reporting (IFRS 8)	255
	Strategic Analysis Tools & Models	262
	Valuations topics	

© ACA Simplified 2018. No copying or reproduction permitted.

Acquisitions – Struggling Company

Assurance

The most recent financial statements may not yet have been audited

The nature of the assurance review will be determined by contractual agreement

The contractual agreement will consider whether an assurance opinion is required, the timescale available to do the work and access to information made available by the administrator

Areas to cover in assurance

Goodwill	enquire whether impairment proposed
Non-current assets	IFRS 13 issues, verify title to assets, analyse charges
Inventories	review age, investigate nature, causes and value of slow moving items, check assets to registration documents, check valuations against trade guides, establish items of consignment inventories
Receivables	review age analysis of receivables, check for normal recovery, use of debt factors in the past
Brand	assess the terms and conditions, have there been other offers?, has the administrator made any attempt to sell the brand name? Incremental cash flows?

Projections and statement of profit or loss

Procedures on projections and statement of profit or loss

Examine year end cut off for revenue enhancement issues

Examine assumptions on which projections are made

Analytical procedures on financial statements to ascertain consistency

Review basis of assumptions for revenue and other changes

Challenge assumptions

Review transactions close to year end and up to date of possible transfer to ensure that ownership and condition of the assets is maintained

Commercial assurance

This process will establish if there are rights, obligations and liabilities that impact on asset value or the future operating of assets

Acquisitions – Struggling Company

Legal review of the terms of contracts

Checking of covenants, preferential interest rates and repayment terms

Ascertain any litigation, contingencies or contractual obligations or penalties

Consider tax issues outstanding

Review market conditions and competitors

Assess viability of different sites/revenue streams

See also	Other Acquisitions topics	
	Bank loans	49
	Change – Definition & Models	73
	Change – Management & Implementation	75
	Marketing Strategies	203
	Overseas Operations topics	
	Prospective Information (ISAE 3400)	226
	Segmental Reporting (IFRS 8)	255
	Strategic Analysis Tools & Models	262
	Valuations topics	

Acquisitions – Synergies and Challenges

Synergies

Main justification for many acquisitions – but check that will actually happen – if not, shareholder value harmed

Revenue synergies

Benefits
- Higher revenues for acquirer
- Higher return on equity
- Longer periods of growth

Sources
- Increased market power
- Marketing synergies – two parties can combine advertising resources and cross-advertise
- Strategic synergies
- Locational synergies

Dangers
- Revenue synergies are harder to quantify than other synergies
- Hard to know how customers will react – will they actually buy?

Cost synergies
- Normally considered to be substantial – but will they happen and will they outweigh integration/redundancy costs?
- Primary source – economies of scale

Financial synergies
- Diversification – gain to shareholders if not already diversified themselves
- Uses surplus cash that otherwise not being used ("cash slack")

Human resources synergies
- Sharing of skills and expertise
- May be able to buy in access to information, techniques and networks

Accounting impact of an acquisition

Subsidiary – consolidate in debts – affects gearing but could increase profits (100% of subsidiary)

Associate – debts not consolidated in but profits boosted (by lower amount than a subsidiary: lower % owned)

Challenges – Integrating a Small Business with a Listed Company

Small business

May be owned by small group of shareholders or even a family

May have significant amount invested

May be important to self-esteem/pride of family members – primary objective not purely financial

May not be interested in maximum short term returns

Listed business

Needs to ensure high returns for shareholders immediately (stock market oversight)

Primary objective likely to be wealth maximisation – purely financial aims

See also	Other Acquisitions topics	
	Bank loans	49
	Change – Definition & Models	73
	Change – Management & Implementation	75
	Marketing Strategies	203
	Overseas Operations topics	
	Prospective Information (ISAE 3400)	226
	Segmental Reporting (IFRS 8)	255
	Strategic Analysis Tools & Models	262
	Valuations topics	

Agreed Upon Procedures

Examination example points

For a good example, see **SBM July 2016 past paper** (model answer page 14) (worth **14 marks**)

In an AUP engagement, the practitioner provides a report on factual findings from procedures agreed in advance with the relevant party or parties.

Procedures and tests should be sufficiently detailed so as to be clear and unambiguous and discussed in advance to ensure that they are useful for the purposes.

The practitioner is required to comply at a minimum with ISRS 4400 *Engagements to Perform Agreed Upon Procedures on Financial Information*

The AUP report does not express a conclusion and is therefore not an assurance engagement – it will not provide recommendations based on the findings – the relevant parties are instead requested to review the procedures and findings and to use the information to draw their own conclusions

The value of the AUP process is in providing objective testing by a practitioner with relevant expertise – testing is independent and also protects confidentiality (practitioner is bound by the Code of Ethics for Professional Accountants under ISRS 4400) – saves one of the parties carrying out the procedures themselves (time and money saving)

Example of AUP performed on a licensing agreement (SBM July 2016 past paper)

Procedures on the contractual terms such as number of bags sold, number of customer complaints about product quality and the number of customer complaints about service quality

Benefit is that the engagement provides evidence of compliance with the terms of the licensing contract: ensures correct royalty payments and monitoring of quality control issues

The confidential nature of AUP might be the only way to give the parties enough confidence to allow the procedures to be carried out at all

General notes

Agreed upon procedures are procedures of a standard audit nature but which have been **specifically agreed upon by the auditor, entity and any appropriate third parties for a purpose other than preparation of a statutory audit.**

A difference with statutory audit is therefore that there must be **agreement on the procedures to be applied** (hence the name "agreed upon" procedures) whereas in a statutory audit it is the auditor who determines which procedures to use.

A second difference is that the recipients of the report containing the "agreed upon" procedures are **left to form their own conclusions – the auditor/practitioner does not offer a conclusion**, unlike in a statutory audit (or other types of assurance).

Agreed Upon Procedures

Agreed upon procedures are governed by **ISRS 4400**. Note that ISRSs have not been adopted in the UK.

In setting up the agreed upon procedures, agreement should be reached on the following matters:

- Nature of the arrangement as not constituting an audit or review i.e. no assurance is expressed at all

- Purpose of the engagement

- Identification of the financial information to which the agreed upon procedures will be applied

- Nature, timing and extent of the specific procedures to be applied

- Anticipated form of the report

- Limitations on distribution of the report

The report of factual findings should contain:

- Identification of specific financial or non-financial information to which the agreed-upon procedures have been applied

- Statement that the procedures performed were those agreed upon with the recipient

- Statement that the engagement was performed in accordance with the ISRSs applicable to agreed upon procedure engagements or with relevant national standards or practices

- If the auditor is performing the agreed upon procedures, a statement that the auditor is not independent of the entity

- Identification of the purpose for which the agreed upon procedures were performed

- A listing of the specific procedures performed

- A description of the auditor's factual findings including sufficient details of errors and exceptions found

- A statement that the procedures performed do not constitute either an audit or a review, and, as such, **no assurance is expressed**

- A statement that had the auditor performing additional procedures or an audit/review then other matters may have been arisen and reported

- A restriction on use of the report to only those parties that have agreed to the procedures which have been performed

Agreed Upon Procedures

- A statement that the report relates only to the elements, accounts, items or financial and non-financial information specified and does not extend to the entity's financial statements taken as a whole

Again, **no assurance or opinion is offered** – there is only a reporting of **factual findings**

See also   Acquisitions – Due Diligence   26

Assurance – General Points (ISAE 3000)

ISAE 3000 distinguishes between 2 types of assurance engagement:

reasonable assurance engagements – these engagements aim to reduce engagement risk to an **acceptably low level** – the **conclusion** is expressed in a form that conveys the practitioner's **opinion** on the outcome of the measurement or evaluation of the underlying subject matter against criteria

limited assurance engagements – these engagements give a **lower level of** assurance than reasonable assurance engagements – the nature, timing and extent of procedures carried out would be **limited** – even so, the level of assurance should still be **meaningful** in the judgement of the practitioner, meaning that it is likely to **enhance** the **intended user's confidence** about the subject matter information

Assurance	Level of risk	Conclusion	Procedures	Example
Reasonable	Low	Positive expression – an opinion is expressed	High	"The management has operated an effective system of internal controls"
Limited	Acceptable	Negative expression – no opinion is offered, conclusion only notes whether matters have come to attention indicating material misstatement	Limited but still meaningful	"Nothing has come to our attention indicating significant deficiencies in internal control"

Elements of an assurance engagement

- a 3-party relationship involving a practitioner, a responsible party (the client entity) and an intended user
- subject matter
- suitable criteria
- evidence
- an assurance report – written report containing the practitioner's assurance conclusion which is issued to the intended user in a form appropriate to the engagement (reasonable assurance or limited assurance)

Process at the end of an assurance engagement

The practitioner must express a conclusion **in writing** in an assurance report – the report should include the following elements:

Assurance – General Points (ISAE 3000)

1. description of the **level of assurance** obtained

2. subject matter information evaluated against **criteria** (for example, "The company's internal controls operated effectively in terms of criteria X in the period")

3. **identification** of the applicable criteria

4. description of **significant inherent limitations** (for example, noting that a historical review of internal controls does not provide assurance that the same controls will continue to operate effectively in the future)

5. if the applicable criteria are designed for a **specific purpose**, there should be a **statement** alerting readers to this fact – this statement should indicate that the subject matter information may **not** be suitable for another purpose

6. **responsible** parties and their **responsibilities** as well as the **responsibilities** of the **practitioner**

7. statement that the work was performed in accordance with a **relevant specific ISAE** or in accordance with **ISAE 3000 for general assurance work**

8. an **informative summary** of the work performed

Level of assurance possible

Absolute assurance is generally **not** attainable as a result of factors such as:

- use of **selective testing**
- the **inherent limitations** of control systems
- the fact that much of the evidence available to the practitioner is **persuasive** rather than **conclusive**
- the use of **judgement** in gathering evidence and drawing conclusions based on the evidence
- in some cases, the **characteristics of the subject matter**

Types of conclusion

An **unmodified opinion** is possible where the practitioner concludes:

in the case of a **reasonable** assurance engagement, the subject matter information is prepared, in all material respects, in accordance with the applicable criteria

in the case of a **limited assurance** engagement, that, based on the procedures performed and the evidence obtained, no matter has come to the attention of the practitioner that causes them to believe that there may be a material misstatement of the subject matter information as compared with the applicable criteria

A **modified conclusion** will be issued when the above **does not apply**.

Assurance Engagements on Greenhouse Gas Statements

Regulated by ISAE 3410 *Assurance Engagements on Greenhouse Gas Statements*

All businesses emit greenhouse gases, either directly or indirectly.

As the public has been seeking greater confidence in greenhouse gas emissions, ISAE 3410 has been created to enhance this confidence.

Reasons for preparing a greenhouse gas statement include:

> may be required under a regulatory disclosure regime

> may be required as part of an emissions trading scheme

> company may wish to make voluntary disclosures

An engagement performed in accordance with ISAE 3410 must also comply with the requirements of ISAE 3000.

An engagement under ISAE 3410 can provide either limited assurance or reasonable assurance, based on the circumstances (such as the requirements of law or regulation). ISAE 3410 does not itself specifically require the level of assurance to be limited or reasonable.

The key stages are the same as for any assurance assignment and include planning, obtaining an understanding of the entity, identifying and assessing the risks of material misstatement, obtaining written representations and forming an assurance conclusion.

The understanding required to perform a limited assurance engagement will be less than that required for a reasonable assurance engagement – in particular, for a limited assurance engagement there is no requirement to obtain an understanding of control activities relevant to the engagement or to evaluate the design of controls and determine whether they have been implemented.

Similarly, risk assessment procedures will be less extensive in a limited assurance engagement – assessment of the risks of material misstatement would not need to be performed at the assertion level in such an engagement.

Reporting will be similar to other assurance reports and should include a title, addressee, identification and description of the level of assurance, description of the entity's responsibility, identification of the applicable criteria, a description of the practitioner's responsibility and an overall assurance conclusion.

In relation to reporting, the following points must be included:

> a statement that the quantification of greenhouse gases is subject to inherent uncertainty

> a statement that the firm applies ISQC 1

Assurance Engagements on Greenhouse Gas Statements

a statement that the practitioner complies with the IESBA Code or other professional requirements

a statement that the engagement was performed in accordance with ISA 3410

if the practitioner expresses a conclusion that is modified, the report must include a section that provides a description of the matter giving rise to the modification and a section containing the modified opinion

Appendix 2 of ISAE 3410 includes illustrative examples of reports for both reasonable and limited assurance engagements.

See also Sustainability Reporting and Social Reporting 269

Assurance Reports on Controls at a Service Organisation

Definition of a service organisation – a third party organisation that provides services to user entities that are part of those entities' information systems relevant to financial reporting

Regulated by ISAE 3402 *Assurance Reports on Controls at a Service Organisation*, which expands on how ISAE 3400 is to be applied in a reasonable assurance engagement to report on controls at a service organisation

ISAE 3402 is to be applied in a reasonable assurance engagement to provide a report to user entities and their auditors on the controls at a service organization.

ISAE 3402 rules only apply where the service organisation is responsible for, or otherwise able to make a statement about, the **suitable design of controls**.

This means that ISAE 3402 does not apply where the assurance engagement is to:

> report only on whether controls at the service organisation operated as described, or

> report on controls at a service organisation other than those related to a service that is likely to be relevant to user entities' internal control as it relates to financial reporting

The 2 types of reports – Type 1 and Type 2

A Type 1 report is a report on the description and design of controls at a service organization.

In a Type 1 report, the service auditor will express his opinion as to whether the description fairly presents the service organisation system and that the controls related to the control objectives stated in the description were suitably designed.

A Type 2 report is a report on the description, design **and operating effectiveness** of controls at a service organization.

In a Type 2 report, in addition to the points reported on for a Type 1 report, the service auditor will **also** express an opinion as to whether the controls tested **operated effectively** throughout the specified period.

Where the auditor cannot agree with the details of the report or is unable to obtain sufficient appropriate evidence, a modified report must be issued.

ISAE 3402 states that the objectives of the service auditor are to obtain reasonable assurance about, and report on, whether, in all material respects, based on suitable criteria:

> the service organisation's description of its system fairly presents the system as designed and implemented throughout the specified period or as at a specified date

> the controls related to the control objectives stated in the service organisation's description of that system were suitably designed throughout the specified period

Assurance Reports on Controls at a Service Organisation

where included in the scope of the engagement, the controls operated effectively to provide reasonable assurance that the control objectives stated in the service organisation's description of its system were achieved throughout the period

The following procedures are **required** under ISAE 3402:

consider acceptance and continuance issues

assess the suitability of the criteria used by the service organisation

consider materiality with respect to the presentation of the description, the suitability of the design of controls and, in the case of a Type 2 report, the operating effectiveness of controls

obtain an understanding of the service organisation's system

obtain evidence regarding the service organisation's description of its system, whether controls implemented to achieve the control objectives are suitably designed and the operating effectiveness of controls (when providing a Type 2 report)

determine whether, and to what extent, to use the work of internal auditors (where there is an internal audit function)

The service auditor must request the service organisation to provide written representations addressed to the service auditor. Written representations must include:

reaffirmation of the statement accompanying the description of the system

that it has provided the service auditor with access to all relevant information access

that it has disclosed to the service auditor (to the extent that it is aware) any non-compliance with laws and regulations, fraud or uncorrected deviations, design deficiencies in controls, instances where controls have not operated as described and subsequent events

The content of a report under ISAE 3402 is similar to that for any other assurance report and it will include a title, addressee, identification of the service organisation's description of its system, identification of the applicable criteria, responsibilities of the service organisation, a statement that the firm applies ISQC 1, a statement that the practitioner complies with the IESBA Code or other professional requirements, summary of the practitioner's procedures and statements on the limitations of controls.

The report must also contain the practitioner's opinion, expressed in a **positive** form.

See also	Internal Controls	177
	ISAE 3402 – example answer points	184

Balanced Scorecard

The 4 perspectives in the Balanced Scorecard

1. **Customer** – targets based on issues that matter to customers such as cost, quality and delivery, customer satisfaction

2. **Internal business** – improving internal process and decision making

3. **Innovation and learning** – ability to maintain competitive position through the acquisition of new skills and the development of new products

4. **Financial** – growth, profitability, market share and shareholder value

Problems with the Balanced Scorecard approach

Managers may not **understand** the measures used (especially if they are not financial specialists)

May be difficult to gain an **overall impression** of the results provided – hence hard to use the results for control action or as a means of determining the levels of bonus

Measures such as production development and cost reduction will **conflict** – may be difficult to determine the balance that will achieve the best results

Care must be taken in **selecting the correct measures** and ensuring that these do not lead to the wrong outcomes

Interpretation is still needed so there will be some **subjectivity**

Managers must be **genuinely committed** to the scorecard or it will not work

Does not provide a single aggregate summary performance measure (unlike ROI or ROCE)

No direct link to creation of shareholder value (unlike EVA®)

Does not necessarily cause the cultural change needed

Requires the organisation to start thinking in a more long term manner, which may be difficult but also risks distracting the business from day to day operational issues

See also		
	Change – Definition & Models	73
	Change – Management & Implementation	75
	Critical Success Factors	92
	Key Performance Indicators	194

Bank Loans

Why use loans rather than other financing methods such as sale of assets, leases or equity?

Advantages

Certain amount received (compared to sale of assets or issue of equity)

Fixed and known repayment schedule (less so if a variable rate of interest applied), which is helpful for planning (compared to an overdraft)

Allows terms of financing and expenditure to be matched to avoid any problems

Disadvantages

Increases gearing (could lead to impact on valuation)

Covenants may need to be offered (loss of control)

Debt capacity

An advantage of degearing now is that if profitable investment opportunities were to present themselves in future, the entity would find it easier to raise debt in order to take advantage of the opportunity – reducing gearing preserves the entity's "debt capacity"

See also	Acquisitions – Financing	29
	Bonds (Loan Notes) v Bank Loans – Comparisons	60
	Loan Decision by a Bank	202
	Overseas Operations – Financing	215

Big Data – audit and data analytics

Data analytics does not relate only to "Big Data"

Data analytics is the process of collecting and examining data in order to extract meaningful business insights, which can be used to inform decision-making and improve performance – can be applied to internal data and external data

Data such as sales or purchases data (part of a company's traditional accounting records) could not really be described as "Big Data"

Data analytics should help both internal and statutory auditors to perform their work by monitoring large, complete data sets rather than testing samples as they may historically have done

Audit data analytics could be used to help the auditor identify trends, correlations and deviations from expected outcomes and/or potential risks in a client's data or control systems

Dashboards and graphics can be used to highlight unusual results – the current year figures could be compared with prior years to gain a deeper understanding of any outliers, variations or trends and to help an auditor determine what further audit tests might be needed to gain assurance over the figures

See also   Big Data topics
Cloud computing 76
Cyber security 95
Digital Strategies 120
Digital Transformation 123

Big Data – ethics

Significant ethical and privacy issues – individuals have a right not have their information shared

Collecting and selling data has become a business with some entities such as data brokers collecting massive amounts of data about individuals – this is likely to be unethical if it is not gathered with their consent

Must ensure compliance with data protection legislation and rules

Likely to be an ethical duty to prevent breach of security and therefore loss of data on customers

Should ensure that data is cleansed and anonymous wherever possible

Increase governance issues within the business to police the correct use of data within the organisation, including respect of legal rules

Overall there is a definite trade-off between privacy and utility of data

See also	Big Data topics	
	Cloud computing	76
	Cyber security	95
	Digital Strategies	120
	Digital Transformation	123

Big Data – general

High-volume, high-velocity and high-variety information assets that demand cost-effective innovative forms of information processes for enhanced insight and decision-making (Gartner)

Also defined as "datasets whose size is beyond the ability of typical database software to capture, store, manage and analyse" (McKinsey) or "the practices and technologies that close the gap between the data available and the ability to turn that data into insight" (Forrester Research)

Exploiting Big Data properly requires skills in computing and manipulation of data, statistical skills to build models and knowledge of business areas to ask the right questions and enable interpretation of the results

This requires teamwork between specialists in IT, data science and different business functions – if organisations do not currently have sufficient staff with the necessary skills, they will either need to recruit additional staff or train existing staff before they are able to take advantage of Big Data

The 4 Vs of Big Data

Volume – large scale or amount of data

Velocity – speed with which "real time" data can now be gathered

Variety – variety of sources and a variety of formats (numerical, narrative, structured, unstructured)

Value – uncertainty regarding reliability so value can vary

Using Big Data

Not just for larger organisations – now much easier for small organisations to use the information due cloud software and lower cost hardware

Confers competitive advantage by providing insights that would otherwise not have been recognised

Ensures that the organisation can keep up with other organisations who are using the same processes

Drives innovation

Allows faster and deeper insights into customers

Analyses information from as many sources as possible

Benefits of Big Data according to McKinsey

Creating transparency

Performance improvement

Market segmentation and customisation

Decision-making

New products and services

Big Data – general

Competitive Benefits of Big Data

Software and hardware advances have led to improvements in processing and storage capability which mean that it is economically viable for businesses to collect and process data from many sources:

> Clickstream data such as searches, sites visited, goods viewed and actual transactions
>
> Social media data such as status updates, comments and likes, photos and videos
>
> Mobile technology is providing more opportunity to create social media and internet data and generates new data about the location of individuals
>
> Open data such as geospatial data or transport data
>
> The internet of things, resulting from computer chips and sensors being embedded in physical assets such as machines or domestic appliances

Current technology means that small companies can also benefit from Big Data analytics

For example, a business could use pattern recognition software to review CCTV footage (used primarily for crime prevention purposes) to understand customer footfall and which areas of the shop people go to, what products they look at and the conversion rates from looking at a product to buying it

The company could also use tools such as "Social Mention" which allow it to track comments made about it on social media and even to provide analysis of those comments

Better quality data should improve managers' ability to monitor and control business activities – it should lead to more accurate reporting, particularly when supported by dashboards that enable continuous monitoring and real-time insight into operations

Having a more detailed understanding of customer behaviour can also be useful in relation to strategic decisions – understanding the customer base of a target business could be an important element in an investment decision: customer loyalty rates could give a valuable insight into the value a business can generate from its customers

To benefit from data, businesses need to move from simply "having it" to getting insight from it and doing something differently as a result

The automation of use of Big Data could help organisations to automate non-routine decision-marking

Computers can hold far more information than humans and can quickly and accurately work through the possible scenarios without making mistakes or suffering from fatigue

Potential Limitations of Big Data

Correlation and not causation – Big Data analysis is good at spotting linkages but does not focus on explaining the cause of any trends and patterns

Sample population may not be representative

More data does not necessarily mean more benefit

Data silos – different parts of the business may not share data sufficiently or efficiently

Increased automation of analysis could lead to risks:

> How will the business know if something has gone wrong?
>
> How will the business correct potential errors?
>
> Will computers actually be better decision-makers than humans? In some scenarios, human knowledge remains vital

Importance of Data Cleansing

Data cleansing may be required if there is a risk that data may be inaccurate, inconsistent or out of date

The risks here are greater for Big Data as the new sources of data could be unreliable or become outdated very quickly

Blind analysis of large scale data sets is likely to lead to significant mistakes

High quality data is achieved by removing inaccurate records before analysis is carried out – this process is called data cleansing

In situations where data is being used to identify more general trends, accuracy may be less important – the data will still correctly identify general trends, even if some of the individual data items are unreliable

See also   Big Data topics
	Cloud computing	76
	Cyber security	95
	Digital Strategies	120
	Digital Transformation	123

Big Data – impact on business models

Big Data can be described in relation to the 4 "V" characteristics:

volume – the bigger the amount of data, the more potential insights it can give in terms of identifying trends and patterns

velocity – the rate at which data flows into an organisation and with which it is processed to provide usable results

variety – the range of data types and sources from which to draw insights – in particular, Big Data combines structured and unstructured data (unstructured data means content such as conversations on social media, photographs or online video postings, and can be contrasted with structured data, which is more traditionally associated with computer storage such as database or spreadsheet information)

Volume and variety present challenges – large data sets are impossible to **capture**, **store** and **process** with standard technology: the sheer **volume** of data can end up **slowing down** a company's **systems** – it can also be a complex challenge to **turn the data into useful information**

value – uncertainty regarding reliability so value can vary

Benefits of Big Data (according to the consultancy firm AT Kearney)

faster decisions – Big Data can provide more frequent, and more accurate, analysis which helps speed up strategic decision-making

better decisions – Big Data can estimate the impact of decisions using cross-organisational analysis and can help to quantify the impact of decisions

proactive decisions – use of predictive analytics to forecast customer market dynamics can help shape decisions

Big Data and competitive advantage (according to the consultancy firm AT Kearney)

Customer insight – Big Data puts the customer at the **heart** of corporate strategy by allowing the company to optimise product offerings in response to changing patterns of consumer demand

Big Data allows retailers, for example, to analyse data points regarding individual products at a **particular time and location** rather than at a more **generalised** store level or product group level as in the past

Insights from the analysis can be used to optimise product assortments by location, time and profitability

Product innovation – an increased level of feedback on how machines are operating through a new breed of connected, intelligent monitoring machines can be used to optimise performance and to forecast maintenance needs

Big Data – impact on business models

Integration of the data generated by these intelligent monitoring machines could be a source of **competitive advantage** for a company which generates the data: customers may switch to such a company if it can **demonstrate improved performance and better management of maintenance** of its own products

Collecting data – the collection of data itself could generate revenues if that data can then be sold onto client companies, subject to Data Protection laws

Similarly, data, and the related analytics, are a **product in their own right** – technology and analytics firms have emerged to provide insights from the data

Simulations – Big Data sets could be valuable in helping companies to run experiments or test hypotheses regarding new products

Operations – detailed, **real-time information** from sensors or radio-frequency identification (RFID) can improve supply chain performance – processes, materials and asset movements can be monitored in real-time – retailers will be able to **monitor stock levels of all products** rather than focusing attention on, for example, the top 100 products which tend to be over- or under-stocked – companies can make use of pricing, promotion and loyalty card data to create deeper insights into what customers buy, and when, allowing retailers to build a **predictive model of distribution** to limit overstocking

It should be noted that Big Data and data analytics are simply a **means to an end** – they are tools which help organisations identify, and then implement, solutions which generate value, or **competitive advantage** – but **only if the data is used in the right way**

Points from SBM November 2017 Mock 2 (Q1 – 7 marks)

Examples of the impact of Data Analytics on a restaurant chain

Demand and pricing

Demand at **individual** restaurants can be **forecast more accurately** – demand could be monitored by menu category at individual restaurants to enable **better planning**

Performance of **individual** restaurants can then be **monitored** more carefully to detect variations – underperforming restaurants can be **targeted for improvement** to ensure that targets are met

Data can then be **aggregated** to enable local and regional management to detect sales trends over time

Comparisons can be made to **rival** restaurants and pricing – potential customers are likely to perform this comparison themselves so such external data will be very useful when entering a new market or region

Operational management

Data analytics will allow managers to **monitor demand for different products in detail** and make informed decisions as a result

Detailed data in **real time** (or near to real time) will help managers to identify which product lines are selling better than others and to respond to this by **changing the mix of products** they offer – it will also allow managers to increase the amount of popular product lines **ordered from suppliers**

Demand on **different** days and at **different** times can be **predicted more accurately** – this will help with staff planning and the ordering of items from suppliers

Customer relationship management

Using data analytics to gather insights from **unstructured data** on social media sites may provide more reliable and informative results than traditional methods such as formal customer surveys – **recurring themes in social media comments** could help to highlight **specific areas for improvement** or allow the company to obtain a **better understanding of customer requirements** – areas of outstanding performance might also be highlighted, allowing the company to take action to **maintain** such performance

Comments will provide information on **what is important to customers** – people are more likely to comment upon something which is important to them

Customer segmentation

Data analytics could be used to identify **different groups of customers** – **targeted** marketing strategies can then be developed and tailored for different customer types, increasing the effectiveness of marketing promotions

Segmentation of customers may also help **increase customer loyalty and retention**

Points from Business Strategy (Professional Level) March 2017 past paper (Q3 – 9 marks)

Big Data encompasses information from multiple internal and external sources – examples from the question Exhibit were then given

Companies can analyse the data and use it to adapt their products to meet customer needs and to find new sources of revenue

The 4 Vs were then defined and applied to the scenario

Use of Big Data can provide a competitive advantage in **marketing & sales**, **inventory & pricing** and **customer service**

> **Marketing & sales** – can establish a customer loyalty scheme to collect data on needs and buying habits – this could be analysed by Data analytics software – social media can be used to gain insights – marketing can be more targeted and can promote related/similar products to those purchased or based on recommendations

> **Inventory & pricing** – can provide a tailored experience and help predict inventory requirements – could help negotiate favourable rates with suppliers as a result – trends can be identified in real time to improve inventory and pricing decisions e.g. automatically offering a price reduction if something is not selling well – discounts could be sent to customers who have not purchased for some time – competitor pricing can be monitored

Big Data – impact on business models

Customer service – feedback can be left and made public via social media – this can help the company to proactively deal with potential issues and respond quickly to any complaints

Practical considerations include connections to IT strategy, cost, skills required, time, impact on customers through any disruption to website code and data protection and security

Data protection and security was given most emphasis in the question – collecting and holding personal data has legal and security implications – the Board must ensure that appropriate controls are in place to prevent customer information falling into the wrong hands and to ensure compliance with the Data Protection Act – accountancy firms and legal advisers can assist here

See also

Big Data topics	
Cloud computing	76
Cyber security	95
Digital Strategies	120
Digital Transformation	123

Bonuses – Audit Procedures

Verify managers' bonuses paid to salary records

Recalculate managers' bonuses

Examine the basis for allocating assets and other key variables to see if accounting policies have been correctly applied

Ascertain whether the level of bonuses is dependent on any other factors and verify these elements by recalculation or inspection of documentation

Ascertain whether managers' bonuses have been authorised by the board

Perform work on the income statement to include checks over cut-off expenditure for the year and also ascertaining whether any significant sales near the year end have influenced the bonus

Examine refunds and credits to customers after the year end to see if there have been any issues

Compare levels of key variables with the previous year and obtain explanations for significant changes

See also   Remuneration Strategies   238

Bonds (Loan Notes) v Bank Loans – Comparisons

Elements of a comparison – look for **differences** between the 2 instruments relating to:

Interest rates

Fixed or variable interest rate? (Plus interaction with expectations of future rates – if future rates are expected to rise, then beneficial to have a fixed rate … and vice versa)

Issue costs (tend to be higher for bonds)

Time period of the instrument and refinancing risk – shorter time may need renewing

Cash flow/liquidity benefits in paying later (e.g. zero coupon bond) – but will there be a large payment at the end rather than gradual payments over time as with a bank loan?

Interest rate risk

Fair value risk

Gearing – both types increase gearing, but how much and how volatile will interest rates be?

Covenant risk

Availability risk – bonds may not be taken up or not taken up in full (use underwriting) and bank loans may not always be offered

Do not forget to give a reasoned conclusion and recommendations about which option is best, making scenario-specific points

Financial reporting

IS – effective rate of interest

SFP – liability based on opening amount plus interest less cash paid – assess whether a current or non-current liability

SCF – cash actually paid

Bonds – Standard Narrative Points

Discuss cash flow and immediate business impact versus Effective Interest Rate and financial reporting impact

Consider timing – a zero coupon bond has no payments until the final day but then has a large single cash flow including the premium amount

Bonds (Loan Notes) v Bank Loans – Comparisons

Consider impact of exchange rate if applicable

Risk versus cost – perhaps one bond has a cheaper financing costs but is there more risk from a covenant, for example?

See also Acquisitions – Financing 29
Bank Loans 49
Loan Decision by a Bank 202
Overseas Operations – Financing 215

Branding and Rebranding (IFRS 13)

What is needed to create a strong brand?

Genuine commitment by key stakeholders and Board support

Detailed research to understand the position and market

Time – needs to be established for some time (NB QB question suggests less than 5 years not enough) – a brand can only be developed over time

Product quality

Reputation for good customer service

Ethical business practices including concerns for health and safety and relevant legislation

Avoid reputation risks – identify these in advance and take action

Marketing including advertising

Should a strong brand be built or should we wait? (According to QB)

If a fairly new company and a relatively small competitor in the market, brand strategy may be a longer term issue

May be important to build quality, service and reputation just to keep the business going rather than specifically to create a strong brand image

Brand Valuation under IFRS 13

Internally generated brands are not recognised as intangible assets under IAS 38 and so will not be recorded on the SFP but there may be a need to value before an acquisition or disposal (to help management determine a suitable price to pay/receive) and then if the acquisition/disposal takes place that value may be needed for financial reporting purposes as well

IFRS 13, paragraph 9: fair value is "the price that would be received to sell an asset or paid to transfer a liability in an orderly transaction between market participants at the measurement date"

IFRS 13 requires us to determine FV based on "highest and best use" from a market participant's perspective – acquirer permitted to assume that current use is highest and best use without searching for alternatives unless market or other factors suggest otherwise

Level 1 inputs – quoted prices in an active market – not normally relevant as a brand is unique

Level 2 inputs – other observable prices e.g. in non-active markets such as a recent bid

Level 3 inputs – unobservable inputs, including internal company data

Methods set out in IFRS 13:

Market basis – market price and other market transactions – difficult if brand is unique

Income basis – present value of **incremental** income generated by the brand, considering value including any possible price premium effect and additional sales

Branding and Rebranding (IFRS 13)

Cost basis – current replacement cost of the brand, which might be estimated as the present value of the advertising and other expenditure needed to set up an equivalent brand, including an allowance for risk and how expenditure could replicate the brand in varying market conditions (this requires a large amount of judgement and estimation, hence apply **professional scepticism** – see page 224)

FR implications of rebranding via an acquisition

IFRS 3 *Business Combinations* applies

May give rise to 2 different types of intangible asset: trade names and goodwill

Trade names

Acquiring other brand names means that future economic benefits are attributable

The trade names are also separable and identifiable

So prior to rebranding, there may be right to carry as separate intangible assets under IAS 38

Following the rebranding it is unlikely that the trade names will continue to have any separate value

Any remaining amounts will have to be written off and charge to profit or loss

Goodwill

An asset which is initially measured at cost (being the excess of consideration over fair value of all identifiable assets, liabilities and contingent liabilities)

These assets would include the trade names of the acquired chains of retail outlets

Measured at cost less impairment losses and is not amortised but tested annually for impairment

Rebranding should not affect goodwill as this is an historic amount and is not remeasured just because of a change in business activities

However there may be impairment considerations in the case of those acquired businesses which have already been identified as underperforming

Impairment tests should be carried out under IAS 36 by allocating the goodwill to cash generating units and testing these by comparing the carrying amount of the unit, including the goodwill, with the recoverable amount

Look out for a possible **gain on a bargain purchase** – this occurs if the purchaser pays less than the FV of the net assets acquired – this has been quite common in SBM mocks and was also common under the previous Business Change syllabus

If a gain on a bargain purchase occurs, IFRS 3 requires the entity to reassess the identification and measurement of assets and liabilities acquired and, if a gain on a bargain purchase still occurs after this reassessment, to recognise immediately in profit or loss any gain on a bargain purchase (negative goodwill) remaining after the reassessment

Branding and Rebranding (IFRS 13)

FR implications of rebranding with significant business changes

IAS 16 PPE issues? Cost of refits and changed signage for the new brand should be capitalised as non-current assets in line with IAS 16 – depreciate over a reasonable number of years (e.g. the standard refit period of the company) and charge to profit or loss

Disposal issues? Write off capital assets no longer used under IAS 16 rules or perhaps profit or loss on disposal if can be sold? Charged to profit or loss

Marketing costs should be expensed as incurred and charged to profit or loss

Development costs – consider whether these can be capitalised or not

Exam tip – Do not forget the obvious points on how something is treated in the IS or SFP – the client still needs to know this

Social Media and Brand Value

With the advent of social media and its ability to influence public opinion, a brand's value/company reputation can be affected very rapidly by adverse comments about it

Acquisitions and Brand Value

If an acquiring company does not research a brand properly, it could risk overpaying for assets which have lost their value or which may not translate effectively into the business environment facing the post-acquisition group – this is particularly important in marketplaces facing the threat of new entrants or the disruption of business models

Therefore due diligence should take place before the final decision to acquire a brand is taken

See also	Acquisitions topics	
	Cash Flow Forecasts – Evaluation	72
	Marketing Strategies	203
	Valuation topics	

Brexit

Exam tip – whilst you may gain some credit for mentioning Brexit, we do not recommend that you write more than a couple of sentences maximum unless the question strongly indicates that it is a major issue in the specific question being asked – also ensure that your own personal political views do not influence your points!

Could have an impact on various elements of the PESTEL framework

Could affect the attractiveness of the UK as a business location

Arguments of those who voted to leave the EU

High levels of immigration

Excessive bureaucracy

Desire for the UK to negotiate its own way in the world

Decline in the value of the pound could drive higher exports

Arguments of those who voted to remain in the EU

Easier selling of goods and services to other EU countries

Economic benefits provided by a migrant workforce

Easier for UK businesses to send money, people, products and services around the world

Could cause economic harm as the UK may lose access to markets and trade deals

Decline in the pound and stockmarkets – the UK lost its AAA credit rating

Decline in the value of the pound to the lowest levels against the dollar since 1985, increasing costs

Strong sense of uncertainty created

Article 50 allows 2 years for the two sides to agree terms

The terms of Britain's exit will have to be agreed by 27 countries, involving the unravelling of 43 years' worth of treaties and agreements – this process will take a long time – a new trade deal between the EU and the UK needs to be set up

On 2 February 2017, the UK government released its White Paper which outlined its approach to leaving the EU – this document covered the UK's exit from, and new relationship with, the EU, along with its strategic aims

The demands of other EU member countries will determine what Brexit finally looks like – it is probable that the 2 years allowed under Article 50 will not be enough time to get all the new arrangements in place

In the meantime, EU law still applies in the UK for as long as it remains a member

Business Plans

Elements

Statutory data

Executive summary

Marketing

Product/service details

Management team

Plant & equipment

Start-up costs

Business plan

Summary

Appendices

Constructing a business plan

Cash flows really are key here

Cash inflows

Cash sales
Cash from receivables
Interest receipts
New finance issues

Cash outflows

Payments to payables
Capital expenditure
Loan repayments
Interest payments
Tax payments
Dividend payments

Check for timing differences and the impact on the business

Evaluating a Business Plan

Are the sales and revenue forecasts reasonable and achievable? Compare to external data and estimates, looking at capacity and consideration of any limiting factors

Are costs understated and has account been taken of inflation (meaning specific inflation rates for the different elements of cost, and not just the general overall rate)? Do the costs reflect expansion possibilities?

Are market share projections realistic? This could be assessed again external market research data

See also	Change – Definition & Models	73
	Change – Management & Implementation	75
	Professional Scepticism	224
	Prospective Information (ISAE 3400)	226

CAPM

$k_e = r_f + \beta_e (r_m - r_f)$

Based on the principle that risks and rewards of investment need to be appropriately balanced

The model calculates the reward expected from a given security, considering the risk of that security – this indicates the market price required

Total risk is made up of systematic and unsystematic risk

Unsystematic risk is unique to the security and therefore not to the economic system/market (hence **un**systematic risk) – this may relate to the nature of the company and its activities

Systematic risk is based on the risk associated with general market and economic factors

The average risk of all securities is measured by a beta value of 1

If the beta is more than 1, then the security is more risky than average and vice versa

Risk works in both directions – if the market were to rise by 10% overall, then an asset with a beta of 1.5 would rise by 15% because its risk is 1.5 times the average market value

Unsystematic risk is unique to the particular company being considered – this can be diversified away by investing in a greater range of companies

Systematic risk cannot be diversified away – the economic system is inherently risky and this cannot be avoided

Worked Example

Example plc has a beta of 1.8. The risk-free rate of return is 4% and the average market return is 8%.

Explain what each of these figures means and calculate Example's cost of capital using CAPM. Explain what CAPM is doing.

Beta of 1.8 – this means that the required return on Example plc's shares will change by 1.8 times the change in the return required for the market in general (increase or decrease). This suggests that Example plc has relatively volatile and high risk shares.

Risk-free rate of return of 4% – this means that investors can get a return of 4% by investing in the safest asset class available (probably government bonds). This is therefore the minimum rate of return an investor can achieve at no risk – shares, which involve higher risk, must therefore offer more.

Average market return of 8% – this means that the market is generally paying 8% on the cost of shares.

Cost of capital = 4% + (1.8 x (8% - 4%)) = 11.2%

The 4% at the start of the equation sets the minimum possible cost of capital (the minimum an investor will demand, given that they can get 4% on risk free government bonds).

By finding 8% - 4% in the brackets we are saying that the premium for investing in the market in general is a further 4%. We then multiply this by 1.8, which is the specific beta of Example plc, to adjust this risk premium up for the specific case. This means that investors should require 7.2% for investing in Example plc, on top of the 4% risk free element.

Degearing and Regearing Example

Apply the formula

$\beta e = \beta a [(E + D(1 – T)) / E]$

Example

A company is considering a new business venture: the company has a debt:equity ratio of 2:3 which will remain in place after the new project starts. A company in the prospective area has an equity beta of 1.20 and a debt:equity ratio of 1:2 and the taxation rate is 20%.

We have all the figures except βa, the asset beta for a company in the new market sector (i.e. the pure beta which is not affected by the financing structure used). So we first extract this and then run the formula again with our company's data

Ungear to find βa for the market sector

$1.2 = \beta a [(2 + 1(1-0.20)) / 2]$

$1.2 = 1.4 \beta a$

$\beta a = 0.857$

Regear to find βe for our company

$\beta e = 0.857 [(3 + 2(1-0.2)) / 3]$

$\beta e = 1.314$

Limitations of CAPM

Forecast figures should really be used to look at future excess return but in practice historical returns are used

Need to determine a risk-free rate – in practice interest rates vary with the term of the lending so this is harder to do than it may seem

Errors in statistical analysis used to calculate beta values

Historical betas may be a poor basis

Beta values change over time

CAPM

Model is unable to forecast accurately returns for companies with low price/earnings ratio or to take account of seasonality month of the year or day of the week effects

Financial managers should use betas for industrial sectors rather than individual company betas as then measurement errors will tend to cancel each other out

CAPM fails to take into account the ways in which returns are paid – investors may prefer dividends or capital gains and will invest in the relevant companies accordingly

See also   Valuations topics

Cash Flow Forecasts – Evaluation

Check for any **material omitted figures**

Check for any **material underestimates**

Consider whether the **forecast is full enough** – does it extend beyond gross profit activities or operating activities to include all relevant cash flows (e.g. CAPEX and taxation)?

Have any **finance costs** been omitted? (e.g. if there is not enough cash to make necessary purchases, credit will be needed but has this been allowed for in the model?) Consider an appropriate interest rate, taking into account the changes being considered (e.g. a higher gearing rate may increase the interest rate charged)

Has **enough been allocated to key categories** such as the advertising spend, administrative costs, new staff costs and CAPEX, etc?

Do **cost savings and synergies appear unrealistic**?

Do **variable costs change in line with activity** (e.g. staff costs, material costs, taxation figures)?

Use your professional scepticism – are there any reasons to think that the forecast could be biased (intentionally or otherwise)? Has the forecast been prepared by a manager who is keen to retain his or her job, for example, and has it therefore been estimated too generously?

See also		
	Business Plans	67
	Prospective Information (ISAE 3400)	226
	Valuations – Free Cash Flow Model	293

Change – Definition & Models

CAMPS – change affects:

Costs
Accounting treatment
Markets
People
Systems

Factors promoting change

External – competitor behaviour, buyer behaviour, technology, economic events

Internal – changes in leadership style, individuals, groups, stakeholders, response to external events

Levels of change

- Strategic
- Process/operational

Types of change

- Predictable v unpredictable
- Adaptive/minor v fundamental/major
- Incremental v transformational

Barriers to change

- Groups and group thinking
- Culture
- Individuals, especially powerful or important individuals
- Personnel
- Stakeholders, including groups of stakeholders

Lewis & Schein

Unfreeze	create motive for change to remove individual and group barriers
Move	identify new behaviour and communicate and/or create new culture
Refreeze	consolidation and reinforcement of new behaviour

Change – Definition & Models

Types of reinforcement

Positive – praise and reward

Negative – sanctions and punishment for those who deviate

Gemini 4 Rs

Reframe

Restructure

Revitalise

Renewal

See also Big Data topics
Change – Management & Implementation

Change – Management & Implementation

General overview of change process

Determine need or desire for a particular change

Prepare a tentative plan which considers alternatives (brainstorming)

Analyse probable reactions

Take a decision from alternative options

Establish a timetable

Communicate the plan

Implement the change

Review the change, via continuous evaluation

Communication of the plan – possible stakeholders and their concerns

Shareholders	share price, profits, dividends
Staff	job security and earnings
Management	involvement, impact on power and control
Customers	availability of product, quality, price, reliability including delivery
Financial press/analysts	how and why decision has been made, impact on share price and profits

Project life cycle model

Define – identify the need served

Design – find an approach that leads to maximum added value

Deliver – develop a clear and feasible timetable

Develop – post-implementation review to determine whether the change in processes was as efficient as it could be and that expected value is being obtained

See also	Big Data topics	
	Change – Definition & Models	73

© ACA Simplified 2018. No copying or reproduction permitted.

Cloud computing

Cloud computing can be defined as "a model for enabling ubiquitous, convenient, on demand access to a shared pool of configurable computing resources that can be rapidly provisioned and released with minimal management effort or service provider interaction"

In effect, cloud computing is access to business services through the internet – this includes **software as a service**, **a platform as a service** or **infrastructure as a service** (for example, data storage and backup).

Benefits of cloud computing

cost effectiveness – removes the **capital cost** required for buying hardware and replaces this expenditure with revenue costs for the services that an organisation uses

flexibility – allows companies the capacity to **scale up or down** as required, which could be ideal for businesses with growing or fluctuating demand

speed – establishing a cloud-based approach to data storage and management can be done **faster** than establishing the same technology in-house

accessibility – data is accessible **anywhere around the world** where there is internet connectivity – this can promote more effective collaboration between teams at different locations, including by improved document control through **central storage of a single version of files** (reducing the risk of conflicting versions, formats and so on if colleagues send multiple documents by email rather than using a centrally-stored, single document cloud approach)

availability – cloud computing is available **both** to **larger** organisations and **very small** entities alike – **small companies** can then adopt the latest cutting-edge technology **without the need for significant capital investment**

automatic software updates – these are rolled out on a **regular and automatic basis** by the cloud service provider so organisations **do not have to worry about updating** system software or systems themselves

Risks of cloud computing

entrustment of data – company data must be entrusted to the cloud so it is essential that the service provider's infrastructure is **secure** – there is an **increased risk** that the data held by the service provider may be **stolen**, **lost** or **corrupted** (not only by hackers but also by the service provider's own staff)

outages – even the best cloud service providers can suffer **technical issues** or there could be more serious **connectivity** issues preventing an organisation from connecting to the cloud so it will be important to have a **plan** to deal with such **disruption**

lack of diminishing marginal cost – if a company invests in its own capital infrastructure and significantly increases demand, it will be able to **spread the initial fixed cost over a larger and larger volume of output** whereas if it uses a cloud computing service then it could be **locked into** increasing costs as it grows because the service provider may not necessarily provide any **discount** for very large volumes of activity

Cloud computing

Issues to consider before transferring information to a public cloud (ICAEW paper *Security and Assurance in the Cloud*)

Data privacy, risk and security – if the information is **critical** to the business, or an organisation **cannot be reassured** that information will be adequately **protected**, then information should probably **not** be moved to the cloud – the organisation should also consider if there is a practical way to **encrypt** sensitive information before it is **uploaded** to the cloud

Access and identity – the potential cloud service provider should be asked about how it **controls** access to data – in particular, the organisation will need to know how staff and customers are **identified** and **given access** – if data is held in an environment alongside data from other clients, there must be effective **access separation** and **confidentiality protection**

Resilience and business continuity – the organisation should ask how the service provider deals with **outages** and **backups** of data

Regulatory compliance – the organisation should consider any **regulatory** or **legal** restrictions which could affect a move to the cloud: for example, are there any restrictions which require the organisation to process (or not process) information in a specific jurisdiction or country?

Assurance – the organisation should consider seeking **assurance** from potential service providers around key aspects of the service they provide in relation to their plans for data security, service outage, recovery and other key issues before entering into any contract with them – **the organisation should work through a comparative evaluation of the different providers on the market**, identifying the provider which best fits its needs, rather than simply engaging the first provider that it finds – the organisation may wish to request that an assurance report on the service provider's systems be carried out under ISAE 3402

Cloud computing versus owned technology

The **balance** between **benefits** and **risks** (see above) becomes critical for senior management

Organisations with IT staff that possess the levels of **expertise** required to manage an IT system may prefer to **retain** data storage and data management **in-house**

Complex data **compliance** requirements or a **risk-averse** attitude will make **in-house** management more likely

For organisations (particularly **smaller** and **medium-sized** entities) that need a multi-national or global presence but **lack the necessary IT expertise and resources** to manage their data and infrastructure in-house, a **cloud-based** approach may be appropriate

A related question is: **what data** will be stored in the cloud? Will **personal data** be part of the data accessed or stored in a cloud computing service? An organisation must **still comply** with data protection laws even if it uses external providers – the **organisation** is likely to be considered to be the "**data controller**" for legal purposes, with the **cloud service provider** simply being the "**data processor**"

Cloud computing

Assurance over cloud services

ISAE 3402 provides guidance regarding any assurance work over the services provided by another organisation – see our notes on **ISAE 3402 – example answer points** starting on page **184** of these Exam Room Notes.

Under this standard, the objectives of the service auditor are to obtain **reasonable assurance** about whether, in all **material** respects, and based on suitable **criteria**:

- the service organisation's **description** of its system **fairly presents** the system as designed and implemented throughout the specified period or as at a specified date

- the **controls** related to the control objectives stated in the service organisation's description of its system were **suitably designed** throughout the specified period

- where included in the scope of the engagement ("**Type 2 report**"), the controls **in fact operated effectively** to provide reasonable assurance that the control objectives stated in the service organisation's description of its system were achieved **throughout the period analysed**

Security and the cloud (ICAEW document "Cloud adoption – Understanding the risk of cloud services")

It is **impossible** to **guarantee** that data can be **totally secure** – the level of security deemed necessary will depend on the value of the data in the users' eyes

The following questions should be asked as best practice:

-is the platform regularly tested by third-party "**penetration testers**" for potential vulnerabilities? Do such testers vigorously test the platform to determine whether an attacker could gain unauthorised access?

-what is the process in the event of a **security breach** being determined?

-is data held on the platform stored in an **encrypted** format?

-is **payment data** held on a platform which complies with the payment card industry's data security standard (**PCI DSS**)?

-is the platform protected against "**denial of service**" attacks, where attackers could prevent access to the service indefinitely by flooding the platform with erroneous traffic or requests for information?

See also	Big Data topics	
	Cyber security	95
	Digital Strategies	120
	Digital Transformation	123

Compilation Engagements

Collection, classification and compilation of financial information. In this type of engagement, the accountant is using his or her **accounting** expertise rather than **auditing** expertise. The process is governed by **ISRS 4410**.

Example outputs from this process include historical financial information, pro forma financial information and prospective financial information including financial budgets and forecasts.

There should be agreement on:

- the intended use and distribution of the financial information and any restrictions on its use or distribution

- identification of the applicable financial reporting framework

- the objective and scope of the engagement

- the responsibilities of the practitioner, including the requirement to comply with relevant ethical requirements

- the responsibilities of management for the accuracy and completeness of the information and records and documents

- the expected form and content of the practitioner's report

The practitioner works to **obtain an understanding of the entity's business and operations**, including the accounting system and records and the applicable financial reporting framework. **The specific nature of the work varies considerably, depending on the nature of the engagement.**

If the practitioner becomes aware that the information provided by management is incomplete, inaccurate or otherwise unsatisfactory then the practitioner must bring this to the attention of management and request additional or corrected information. The practitioner must withdraw from the engagement and inform management/those charged with governance if management fail to provide this information and the engagement cannot be completed or if management refuse to make the amendments proposed by the practitioner.

The practitioner obtains an acknowledgement from management/those charged with governance that they take responsibility for the information in its final form. The practitioner's report should contain the following elements:

- a statement that the practitioner has used the information provided by management

- a description of the responsibilities of management or those charged with governance

Compilation Engagements

- identification of the applicable financial reporting framework and any special purpose financial reporting framework

- identification of the financial information, including the titles of each element of the financial information

- a description of the practitioner's responsibilities in compiling the financial information

- a **description** of what a compilation engagement entails

- explanation that the compilation engagement is **not an assurance engagement** and therefore the practitioner is not required to verify the accuracy or completeness of the information provided by management

- explanation that the practitioner does not express an audit opinion or a review conclusion on whether the financial information is prepared in accordance with a financial reporting framework

- an explanatory paragraph which describes the purpose of the financial information and which draws the attention of readers to the fact that the information may not be suitable for other purposes, if it is the case that a special purpose framework has been used

Suspected non-compliance with laws and regulations

Under ISRS 4410, the practitioner should always consult internally, obtain legal advice and consult with the regulator or professional body in order to understand the implications of different courses of action

Convertible Bonds

Split into equity and liability elements

Comment on need to unwind the liability element (look out for time apportionment here) and consider whether it is a current or non-current liability

Use round thousands to make the calculation quicker – the examiner just wants to see the principle

Worked Example

Show the split accounting of the following compound instrument:

Issue of 10,000 6% convertible bonds at par of £100

Each bond is redeemable at par or convertible into 4 shares in 2 years

The market rate of interest for similar debt without the conversion option is 8%

The value of the bonds is £100 x 10,000 = £1m

Annual interest is based on the **nominal or coupon** amount of 6%, so £60,000 per year

Always discount at the market rate of interest EXCLUDING the conversion option

So discount the cash flows at 8%

In this case, there will be three cash flows: £60,000 interest in year 1, £60,000 interest in year 2, and £1,000,000 redemption in year 2

The PV of these flows gives us the liability element

The balancing figure is the equity element

	Cash flow @ 6%	DF @ 8%	PV
Year 1	60,000	1/1.08	55,556
Year 2	1,060,000	1/1.08/1.08	908,779
Liability element			964,335
Equity element Balancing figure			35,665 (B)
Total proceeds			1,000,000

There will be impacts on the financial statements in the intervening period before conversion

profitability/income statement
finance cost on the unwinding of the liability element (check for time appointment issues)

statement of financial position
liability element will increase due to unwinding, increasing gearing

Convertible Bonds

Narrative points

Likely take up in the market – are the terms attractive?

Investors are generally willing to accept a lower interest yield

Unusual instruments – not many real world issues

Advise client to take advice from an investment bank

See also		
	Acquisitions – Financing	29
	Bank Loans	49
	Bonds (Loan Notes) v Bank Loans -- Comparisons	60
	Finance – Sources for SMEs	131

Corporate Governance – Definition and Concepts

Corporate governance can be defined as "the system by which organisations are directed and controlled". We would advise you to start your answer with this definition, before applying this to the scenario given.

CG is used to:

- Reduce risk

- Specify distribution rights and responsibilities between different stakeholders

- Specify rules and procedures for corporate decisions

- Provide a structure through which objectives are set

- Provide a framework for ethical and other safeguards

- Promote new investment and confidence in companies

Fundamentally, as a matter of good governance the board should have clear strategic objectives

The board should also establish its risk appetites and framework for considering risks

Indicators of CG problems

- Domination by a single individual

- Lack of involvement of the Board

- Lack of an adequate control function, including internal audit

- Lack of supervision due to systems deficiencies or a lack of segregation of key roles

- Lack of independent scrutiny by the external auditors

- Lack of contact with shareholders

- Emphasis on short-term profitability rather than long term investment

- Misleading accounts and information

- Persistent board disagreements between Executive Directors and NEDs

Evaluation of Corporate Governance Mechanisms

- **Reviewing minutes** of the meetings of the board of directors

- **Reviewing supporting documents** prepared for the board of directors

- **Making inquiries of certain directors** and the company secretary

- **Attending meetings of the audit committee** at which the annual report and accounts are considered and approved

- **Making appropriate enquiries** and reviewing the statements made by the board

- **Reporting by exception** if problems arise such as the board summary not reflecting the auditors' understanding of that process or there has been a failure to disclose or conduct an annual review

Key Points in the April 2016 update to the UK Corporate Governance Code

The audit committee is required to have "competence relevant to the sector in which the company operates"

The audit committee report within the annual report must provide "advance notice of any retendering plans"

The provision that FTSE 350 companies are expected to put the audit out to tender at least every 10 years has been removed – but note that this has been replaced with the EU Audit Regulation and Directive requirements for mandatory tendering and rotation of the audit firm.

Corporate Governance Concepts

Leadership	The role of the board
	Division of responsibilities
	The Chairman
	NEDs
Effectiveness	Composition of the board
	Appointments to the board
	Commitment of time
	Development
	Information and support
	Evaluation
	Re-election
Accountability	Financial reporting
	Risk management and internal control
	Audit committees and auditors
Remuneration	The level and components of remuneration
	Procedure
Relations with stakeholders	Dialogue with shareholders
	Constructive use of the AGM

See also Corporate Governance – Past Paper Points 86
Corporate Governance – The Board and NEDs 87

Corporate Governance – Past Paper Points

Summary of Key Corporate Governance Points (see past paper review in *Smashing SBM*™)

- Ensure that you can offer a **brief definition of CG** and **explain why it is necessary**

- Ensure that you can spot the **warning signs** or "**red flags**" which could indicate a **CG problem**

- Consider mentioning the **basic aspects of the UK Corporate Governance Code** but check whether this will apply in the scenario (if not (for example, an AIM-listed company), then just apply the same concepts but state that the Code would be "best practice", so many stakeholders may wish to see the Code followed anyway)

- Indicate the **roles of the Board and NEDs** (including **advantages and disadvantages of NEDs**)

- Indicate **procedures** relating to the **testing of CG at the Board level**

- Consider **stakeholders and their interests**, applying **scepticism to any proposed changes**

- Look at the **existing and potential balance of power**, always considering the **key cut off points of 75% and 50% shareholdings**

- Discuss some possible ways of **improving CG** and the **operation of Boards**

- **Identify different stakeholder groups** and try to provide some **different points for each group**, perhaps under headings, to show the impact of a CG change

Going concern – listed companies

The UK Listing Rules require premium listed companies to include in the annual report a statement that the company is a going concern

The UK Code of Corporate Governance requires directors to state whether they consider it appropriate to adopt the going concern basis of accounting – any material uncertainty should be disclosed

A company's strategic report must include a description of the principal risks and uncertainties facing the company – there should be a statement about how these are being managed or mitigated and a statement about the longer term viability of the business

See also		
	Corporate Governance – Definition and Concepts	83
	Corporate Governance – The Board and NEDs	87
	Shareholding Percentages – Narrative Comments	259

Corporate Governance – The Board and NEDs

The Role of the Board

- **decisions on fundamental matters** to the business such as mergers and takeovers, acquisitions, investments, capital projects, bank borrowing facilities and loans

- monitoring the **Chief Executive Officer**

- overseeing **strategy**

- monitoring **risks and control systems**

- monitoring the **human capital aspects** of the company regarding succession, morale, training and remuneration

- ensuring that there is **effective communication of its strategic plans**, both internally and externally

Non-Executive Directors – Roles, Advantages and Disadvantages

The **roles** of NEDs are:

- **Strategic** – NEDs contribute to, and challenge, strategy

- **Performance** – NEDs scrutinise performance of management in meeting goals and objectives

- **Risk** – NEDs should ensure that financial information is accurate and that controls are robust

- **Remuneration and succession** – NEDs should be responsible for determining appropriate levels of remuneration for executives and should be key figures in the appointment and removal of senior managers and in succession planning

Some **advantages** of having NEDs on the Board include[3]:

- possess **external experience and knowledge** which executive directors do not have

- can provide a **wider perspective**

- **provide comfort to third parties** such as investors or creditors

- can play **certain important roles** such as father-confessor (being a confidant for the chairman and other directors), an oil-can (making the Board run more effectively) and acting as high sheriff (removing the chairman or chief executive if necessary).

---

[3] If your SBM client is relatively small and perhaps family-owned, then the client will be missing out on these advantages so this should give you something to discuss.

- **dual role** as full Board members but also having a strong, independent element

Some **problems** with having NEDs on the Board include:

- may **lack independence**

- may not include people **other than those proposed by the Board**

- the **best candidates for an NED role might naturally work at the best-run companies** anyway i.e. companies that do not need any input from good NEDs

- may have **difficulty in imposing their views** on the Board

- may not **pay enough attention** to preventing trouble or advising on the early warning signs of a problem

- **limited amount of time** to devote to the role

Independence of NEDs

When assessing the independence of NEDs, consider:

- whether the NED has been an **employee of the company in the last 5 years**

- whether the NED has had a **material business relationship** with his or her company as a result of serving in a senior role with another company

- whether the NED receives **additional remuneration** apart from a director's fee or participates in share options or pension schemes

- whether the NED has any **close family ties** with the company's advisers, directors or senior employees

- whether the NED holds **cross-directorships** or has significant links with other directors or through involvement in other companies or bodies

- whether the NED has a **significant shareholder**

- whether the NED has **served on the Board for a substantial period of time**

Establishing an effective Group Control Framework

Ensure that each subsidiary has both responsibility for performance and the ability to control that performance – e.g. if the subsidiary will be monitored based on ROCE then the subsidiary should have control over its capital base and have the ability to borrow funds

Consider the alternatives of centralised control on a divisionalised basis or giving more autonomy to the management of the subsidiary for local decisions (while maintaining accountability to the parent Board for overall performance)

A more localised decision-making should lead to more rapid decisions being made

A more localised decision-making could also incentivise managers to improve performance as their actions can now impact on that performance

The main Board should set clear objectives and monitor achievement of these objectives – the subsidiary should have control over the means required to achieve objectives

Listed Companies and Going Concern

The UK Corporate Governance Code requires the Board:

- To make disclosures on the going concern basis of accounting and material uncertainties in the financial statements

- To disclose principal risks and uncertainties, which may include risks that might impact solvency and liquidity

- To take a broad view, over the long term, of the risks and uncertainties that go **beyond** the specific requirements of accounting standards – narrative disclosures should consider going concern over a period which **exceeds** the time period specified in accounting standards

- To explain the risk management and control processes in place that will underpin their assessment and that the degree of formality of this process is consistent with the size, complexity and particular circumstances of the entity

See also   Corporate Governance – Definition and Concepts   83
Corporate Governance – The Board and NEDs   87

Corporate Social Responsibility (CSR)

Why apply CSR?

Ethically correct approach

Could have strategic value – promoting image of the company to customers

Analysis Frameworks for the Examination

Stakeholders – always consider a **range** of affected stakeholders – for example:

- Employees
- Shareholders
- Customers
- Government
- Local residents
- Supply chain

Risks – consider the potential risks from not following CSR – for example:

- Legal risks – costs, fines
- Reporting risks if CSR is reported (e.g. quoted) – will breach reported commitments
- Reputation risk – poor reputation will mean stakeholders do not want to deal with the company

Other Exam Tips

A business is a business – it is not a charity and it is not the government – it is not responsible for making everyone happy at all times – **consider the limits of CSR**: is the company always responsible to all stakeholders or are there limits?[4] This consideration will add valuable **nuance** to your answer.

Corporate Social Responsibility versus Sustainability

Correct to distinguish the terms as they are different but related

Sustainability can refer both to protecting resources such that future generations can enjoy a prosperous existence and also to how a business can ensure that it develops and succeeds commercially

Corporate Social Responsibility focuses more on ethical responsibilities – the first meaning of sustainability (environmental) may be one of these but there will be further CSR responsibilities in addition such as responsibilities to its work force, helping local communities and promoting the interests of society more generally – CSR is about the company being a good citizen in its society

See also	Corporate Governance topics	
	Ethics topics	
	Stakeholders and Stakeholder Management	261

---

[4] Example from an SBM past paper: a commitment to provide employment to a specific group of employees 10 years ago arguably no longer has implications for the same business today.

Costs of Quality

Prevention costs – costs to prevent non-conforming units being produced

Appraisal costs – costs to ensure that materials and products that fail to meet quality standards are identified prior to shipment

Internal failure costs – costs of scrappage and costs incurred in correcting errors caught at the appraisal stage but before delivery to the customer

External failure costs – costs arising from inadequate quality discovered after the transfer of ownership from the supplier to the purchaser (complaints, warranty claims and recall costs)

Problems with using a Costs of Quality approach

Really it is external costs that matter – these are what will lose future business so the other costs are actually just ways of minimising external costs so there will be a trade off between the costs of the other 3 areas and the impact on external costs

There are also trade offs between the other 3 types of cost – e.g. spending more to prevent problems (prevention costs) is likely to leave a lower budget available for appraisal and internal failure costs

Must evaluate the benefits and costs of the quality control costs rather than assuming that it is always sensible to spend more to get a quality improvement … but the negative impact on customer goodwill is hard to measure

See also	Supply Chain Improvements	267
	Working Capital	305

Critical Success Factors

"Key goals/issues vital to the success of an organisation (sometimes associated with product features, but can be applied more broadly)"

Some example CSFs

Note – ensure these are relevant to the scenario as CSFs will vary widely depending on what industry we are looking at – the below are just some suggestions

High levels of customer service

Wide product range

Speed of product delivery

Quality products

Staff training and development

Use of CSFs

Identification of CSFs helps alert management to things that need controlling

CSFs can be turned into Key Performance Indicators for periodic reporting

CSFs can guide the development of information systems

Can be used for benchmarking organisational performance internally

See also		
	Balanced Scorecard	48
	Key Performance Indicators	194

Currency Risks

Mnemonic TET

Transaction risk — adverse short term movements during ordinary progress of business

Economic risk — effect of exchange rates over the longer term on international competitiveness of a company

Translation risk — risk of exchange losses when translating foreign branches/subsidiaries into home currency

Commercial impact of a change in exchange rates

A significant decline in sterling will make imports of raw materials and commodities (often priced in non-sterling currencies such as the US dollar) more expensive

Manufacturers in the UK then face a choice – either try to pass on the higher costs to consumers by increasing their prices or keep prices unchanged and absorb the higher costs themselves through lower profit margins

But a decline in sterling could benefit UK exporters – if sterling declines in value then other currencies must be rising in value so each time we earn a unit of foreign currency then this will translate into more units of sterling than previously – alternatively if we are happy to continue to earn the same number of units of sterling, we can cut our foreign currency price to do so at the new lower exchange rate: cutting prices will help to penetrate the market

See also Hedging topics
Overseas operations topics

Customer Relationship Management (CRM)

CRM involves the use of database technology and IT systems to help an organisation develop long-term and mutually valuable relationships with its customers

An effective CRM system involves a comprehensive database which can be accessed whenever the customer interacts with the company

This could include website transactions, contact with sales teams, queries and other order processing functions

All employees in customer facing processes should coordinate their efforts so that the customer receives a consistent and suitable service such as targeted marketing – this means that employees in sales, customer service and marketing will need to work well together

Benefits of CRM

Specialised software and hardware can be used to help the company provide the products its customers want, provide better customer service, help the marketing team to cross sell products, to attract new customers and to understand its existing customers better

Ability to track a customer's account history to help personalise products and services for that customer

Ability to measure marketing campaigns, analysing customer clicks and subsequent sales

Provides an ability to "mine" data to identify purchasing and other trends

Allows transaction information to be aggregated to provide KPIs for the business

Helps with forecasting by using sales history to generate sales projections

Could help to promote sales growth

See also	Big Data topics	
	Digital Transformation	123

Cyber security

Controls relating to cyber security need to incorporate **external** factors and so must move beyond traditional approaches based on **internal controls** to maintain the confidentiality, integrity and availability of data:

- Potential threats can now come from **around the world** (organised criminals, corporate spies, disgruntled or careless employees)

- Security weaknesses can be found **throughout a supply chain** rather than just within a single business – the disparate nature of data storage across servers, cloud storage and mobile devices provides a range of access points for attackers to exploit

- The impact of security failures could affect **every aspect** of a business: disruption of operations and customer service, interference with production, damage to brand and reputation, theft of intellectual property or commercially-sensitive information and regulatory fines

The "four flags" which should be considered in relation to cybersecurity (ICAEW report *Audit Insights: Cyber Security*)

1. Businesses should consider "cyber" in all their activities

Businesses need to **manage risks** to ensure that they can **exploit the opportunities** of technology in a **secure** and **sustainable** way – therefore, businesses should treat **cyber security as a business risk** rather than as a technical risk, considering the implications for cyber security of **all** their **strategies** and **operations**

This approach could be particularly relevant to organisations considering a **change in supply chain arrangements** or considering an **acquisition**

Having a plan in place to deal with cyber security issues could provide the organisation with a **competitive advantage** against competitors in the market – the organisation could be seen to be a trusted partner for suppliers and strong security capabilities could be a way of improving its **reputation** with customers

2. Businesses need to accept that security will be compromised

Businesses must concentrate on **intelligence and monitoring**, **detection** and **response**

1. **Intelligence and monitoring** – intelligence on threats can be gathered from a **variety of sources** such as social media or information-sharing schemes with trusted partners or the government

2. **Detection** – hackers can sometimes breach systems for **weeks or months before detection** – data analytics can be important in this respect by identifying **abnormal activity** such as high levels of data downloading or access from unusual places

3. **Response** – an organisation may need to manage a **variety of stakeholder concerns** to limit the impact of the breach – this could include **communicating** with customers who may have been affected and ensuring **compliance** with any **regulatory** requirements – **investors** may also need to be kept informed

Cyber security

Given the growth in social media, a business which does not respond effectively is likely to face **substantial public criticism which could damage its reputation**

3. Businesses should focus on their critical information assets

Instead of trying to do **too much** by protecting **everything**, businesses should **prioritise** their information assets – organisations should identify **where** breaches would have a **substantial** impact on the competitiveness and sustainability of their business and **focus** their security on these areas

4. Most businesses don't get the basics right

According to the ICAEW report, up to **80%** of security breaches could be prevented by implementing **basic good practices**

Complex IT environments, and **lack of expertise**, are both reasons that basic good practices are not implemented in practice

However, **people** are always the **weakest link** in implementing effective security – human failings are being exploited by attackers to gain access to confidential information

ISO 27001

The International Organisation for Standardisation standard **ISO 27001** establishes **best practice** for an information security management system and **identifies** the **requirements** for **establishing**, **implementing**, **maintaining** and **continually improving** such a system

Complying with **ISO 27001** should help an organisation **improve** its **defences** against cyber attacks and increase the **confidence** that **customers** and **other interested parties** have in the organisation's systems

ICAEW 10 steps to cyber security

1. **Allocate responsibilities** – responsibility should rest with a senior manager who has a broad view of all the risks and how to tackle them – other individuals can then be assigned specific roles

2. **Protect your computers and your network** – firewalls should be used to protect against both outside attacks from hackers and to manage the internet activity of staff by blocking access to sites which could cause risks

3. **Keep your computers up-to-date** – the latest patches from software providers should always be applied – a single vulnerable computer network puts all other computers at risk

4. **Control employee access to computers and documents** – use specific user accounts and passwords with a unique username in each case to regulate access

5. **Protect against viruses** – ensure that up-to-date antivirus software is installed and that it regularly scans computers for threats

6. **Extend security beyond the office** – ensure that laptops, phones or tablets used outside the office are also covered by antivirus software, password protection and firewalls – ensure that sensitive data is kept encrypted – ensure that employees are reminded of the dangers of connecting to unencrypted public wifi

Cyber security

7. **Don't forget disks and drives** – removable disks and drives such as USB sticks can introduce malware into computers and could also be lost when containing sensitive information – antivirus and anti-malware software should be applied to such disks and drives and not just to computers

8. **Plan for the worst** – consider whether external help would be required and whether key customers or suppliers would need to be contacted – consider whether some functions can continue to operate using other computers while systems are repaired – ensure there is a clear plan identifying who is responsible for doing what in an emergency

9. **Educate your team** – ensure everyone in the business is aware of the importance of security matters and how to ensure that security can be upheld – for example, by keeping passwords safe and changing them regularly – staff should be reminded not to click on web links or email attachments from unfamiliar sources – employees should be trained to watch out for social engineering or "phishing" where hackers try to trick staff into revealing details

10. **Keep records – and test your security** – keep a record of the hardware and software an organisation uses to help build up a picture of the organisation's security status and to spot potential weak points – apply good record-keeping to effectively test systems on a regular basis

The importance of the weakest link

Ultimately, any organisation is only as secure as its **weakest link** – regular testing will help ensure that no weaknesses get overlooked

Responsibilities of senior management regarding cyber security

Senior management now has to do more than in the past to promote an awareness of cyber security – this may involve:

1. **employing** a **Chief Information Security Officer** to help communicate the threats posed by cyber risks

2. **reorganising roles and responsibilities** to ensure there is **accountability** for cyber security matters within the organisation

3. **learning** from **past** security **breaches**

4. **determining** the organisation's **tolerance** to cyber risks

5. ensuring that **Non-Executive Directors** play an active role in promoting cyber security – this may involve **keeping their knowledge** about the evolving nature of cyber risks **up-to-date** and **challenging the Executive Directors** about whether best practice in cyber security is being followed

See also		
	Big Data topics	
	Cloud computing	76
	Digital Strategies	120
	Digital Transformation	123

Debt Factoring

In a **factoring** transaction, one party transfers the **right to cash to be collected from its receivables** to another party in return for **immediate cash** payment

This allows an organisation with a receivables balance to **receive cash quickly** rather than **waiting** the 30 to 60 days that it can take a customer to pay

The factor advances a percentage of the invoice value and retains the rest of the amount as security against any bad debts – the factor will then also deduct its own fee from the amount paid from the invoice when the invoice is paid by the customer

The **cash advance** rate will typically range from **80%** to **95%** of the invoice value

For financial reporting purposes, the entity will need to determine how to treat its receivables if factoring is in operation

Factoring with recourse

Here the transferor fully or partially **guarantees** the performance of receivables: if the receivables are ultimately not paid then **the factor will not lose out** because the transferor will **pay any shortfall** – the transferor is therefore **not fully transferring the credit risk** to another party

In most factoring with recourse, the transferor **does not allow the transferee to sell the receivables**, in which case the **transferor still retains control** over the asset

In this case, the **criteria for derecognition are not satisfied** and the asset should **not be derecognised**

Instead, the amount advanced by the factoring company should be treated as a **financial liability** in the accounts – effectively a **loan** from the factor

Factoring without recourse

Here the transferor **does not provide any guarantees** about the ultimate performance of the receivables so the **factoring company will bear the loss of any bad debts**

In this case, the entity **has transferred the risks and rewards of the ownership** of the receivables and should **derecognise** them accordingly

Because **risk has been transferred**, this type of factoring is **significantly more expensive** than factoring with recourse

Costs of factoring to a business

Interest – typical interest charges range from **1.5%** to **3%** over base rate

Fees – these fees cover the costs of administration and credit control, and typically amount to between **0.75%** and **2.5%** of turnover

Cost of bad debt risk – in factoring without recourse, there will also be a charge for the cost of bearing the risk of bad debts

See also	Bank Loans	49
	Bonds (Loan Notes) v Bank Loans – Comparisons	60
	Finance – Sources for SMEs	131

Derivatives Calculations – Currency Forward

Reminders

ADDIS – always ADD a discount (and therefore deduct a premium) to the relevant spot rate

Choosing the spot rate to adjust

Spot rates will be quoted on a bid/offer basis such as 1.65 – 1.75

Foreign currency will be received by the company

If the company wishes to exchange foreign currency received **into** sterling, then use the **right hand/higher** spot rate – dividing by the **higher** alternative figure will **minimise** the sterling amount that the bank pays to the company in return for the foreign currency

Foreign currency is required by the company

If the company needs to purchase foreign currency by **paying** sterling, then use the **left hand/higher** spot rate – dividing by the **lower** alternative figure will **maximise** the sterling amount that the customer needs to pay to buy the foreign currency needed

Standard narrative points

Tailored specifically for the needs of the client (value, timing, exchange rate) (contrast with futures and options)

No secondary market exists so hard to get out of the contract if not wanted (contrast with futures and options)

Does not give any flexibility (unlike an option) – what if the foreign customer never pays? We would still have to sell the agreed number of foreign currency units to the bank under the contract – these would need to be purchased in the market at the spot rate, which may be unfavourable

Removes upside risk – we cannot use the spot market at the future date if that is preferable (unlike an option)

Option forward contracts

An option forward contract is a forward exchange contract where the customer can decide precisely **when** to invoke the contract

Performance **must** take place at some time and **cannot be avoided** altogether.

Derivatives Calculations – Currency Forward

Option forward contracts are normally used to cover whole months which **straddle** the likely payment date where the **customer is not sure the exact date** on which they will want to buy or sell currency.

The purpose of an option forward contract is to **avoid having to renew** a forward exchange contract and **extend it by a few days** because this can be **expensive**.

Example option forward contract

A UK company must pay $1m in approximately 2.5 months' time.

The bank will offer a contract which allows the company to choose when, between 2 and 3 months' time, the currency is needed.

The rate applied to the contract will be **either** the **2** or **3-month** rate, **whichever is more beneficial** to the bank.

Derivatives Calculations – Currency Futures

Reminders

Use the futures quote rate when deciding the number of contracts – do NOT use the spot rate at this stage

Only use the spot rate right at the end of the calculation, after you have done everything else in relation to the futures trade

To work out whether the company needs to buy or sell futures, look at the position with different exchange rates, using easy to work with numbers

> e.g. company is going to receive US$2m
>
> > at an exchange rate of $1:£1 this would be £2m
> >
> > at an exchange rate of $2:£1 this would be £1m
>
> Therefore, the company will lose money if the exchange rate number rises (appreciation of the £) – so enter into a futures hedge which will make a gain in that situation – therefore BUY futures now and sell futures if the exchange rate number rises (buying low and selling high generates a profit)

Calculation steps

1. Calculate net amount payment or receivable in the foreign currency

2. Divide the amount from step 1 by the futures quote rate and the contract size (often, £62,500 but check)

> e.g. US$ 1.5m / 1.564 / 62,500 = 16 contracts (rounded up)
>
> Do NOT use the spot rate at this stage

Round the number of contracts to a whole figure – if you round up then you will overhedge, if you round down then you will underhedge

3. Work out whether the futures were sold or bought (see rule above)

4. Calculate the movement in the futures quote from the initial position to the final position (should be given in the question as an estimated future figure) – then multiply this by the number of contracts and contract size

> e.g. (1.564 – 1.582) x 16 contracts x £62,500   (assuming contract size of £62,500)

The gain or loss here will be in the foreign currency

5. Re-calculate the net amount payable or receivable in the foreign currency, allowing for the gain or loss from step 4

> e.g. if the company has to purchase dollars and has made a gain on the hedge then deduct the hedging gain from the underlying dollar purchase as the bank will give the company that

amount of dollars under the hedging contract and so the company does not need to purchase that amount any more

Use the forecast future spot rate at this stage – for advice on selecting the correct spot rate, see below.

Choosing the spot rate

Spot rates will be quoted on a bid/offer basis such as 1.65 – 1.75

Foreign currency will be received by the company

If the company wishes to exchange foreign currency received **into** sterling, then use the **right hand/higher** spot rate – dividing by the **higher** alternative figure will **minimise** the sterling amount that the bank pays to the company in return for the foreign currency

Foreign currency is required by the company

If the company needs to purchase foreign currency by **paying** sterling, then use the **left hand/higher** spot rate – dividing by the **lower** alternative figure will **maximise** the sterling amount that the customer needs to pay to buy the foreign currency needed

Standard narrative points

Not tailored so could lead to under- or overhedging

Requires a margin to be deposited at the futures exchange when the deal is set up (as collateral)

May create liquidity pressure if a margin call is made by the exchange (i.e. the company's hedging position worsens – the exchange may demand further collateral as assurance that the company will be able to pay if the hedging position remains negative from the company's perspective)

Secondary market exists so the company can get out of the deal if not needed (e.g. if the counterparty is going to default) – not possible with a forward

Basis risk exists as the futures quote is at a different rate to the spot rate and will usually move by a different percentage compared to the spot market – therefore unlikely that a perfect hedge is possible

Derivatives Calculations – Currency Options

Reminders

A put option means an option to sell – a call option means an option to purchase

> But check the wording regarding traded options carefully – just because the option price is $1.65 does not necessarily mean that the option is over dollars – the option could be a **sterling** option with a $1.65 exercise price so in this case the put and call terminology is from the point of view of **sterling**

Calculation steps

Note – there are 2 types of option to understand: OTC options and traded options

An OTC or over the counter option is an option over a direct purchase/sale of a specific amount of currency – a traded option is an option to engage in a currency futures trade

OTC options – calculation steps

1. Calculate option premium cost – generally you will multiply the foreign currency amount by the given figure to find the premium cost in sterling – check when this is payable: if it is payable now, add on an interest cost (as the company will lose the opportunity cost of interest income if it has to pay the premium now) – this is likely to require some kind of time-apportionment

2. Apply the exchange rate agreed in the contract to the relevant foreign currency sum

3. Compare this to the spot rate to determine if the option gives a better result – if so, exercise the option – if not, let the option lapse (but state this in your answer)

For advice on selecting the correct spot rate, refer to our instructions on the next page

4. Remember to deduct the premium cost from the final calculation – this must be paid even if the option is not actually exercised

Traded options – calculation steps

1. Calculate option premium cost – divide* foreign currency amount by the exchange rate agreed in the option (**not** the spot rate) and then divide again by the contract size – round the number of contracts – then calculate premium as number of contracts x premium x contract size – if this is a foreign currency amount and payable now, then divide by the relevant **spot rate** (not the exchange rate agreed in the option)

(*Assumes that the exchange rate is quoted as "foreign currency units to £1")

For advice on selecting the correct spot rate, refer to our instructions on the next page

2. Apply the exchange rate agreed in the contract to the relevant foreign currency sum

3. Compare this to the spot rate to determine if the option gives a better result – if so, exercise the option and engage in a futures trade – if not, let the option lapse (but state this in your answer)

For advice on selecting the correct spot rate, refer to our instructions on the next page

Derivatives Calculations – Currency Options

4. Remember to deduct the premium cost from the final calculation – this must be paid even if the option is not actually exercised

Choosing the spot rate

Spot rates will be quoted on a bid/offer basis such as 1.65 – 1.75

Foreign currency will be received by the company

If the company wishes to exchange foreign currency received **into** sterling, then use the **right hand/higher** spot rate – dividing by the **higher** alternative figure will **minimise** the sterling amount that the bank pays to the company in return for the foreign currency

Foreign currency is required by the company

If the company needs to purchase foreign currency by **paying** sterling, then use the **left hand/higher** spot rate – dividing by the **lower** alternative figure will **maximise** the sterling amount that the customer needs to pay to buy the foreign currency needed

Standard narrative points

Offers flexibility – if the counterparty does not pay or the currency is not needed, or if the spot market at the future date is favourable, then the option can simply be left to lapse – "allows the company to protect itself from downside risk whilst preserving the upside potential of [add whether a depreciation or appreciation of sterling is beneficial in the particular case]"

Can be expensive – premium has to be paid even if the option is not used – additional interest cost to consider if the premium is payable up-front

Traded options are not tailored to the specific needs of the client (contract size, maturity date) so can lead to over- or underhedging

> However, OTC options are tailored so these points can be reversed in your answer

Traded options have a secondary market so easy to unwind the hedge if no longer needed – however, the options may be worth less when sold back into the market

> However, OTC options are tailored so there is no secondary market

Basis risk applies if the rate in the option contract differs from today's spot rate (quite likely to be the case) – could lead to under- or overhedging in relation to the movement between today's spot rate and the rate at which the option contract could kick in if exercised

Derivatives Calculations – Summary of Currency Hedging Methods

	Forward	**Money Market**	**Futures**
Tailored?	Yes	Yes	No
Secondary market to "unwind"?	No	Yes	Yes
Transaction cost	Via spread	Via spread on interest and spot rate	Brokerage fees
Complexity	Low	Medium	High
Management costs	Low	Medium	High
Application	Small and medium companies	Banks	Companies with large currency exposures

Derivatives Calculations – Forward Rate Agreements (FRAs)

Reminders

Some questions may have a single FRA interest rate specified – other questions will have 2 alternative rates as a spread such as 3.5% - 2.5%

If a spread is offered, choose the rate that is in the bank's interests i.e. which minimises the amount the bank might have to pay out and maximises the amount the bank might receive

> If the company has taken on borrowing and so wishes to hedge an **increase** in interest rates, then use the higher figure or lefthand side – then if interest rates do rise, the bank will have to pay a lower amount (in our example, only the difference between the market rate and 3.5%, which is better for the bank than the difference between the market rate and 2.5% if interest rates are relatively high)

> If the company is going to start saving and so wishes to hedge a decrease in interest rates, then use the lower figure or righthand side – then if interest rates do **fall**, the bank will have to pay a lower amount (in our example, only the difference between the market rate and 2.5%, which is better for the bank than the difference between the market rate and 3.5% if interest rates are relatively low)

Terminology

The FRA rate may be specified as "4 v 7"

The first figure (lefthand side) states when the FRA will start (so starting in 4 months from now in this example)

The second figure (righthand side) states when the FRA will end (so ending in 7 months from now in this example)

Therefore the time period of the FRA itself is the difference between the righthand figure and the lefthand figure – this will often be 3 months

Remember to pro-rate any annual interest rates for the time period (the difference between the lefthand and righthand side above)

Calculation steps

1. Calculate the amount the company has to pay based on the market rate

2. Calculate the payment to or receipt from the bank – remember to pick the correct rate (see above) and to allow for time-apportionment (often at 3/12)

If the calculation is correct, the net position from steps 1 and 2 should be equal to the FRA rate agreed

Make sure you end by specifying the net amount payment in cash terms i.e. not just the % but the amount of cash that this amounts to (this should be equal to the FRA rate multiplied by the relevant total amount of the loan/saving)

Derivatives Calculations – Forward Rate Agreements (FRAs)

Example FRA calculation

A company intends to take out a £1m fixed rate loan in 4 months for a period of 3 months.

This company is therefore worried about a rise in interest rates and so the bank will offer the lefthand side of the quoted spread (so that the difference between the market rate and the bank's offered rate is minimised if the bank does have to pay anything out)

The following quotes are available:

4 v 6	3.55 - 2.50%
4 v 7	3.58 – 2.52%
4 v 8	3.63 – 2.56%

Illustrate the position if the company has to pay (1) 3% and (2) 4% on the loan.

Solution

The numbers in the "v" quoting system refer to "start month v end month" so if we are starting in 4 months and borrowing for 3 months then our end month is in 7 months so we use a 4 v 7 instrument, using the lefthand side quote.

(1) loan rate is 3%

In this case, the rate is below the rate in the FRA so the company will pay money to the bank – this is the price of protecting itself against high interest rates

Company pays (3.58 – 3.00) x £1m x 3/12 = £1,450 to the bank under the FRA

Company pays 3% x £1m x 3/12 = £7,500 on the underlying loan

Total cost of £1,450 + £7,000 = £8,950 or (£8,950/£1m) x 4 quarters = 3.58% per annum

(2) loan rate is 4%

In this case, the rate is above the rate in the FRA so the company will receive money from the bank under the FRA – this helps the company protect its interest rate against any increase

Company receives (4.00 – 3.58) x £1m x 3/12 = £1,050 from the bank under the FRA

Company pays 4% x £1m x 3/12 = £10,500 on the underlying loan

Total cost of £10,000 - £1,050 = £8,950 or (£8,950/£1m) x 4 quarters = 3.58% per annum

Conclusion

Under either option, the net interest cost is 3.58%, the rate agreed under the FRA.

Standard narrative points

An FRA eliminates downside risk but prevents the company benefiting from upside risk if interest rates in the market move favourably

Derivatives Calculations – FTSE Hedging

Reminders

In most questions, the company will have an existing holding of FTSE shares and will be worried about a decline in value – so it will use a PUT option or SELL futures

> This allows the company to enter into an agreement to sell FTSE shares/FTSE futures at a pre-agreed price – the company will then make a profit if share prices fall because it can purchase the relevant shares in the market at a lower price (sell high, buy low)

Calculation steps – options

1. Calculate the number of contracts – divide the company's portfolio value by (option exercise price x £10)

> For example, £7.5m / (6,454 x £10)

Round the number of contracts – if you round up then you will overhedge, if you round down then you will underhedge

2. Calculate premium cost as number of contracts x £10 x relevant premium from table in the question

3. Calculate gain or loss if options exercised as (option exercise price – FTSE value) x £10 x number of contracts

4. Calculate net position as portfolio value plus gain on options (if applicable) less premium

> As the option should not be exercised if a loss is caused you should never have a loss on the options (just a zero gain after the options are left to lapse as a result of share prices rising i.e. no loss in value on the portfolio to protect against)

Calculation steps – futures

1. Calculate the number of contracts – divide the company's portfolio value by (futures price x £10)

> For example, £7.5m / (6,454 x £10)

Round the number of contracts – if you round up then you will overhedge, if you round down then you will underhedge

2. Calculate gain or loss as (futures price – FTSE value) x £10 x number of contracts

3. Calculate net position as portfolio value plus/minus any gain or loss on the futures

Standard narrative points

May not lead to a 100% efficient hedge due to rounding of contracts

Basis risk may lead to the hedge not being 100% efficient due to the fact that the initial value of the FTSE index may differ from the options/futures exercise price so there will not be exactly the same movement in the FTSE index and the hedging instrument

Futures do not allow the company to benefit from upside risk if the market moves favourably – an option can be left to lapse if the market moves favourably

Futures require a margin to be deposited at the exchange as security and margin calls may subsequently be required if the company's hedge moves significantly out of the money – this may not be good for liquidity

Derivatives Calculations – Interest Rate Futures

Reminders

If the company is worried that interest rates will rise, it should SELL futures – if rates rise from, say, 2% to 4% then the futures quote would fall from 98 to 96 – so profit is obtained by selling high and buying low

If the company is worried that interest rates will fall, it should BUY futures – if rates fall from, say, 4% to 2% then the futures quote would increase from 96 to 98 – so profit is obtained by buying low and selling high

Remember that the gain or loss must be calculated using a 3/12 fraction even if the hedge is not for 3 months – this is because futures are based on a 3 month quoting basis so we always apply 3/12 to the quoted annual rates – we adjust for the hedging periods that are longer than 3 months by buying more futures so the additional length is factored into the calculation already when determining the number of contracts – therefore it would be double counting to also apply a fraction other than 3/12 when calculating the gain or loss

Calculation steps

1. Calculate the number of contracts – divide the amount to be hedged by the contract size and then pro-rate for time if the period is not 3 months

> e.g. (£20m / £0.5m) x 7/3 if we are hedging for 7 months

Round the number of contracts to a whole figure – if you round up then you will overhedge, if you round down then you will underhedge

2. Work out whether the futures would have been bought or sold (see rule above)

3. Determine the gain on the futures as the difference in the final rate versus the futures rate, multiplied by the contract size, number of contracts and **by 3/12 regardless of the time period to pro-rate the annual premium % down to the 3 month rate involved in 3 month futures**

6. Determine the interest cost/income on the underlying loan/savings and then adjust for the gain or loss on the futures to determine the effective rate

> Remember to time apportion upwards to allow for annual rate e.g. multiply by 12/7 if hedging for 7 months

Standard narrative points

Not tailored so could lead to under- or overhedging

Requires a margin to be deposited at the futures exchange when the deal is set up (as collateral)

May create liquidity pressure if a margin call is made by the exchange (i.e. the company's hedging position worsens – the exchange may demand further collateral as assurance that the company will be able to pay if the hedging position remains negative from the company's perspective)

Secondary market exists so the company can get out of the deal if not needed – not possible with a forward

Basis risk exists as the futures quote is at a different rate to the spot rate and will usually move by a different percentage compared to the spot market – therefore unlikely that a perfect hedge is possible

Derivatives Calculations – Interest Rate Options

Reminders

If the company is worried that interest rates will rise, it should purchase PUT options – if rates rise from, say, 2% to 4% then the futures quote would fall from 98 to 96 – so profit is obtained by selling high and buying low – a put option allows the company to engage in a futures SELL trade, which is advantageous

If the company is worried that interest rates will fall, it should purchase CALL options – if rates fall from, say, 4% to 2% then the futures quote would increase from 96 to 98 – so profit is obtained by buying low and selling high – a call option allows the company to engage in a futures BUY trade, which is advantageous

Remember that the gain or loss and option premium must be calculated using a 3/12 fraction **even if the hedge is not for 3 months** – this is because the option is an option to engage in a futures trade – futures are based on a 3 month quoting basis so we always apply 3/12 to the quoted annual rates – we adjust for the hedging periods that are longer than 3 months by buying more futures so the additional length is factored into the calculation already when determining the number of contracts – therefore it would be double counting to also apply a fraction other than 3/12 when calculating the gain or loss, or option premium

Calculation steps

1. Calculate the number of contracts – divide the amount to be hedged by the contract size and then pro-rate for time if the period is not 3 months

   e.g. (£20m / £0.5m) x 7/3 if we are hedging for 7 months

Round the number of contracts to a whole figure – if you round up then you will overhedge, if you round down then you will underhedge

2. Calculate the premium payable by multiplying the number of contracts by the premium % and by the contract size – **finally multiply by 3/12 regardless of the time period to pro-rate the annual premium % down to the 3 month rate involved in 3 month futures**

   e.g. 93 x 0.52% x 0.5m x 3/12

3. Work out whether the futures would have been bought or sold (see rule above)

4. Determine if the option is worth exercising – have interest rates moved in the direction feared by the company?

5. Determine the gain on the futures as the difference in the final rate versus the futures rate, multiplied by the contract size, number of contracts and **by 3/12 regardless of the time period to pro-rate the annual premium % down to the 3 month rate involved in 3 month futures**

6. Determine the interest cost/income on the underlying loan/savings and then adjust for the gain or loss on the futures to determine the effective rate

   Remember to time apportion upwards to allow for annual rate e.g. multiply by 12/7 if hedging for 7 months

Derivatives Calculations – Interest Rate Options

Standard narrative points

Options can hedge downside risk whilst allowing the company to take advantage of upside potential – FRAs and interest rates will lock the company into a particular rate

However, options can be expensive due to the premium cost

Can be traded on the secondary market

Requires a margin to be deposited at the futures exchange when the deal is set up (as collateral)

May create liquidity pressure if a margin call is made by the exchange (i.e. the company's hedging position worsens – the exchange may demand further collateral as assurance that the company will be able to pay if the hedging position remains negative from the company's perspective)

Interest Rate Collars

Consists of a pair of interest rates options – a cap and a floor

A borrower would buy a cap giving the right to borrow at the exercise price for the relevant period – this option is used if the market interest rate increases and therefore cancels out the increased cost of borrowing on the underlying asset

A borrower would sell a floor obligating it to lend at the exercise price for the relevant period – the borrower may have to lend at this rate if the market interest rate falls but the cost of servicing the underlying loan would also be falling, cancelling out the cost

The cost of cap is intended to be offset to some extent or completely by the revenue from selling the floor

The net effect is to create a fixed rate at zero or low cost

Derivatives Calculations – Interest Rate Parity Concept

The interest rate parity equation predicts the forward exchange rate based on today's spot rate, adjusted for interest differentials between countries

The IRP equation assumes that a country with a relatively high interest rate will experience a depreciation in the forward exchange rate to cancel out the benefit of saving at the high interest rate

> If it were possible to lock in a forward rate which did not allow for the relatively high interest rate then everyone would invest in that country at the high interest rate, take out a forward contract and therefore benefit from a risk-free deal to increase interest earnings

> Therefore market forces will lead to the foreign exchange rate depreciating for that country (if there is very high demand for forwards from investors looking to lock in their high interest rate returns then banks will be able to offer less favourable terms)

The IRP equation is calculated as

spot rate x (interest rate in foreign country / interest rate in UK)

Use the average of the bid:offer spread to find the spot rate and the average of the lending and borrowing interest rates to find the interest rate

Example

Spot rate (EUR / £)	EUR 1.19985
Average of lending and borrowing rates in the Eurozone	7.5%
Average of lending and borrowing rates in the UK	9.25%

Forward contract rate per IRP equation = 1.19985 x (1.0075 / 1.00925) = EUR 1.1977

IRP predicts that sterling will weaken from being worth EUR 1.19985 to EUR 1.1977 due to interest rates in the UK being relatively **higher** than in the Eurozone

Question Application

You can use IRP to estimate the expected future exchange rate if you are given interest rate information – this can be used to determine whether exchange rates will move for or against your client (and therefore whether hedging is necessary in the first place)

You can also use IRP as a sense check on the quoted forward discount or premium if this is given in the question

Derivatives Calculations – Interest Rate Swaps

Reminders

You should first calculate the split "difference in differences" to determine what each party to the swap should end up paying on a net basis – this is then entered into the bottom of the Interest Rate Swap pro-forma (see below)

> In other words, in a way, you work backwards when applying the Interest Rate Swap pro-forma

Calculation steps

1. Find the "difference in differences" – find the difference between the fixed rates possible for each party – find the difference between the variable rates possible for each party – find the difference between these 2 figures

   > For example, if party 1 can borrow fixed at 5.2% and party 2 can borrow fixed at 6.4% then the difference in fixed rates is 1.2%

   > If party 1 can borrow variable at LIBOR + 1.2% and party 2 can borrow variable at LIBOR + 1.6% then the difference in variable rates is 0.4%

   > Therefore the difference in differences is 1.2% - 0.4% = 0.8%

2. Split the differences in differences from step 1 equally between the 2 parties (divide the gain by 2)

3. Complete the bottom of the Interest Rate Swap pro-forma working with the party's desired type of borrowing but at a rate equal to the current offer less the split gain from step 2

   > For example, if the party can borrow fixed at 6.4% but the difference in differences is 0.4% then we know that this party should, in the end, obtain fixed borrowing at 6.0% if the swap is set up correctly

4. Complete the other sections of the Interest Rate Swap pro-forma working (see below) with the current rate being paid and then swap rates to ensure that the final result calculated in step 3 is obtained

   > **Tip** – it is often convenient to make one party pay a rate of LIBOR under the swap to cancel the LIBOR element and just leave an easier to work with percentage available – for example, if the company is paying LIBOR + 1.6% already and receives LIBOR under the Interest Rate Swap then this nets to just + 1.6% through the cancellation of LIBOR payment and receipt

Example Interest Rate Swap Calculation

Fortitude plc borrowed at 5.2% last year and can obtain a variable rate of LIBOR + 1.2%

Fortitude plc would like to move to a variable rate form of borrowing.

Veracity plc borrowed at LIBOR + 1.6% last year and can obtain a fixed rate of 6.4%.

Derivatives Calculations – Interest Rate Swaps

Veracity plc would like to move to a fixed rate form of borrowing.

The 2 companies are considering an Interest Rate Swap to allow them to move onto the type of borrowing that they prefer.

Solution

Difference in fixed rates is 6.4 – 5.2 = 1.2

Difference in variable rates is 0.4

Difference in differences is 1.2 – 0.4 = 0.8

Split equally, this means that each company should be able to obtain is preferred type of borrowing at 0.4% less than it can otherwise obtain.

So Fortitude plc should end up with a rate of LIBOR + 0.8% and Veracity plc should end up with a fixed rate of 6.0%

We can therefore enter these amounts into the bottom of the Interest Rate Swap pro-forma first (see below) – the payment in the third row from Veracity to Fortitude is a balancing figure to achieve the target amounts identified above

	Fortitude	Veracity
Paying now	(5.2%)	(LIBOR + 1.6%)
Fortitude pays Veracity	(LIBOR)	LIBOR
Veracity pays Fortitude	4.4%	(4.4%)
Net payment	(LIBOR + 0.8%)	(6.0%)

Remember that the net payment row is actually filled in first, once we know what the correct "target" is i.e. the company's desired type of borrowing, adjusted for the equally split "difference in differences"

Standard narrative points

An Interest Rate Swap costs significantly less than terminating an existing loan and taking out a new one

Interest rate savings are possible by using the principle of comparative advantage

Interest Rate Swaps are available for longer periods than short-term methods such as FRAs, futures and options

Flexible since they can be arranged for tailor-made amounts and periods – can be reversed if not needed

Allows the company to obtain the type of interest (fixed or floating) that the company wants

Derivatives Calculations – Interest Rate Swaps

Can help with cashflow planning e.g. if switching from a variable rate to a fixed rate, where cash payments then become known and fixed in advance

Compare the effective interest rate before and after the swap – clearly state the better deal and quantify the savings obtained

Risk of counterparty default – this should also be considered when evaluating the rate

Are there better alternatives? See our notes on the **Hedging topics**

See also		
	Acquisitions – Financing	29
	Bank Loans	49
	Bonds (Loan Notes) v Bank Loans – Comparisons	60
	Interest Rate Calculations	169
	Option valuation	207

Derivatives Calculations – Money Market Hedging

Reminders

If we are going to receive foreign currency in future, then we can take on an initial foreign currency debt now, allow the debt to grow slightly over time up to the same value as our receivable and then clear the debt when the customer pays

> We therefore take on a foreign currency debt now, convert to sterling at today's spot rate and **save in sterling**
>
> Foreign currency receivable → borrow in foreign currency, save in sterling

If we are going to have to pay foreign currency in future, then we need to start saving in foreign currency now, benefiting from interest income to grow the relevant amount up to the same value as our payable, allowing us to make payment at the future date

> To pay for saving in the foreign currency, we take on a sterling debt now, convert to foreign currency at today's spot rate and **save in the foreign currency**
>
> Foreign currency payable → borrowing sterling, save in foreign currency

Check the terminology – the interest rates are likely to be quoted as "lending" and "borrowing" – this means from the point of view of the **company** so "lending" means that the company lends to the bank (i.e. saves)

Calculation steps

1. Work out whether the first step is to save or borrow – see Reminders above

2. Divide the amount from step 1 by the applicable time-apportioned interest rate to reduce the figure from step 1 slightly – the debt/saving will then grow slightly over time up to the full receivable/payable

Remember to time apportion the quoted annual interest rates (probably by 3/12, 4/12 or 6/12 – check the question)

3. Apply the correct spot rate to the slighted reduced figure created in step 2

4. Apply the applicable time-apportioned interest rate to the figure from step 3

If you used a borrowing rate in step 2, then you must be using a lending/savings rate in step 4

If you used a lending/savings rate in step 2, then you must be using a borrowing rate in step 4

The result from step 4 is the overall cost of the Money Market Hedge

You may wish to compare the sterling cost from step 4 to the foreign currency figure to calculate the equivalent "synthetic" exchange rate that you have created from the Money Market Hedge – then compare with the exchange rates involved in alternative hedging arrangements (if applicable)

Derivatives Calculations – Money Market Hedging

Example of Money Market Hedging calculation (foreign currency payable)

Company needs to pay CU145.6m (a foreign currency) in 3 months

Spot rate today	78.81 – 90.62
Sterling borrowing interest rate	3.6% pa
CU borrowing interest rate	6.6% pa
Sterling lending interest rate	2.9% pa
CU lending interest rate	5.6% pa

Solution

Company needs to have CU145.6m available in 3 months so start saving an amount just less than this (to allow for savings income)

CU savings rate, time-apportioned is 1 + (5.6% x 3/12) = 1.014

    CU145.6m / 1.014 = CU143,589,744

To fund this at the spot rate, we need to borrow sterling at 78.81 (lower or lefthand spot rate as bank will want to maximise the cost of the borrowing by dividing by the lower figure)

    CU143,589,744 / 78.81 = £1,821,974

Sterling borrowing rate, time-apportioned is 1 + (3.6% x 3/12) = 1.009

    £1,821,974 x 1.009 = £1,838,372

    (or you can present the sterling interest cost separately as £1,821,974 x 0.009 = £16,398)

Equivalent synthetic rate = 145.6m / 1,838,372 = 79.2

Standard narrative points

Creates a fixed exchange rate – eliminates downside risk but also removes upside risk of just using the future spot rate if the market has moved in a beneficial direction

If the counterparty fails to pay a receivable then the company would still need to repay the foreign currency debt that it took on as the first part of the money market hedge – this could expose the company to a foreign currency loss (equally, a foreign currency gain could occur)

If the company no longer needs the foreign currency then it would still need a way to repay its sterling debt so it would need to liquidate its foreign currency savings taken on as the first part of the money market hedge – this could expose the company to a foreign currency loss (equally, a foreign currency gain could occur)

Money market hedge can be customised to company's requirements – not a standardised or market product

Digital Strategies

Digital strategy can be defined as "the use of digital technology and digital assets to challenge existing ways of doing things and to restructure accordingly, in particular in relation to the way businesses interact with their customers"

Types of digitisation

Digitisation can affect **products and services** – for example, turning a DVD into a digitally streamed experience

Digitisation can transform the **way** a product or service is **delivered** to the customer – for example, through online commerce rather than a retail store

Digitisation of the **supply chain** – for example, introduction of an inventory management system which connects all retailers, distribution centres, manufacturers and suppliers such that orders placed are fulfilled automatically, smoothing out gluts and shortages

Digitisation of the **wider business environment** – for example, enabling customers to be linked via crowdsourcing platforms, eliminating the need for business intermediaries

Impact of digital disruption (according to the consultancy firm McKinsey)

unconstrained supply – digital technology has reduced transaction costs and therefore sources of supply which were previously not economic are now possible

removal of distortions in demand – customers have more complete information about products – products and services are becoming unbundled in ways that were previously combined by necessity or convenience (for example, customers can now buy individual tracks rather than whole music albums)

making of new markets – supply and demand can be connected in ways which were impossible before (for example, Airbnb has not constructed new buildings but has simply brought people into contact with each other)

creation of new and enhanced value propositions – as markets evolve, the expectations of customers increase (for example, customers now expect instant or at least quicker delivery than in the past) so companies must meet those heightened expectations through digital features, digital automated delivery and distribution models

reimagined business systems – new entrants can surprise incumbents by introducing completely different ways to make money

hyperscale platforms – companies like Amazon span many product categories and customer segments due to their very large scale – this allows such companies to offer customers a unified value proposition across products and services and to gather large amounts of information about customers – this information can be used to identify opportunities to move into new sectors

best-in-class user experience – customers no longer compare a company's online offerings with those of their direct rivals but with, for example, best-in-class operators such as Apple or Amazon – therefore, a firm must offer improved search filter tools, streamlined and user-friendly order processes, smart recommendation engines and customised bundling of products or services in order to compete

Digitisation as a source of competitive advantage

According to the consultancy McKinsey, **to date**, digital strategies have primarily focused on **digital distribution** and **marketing** – in most cases companies have merely been trying to **keep pace** with their competitors rather than using digitisation as a source of competitive advantage (in other words, digital distribution and marketing has become a **threshold competence** rather than a **unique competence**)

To gain **competitive advantage**, digitisation would need to differentiate a business from competitors through investment in other dimensions of digitisation that have seen less adoption such as digitisation of the supply chain – companies must invest in creating a **competitive premium** based on doing things in ways that other companies cannot

Digitisation must be grounded in **broader corporate strategy** rather than being an aim in itself

Digitisation should **not** be seen as a **purely IT strategy** – successful digital transformation involves fundamental changes in **capabilities**, **business processes**, **governance** and **culture**, as well as having purely technological aspects

Mass customisation is one example of a business model which has evolved to take advantage of digitisation: for example, the appliance manufacturer Haier makes its washing machines and refrigerators in China to order – customers specify features they want on their computer and those specifications are transmitted directly to the assembly line

Developing a digital strategy

The company will need to decide whether to **attack** or **defend** in the face of digital disruption

A company operating in a high margin business may not see the need to set up a low-cost innovative proposition but this could lead to problems in the longer term if attackers prove sufficiently attractive to customers to capture market share

New channels/methods and new low-cost entry options are promoted by digitisation

The strategy must **differentiate** the company from competitors

Big Data and marketing

Big Data can be used to **personalise** marketing messages and offers – marketing can be **targeted** more precisely than ever before

Digital Strategies

Real-time data **visualisation** technologies such as **dashboards** enable managers to **adjust tactics** based on live data feeds – for example, sales managers are able to adjust pricing based on online sales, and inventory, data

Big Data increases the **volume** and **variety** of customer **data available to marketers** – for example, online purchase data, click-through rates and browsing behaviour on websites as well as social media interactions

Simply **having** Big Data **does not automatically** give an organisation a marketing advantage, or competitive advantage – it is the **insights** organisations gain from the data and the **quality** of decisions that they make based on that data, which make the difference

If Big Data is used well, it should benefit the organisation in 3 key areas:

1. **customer engagement** – Big Data can provide insight into not only who an organisation's customers are but where they are, what they want, how they want to be contacted and when

2. **customer retention and loyalty** – Big Data can help organisations identify what factors influence customer loyalty, and what encourages them (or discourages them) to continue to purchase from an organisation

3. **marketing optimisation** – Big Data can help organisations determine the optimal marketing spend across different channels because analytics can help organisations measure, in detail, the impact of different forms of marketing

See also	Big Data topics	
	Cloud computing	76
	Cyber security	95
	Digital Transformation	123

Digital Transformation

Digital disruption relates to the impact that new digital technologies have on business as usual

Digital transformation refers to the way in which the impact of digital disruption can be proactively managed

Digital transformation involves understanding the existing information and dataflows in a business and then reshaping business processes and systems to maximise the use of digital technologies

New, underlying and enabling technologies include

> Ever-increasing processing power
>
> Ever-increasing data storage
>
> Improved operating systems and networking infrastructure
>
> The internet as a platform
>
> Increasing reach and bandwidth of broadband
>
> Emergence of open source software
>
> Miniaturisation and the rise of the mobile

Benefits of digital transformation

Can help a business to improve its existing business model and also create new opportunities

Can help add value through increased customer engagement and retention, personalisation of products and services, integration of systems and collaboration with suppliers to speed up fulfilment, and improved quality control processes

The ICAEW (2016) publication Digital transformation – the next steps: a business guide to digital change management suggests that some key areas to consider in relation to the evaluation of a business's current position and its priority areas for change include:

Knowledge management

How well is knowledge managed in the business?

Is there an intranet?

Can information such as business performance information be shared easily?

Efficiency and productivity

Does the business use ERP or manufacturing resource planning systems?

Does the business use cloud technology to be more efficient, flexible and mobile?

Payment and finance

Can the business accept telephone, mobile and online payments?

Does the business use online banking?

Do managers have access to accounts and finance at any time, anywhere?

Is the business' e-commerce system integrated with back office functions?

Customers and marketing

Does the company's website engage customers and add value?

Does the website work with tablets and mobile devices?

Does the business delivery products/services online?

Does the business have a search engine optimised website?

Do you regularly evaluate competitors' products, websites and social media?

Do you have a CRM system?

Do you regularly send out e-communications to customers?

Does the business offer personalised products or services?

How responsive do customers think the business is?

Does the business use social media? Does it have a good online interaction with its customers?

Does the business check all online channels for customer feedback and any issues which could affect brand reputation?

Does the business use information gathered from websites and social media to identify potential new ways of working or potential new products/services?

IT systems

How does the business manage its computer network?

Has it implemented cloud technologies for its infrastructure?

Does the business use technology to collaborate with other businesses?

Governance

Does the business have an IT policy covering use of hardware and software, data protection and internet usage?

Does the business have a disaster recovery plan? Is the plan updated regularly?

Are the business's systems secure and protected from viruses/malware and hackers?

Does the business have measures in place to enable staff to use their own devices securely when accessing organisational data?

See also	Big Data topics	
	Cloud computing	76
	Cyber security	95
	Digital Strategies	120

Disposals and Assets Held for Sale (IFRS 5)

Consider IFRS 5 rules on disposal groups: a group of assets to be disposed of, by sale or otherwise, together as a group in a single transaction – consider IFRS 5 held for sale criteria:

1. Available for immediate sale in its present condition

2. Sale highly probable (**significantly** more likely than not):

    - Management committed to a plan to sell
    - Active programme to locate a buyer
    - Marketed at a price that is reasonable in relation to its current fair value
    - Sale should be expected to take place within one year from date of classification
    - Unlikely that significant changes to the plan will be made or that the plan will be withdrawn

Remember to apply the above criteria by using the scenario – always consider if impairment applies

If there are Assets Held for Sale then very often there may also be a discontinued operation – see below.

Immediately before reclassification as held for sale (IFRS 5, IAS 36)

Review the carrying amounts of assets per IFRS 5 – assess the evidence of **each individual** asset or CGU immediately prior to the held for sale date

Determine if depreciation correctly treated (ceases at the correct time and yearly charge reflects this)

After classification as held for sale (IFRS 5, IAS 36)

Measure at the lower of carrying amount and FV less costs to sell

Impair if the carrying amount is greater than the FV less costs to sell

Test for impairment based on the disposal group as a whole (notice the difference with reclassification as held for sale)

Allocated impairment under IAS 36 in the following order: goodwill and then pro rata over the other assets

No asset shall be reduced below its recoverable amount nor below zero

Discontinued operation (IFRS 5)?

If there is disposal of a cash-generating unit (CGU) which relates to a separate line of business then the entity must provide an analysis of the contribution of the discontinued element separately presented from profit from ongoing operations to help the user assess possible future profitability, cash flows, financial position and earnings-generating capacity

A CGU generates revenue, is material and is operationally distinguishable from the rest of the company.

Ethics – Independence

Potentially very examinable in SBM – you are likely to be working at an advisory firm and will be asked to assist the client further – is this permissible?

Advisory Manager joining a client

Raises independence, self-interest and familiarity threats

Procedures should be in place such that the advisory firm is notified as soon as possible

Consider safeguards such as not having further involvement in the work

Consider discussing with Ethics Partner/Director of the advisory firm

Note – restrictions and safeguards will not be as strong if your firm in the examination is not an audit firm (and normally it will not be)

See also   Ethics – Frameworks and Problems   127

Ethics – Frameworks and Problems

In SBM you are supposed to adopt a nuanced or careful approach – not everything is a disaster and not everything is necessarily an ethical problem

You should always start your answer by stating that it is necessary to **first establish the facts before doing anything further**

Framework 1 – Case Study Approach: IIR Framework[5]

Issue – clearly explain why there is a potential ethical problem, using moral language such as "breach of confidentiality", "breach of distrust", "lack of integrity" and so on

Impact – clearly explain how significant the issue is, considering the different stakeholder groups (and considering that there will likely be differential impact on different groups)

Recommendations – clearly explain how the client should deal with the issue (demonstrating the **Recommendations** Case skills "lens")

Framework 2 – Institute of Business Ethics: TEF Framework

Transparency – is the client being open, honest and upfront with affected parties or is information being unethically withheld for self-interested reasons?

Effect – who is impacted by the issue and how serious is the impact? (Consider different stakeholders and recognise the likelihood of differential impact/effect on each group of stakeholders.)

Fairness – would a reasonable, informed but independent third party view the action as fair to all parties?

Framework 3 – ICAEW Ethical Conflict Resolution: The 6 Steps

Establish the:

1. Relevant **facts**
2. Relevant **parties**
3. Ethical **issues** involved
4. Fundamental **principles** related to the matter
5. Established **internal procedures**
6. **Alternative** courses of action

---

[5] See our book *Cracking Case™ – How to Pass the ACA Case Study* for a detailed explanation of IIR: there is not really any choice over framework in Case Study – IIR is what you **must** use so why not get practising for the future in your preparations for SBM?

Ethics – Frameworks and Problems

Framework 4 – ICAEW Code Principles: The 5 Core Principles

1. Integrity
2. Objectivity
3. Professional competence and due care
4. Confidentiality
5. Professional behaviour

Framework 5 – Threats and Safeguards

- **Self-interest** threat (very common)
- **Self-review** threat
- **Advocacy** threat
- **Familiarity** or **trust** threat
- **Intimidation** threat

Be careful of giving too much of an "auditor approach" to your answer: generally the SBM paper will indicate that the **advisory firm is not the auditor of the client** so **conflicts and threats** will be of a different nature.

Past paper problems and ethical issues raised

Example	Ethical issues	Recommendations
Not informing staff of information	Lack of integrity, unfair, dishonest, broken promises	Inform staff fully, consider using a change agent, use change management models
Appraisal systems	Fairness, lack of objectivity if some managers have more say in decisions, self-interest threat if decide own bonuses	Inform staff fully, prevent individuals deciding own remuneration
Reduction in training costs after making promises	Lack of integrity, lack of professional competence and due care, compromises commitments to customers, broken promises	Implement improved training, discuss with staff
Termination of apprenticeship scheme without notice	Lack of integrity, lack of corporate responsibility	Discuss with staff immediately, legal advice
Possible bribery or inducement	Could fall under the Bribery Act, could be fraud, self-interest threat, failure of fiduciary duty to shareholders	Confirm all facts immediately, seek legal advice, check whether inducement has occurred or is rather a future

Ethics – Frameworks and Problems

Example	Ethical issues	Recommendations
		possibility, speak to the Board, consider disclosing to Police (after taking legal advice), if any doubt, do not act
Transactions on unusual terms	Confidentiality, self-interest threat, deals below market value, lack of integrity	Investigate further to obtain more facts, transparency so the Board is aware of all arrangements, investigate possible inducements or self-interest threats for directors, legal advice to determine if the Bribery Act is relevant
Use of low quality raw materials	Could lead to health and safety concerns, might breach contractual agreement, might breach the spirit of a contract (even if it is legally permissible) damaging business trust, could result in deceptive behaviour if the final product is advertised in a way that suggests that all raw materials used are high quality	Check terms of contract, determine the appropriate disclosure of any change in materials used, ensure customer has appropriate quality assurance procedures in place, provide transparency in any cases of doubt or concern

Compliance with the contractual terms could be an appropriate defence provided that the contract terms are clear and there is a common understanding |

Ethics – Frameworks and Problems

Example	Ethical issues	Recommendations
Accidental receipt of confidential information	Could lead to unintentional breach of confidentiality by the recipient – not a deliberate act	Inform the sender (including the Board if relevant), information should not be passed on to any other parties unless required by law, recipient may be obliged to take further action such as discussing the issues raised with the Board if these are serious (even though it was never intended that the recipient would receive the information)
Director not disclosing a proposed consultancy arrangement with another group company	Transparency particularly in the context of a proposed MBO involving the other group company, conflict of interest as the Director will not want to threaten future income from the consultancy arrangement and so may promote the interests of the other group company over those of the current employer, could be illegal activity if the Director attempts to alter the nature of transactions between the companies on a self-interested basis	Check facts and determine what has actually been finalised and agreed, take legal advice, avoid "tipping off", ensure transparency by informing all affected parties of the full facts, consider excluding the Director from future discussions on the relevant issue, ask the Director not to accept the consultancy arrangement, if the Director is an ICAEW Chartered Accountant consider reporting the Director to the ICAEW Ethics Committee on the grounds of reasonable suspicion of an ethical, legal or other disciplinary breach

See also Ethics – Independence 126

Finance – Sources for SMEs

Owner financing

Equity finance

Business angel financing

Venture capital

Leasing

Factoring

Bank loans

Microfinance

SMEs experience problems in obtaining financing because of the problem of uncertainty and lack of data – they do not have the business history or track record that larger organisations possess

They are also less subject to scrutiny by law so there is less trust

Banks use scoring systems to control exposure to SMEs – these systems may not always identify the correct results

See also	Bank Loans	49
	Bonds (Loan Notes) v Bank Loans – Comparisons	60
	Loan Decision by a Bank	202

Financial Performance Review in SBM – Some Advice

- Use tables of figures, particularly if comparing different years or different business streams, and present such tables at the **start of your answer before the narrative**: the examiners really seem to like this and it also automatically gives you an overview of the position and a range of points to look out for.

- Look out for **exceptionals** – are there any unusual events in only one of the years considered or only one of the business streams considered? If you do not have time to make the adjustments numerically then at least still comment on the issue to get some partial credit.

- **Do not forget the obvious** – mention that revenue declined by X% and mention that profit increased by Y% – just because this is one of your last few examinations, do not assume that every point has to be rocket-science.

- Suggest **causes** – look for reasons for the changes: you do not have to be certain here as anything sensible, based on the scenario date, should score some credit.

- **Margin anomalies** – are the margin movements strange given the revenue changes? Are the margins moving in different directions (GPM up but OPM down)? Why?

- **Revenue versus the market** – does the change outpace the market/industry or is it weaker? Why?

- Compare **volume versus price changes** (if the data allows) – still on the theme of causes, try to assess whether it is a change in price or the change in sales volumes which is driving the overall change (note that this may not always be possible if you do not have price information but you could look at margins)

- If **price has changed**, look at the "**elasticity**" or responsiveness of demand to the changes – was the price change a good decision?

- Consider the **product mix** and any changes

- **Look for any missing figures/provisions etc – but do not go too crazy as there will always be plenty of factors not considered!** Try to stick to MS^2 points – if there has been a legal dispute in the year but there is no provision then this is relevant but mentioning a missing deferred tax balance is probably not material (unless the scenario mentions tax). If CAPEX has increased funded by loans then a lack of change in finance charges is significant but only if the scenario puts some emphasis on CAPEX spend.

- Comment on **margins** but ensure that you add narrative – do not just say that the margin has gone up or down, give some reasons why.

- Look for **patterns** – are all costs up? Was there only one business stream which suffered a loss? Recognising these patterns will help you to understand the big picture.

Financial Performance Review in SBM – Some Advice

- **Exceptions** – is there only one revenue stream that is growing? Is operating profit down, even though gross profit is up?

- **Scenario-specific indicators** – make sure you include plenty of points on these, moving beyond the typical accountant's figures such as gross profit margin and operating profit margin to consider the unique forms of data that are specific to the company in the scenario[6] (for example, revenue per passenger, profit per staff member etc)

- Try to identify the **major drivers of the changes** and also specifically comment that these are the main drivers

- Look for **interdependencies** between streams

- Comment on **particularly high and low margins**

- **Compare changes in monetary figures with absolute underlying numbers** e.g. revenue changes versus changes in passenger numbers

- Consider **fixed costs**, **operating gearing** and **marginal costs**

- Analyse **different cost categories** (but only if there are **material** changes)

- Consider **cash flows versus financial reporting treatment** (providing the perspective of the "Accountant in Business")

See also   Q1 – Technique Reminders   231

---

[6] In the July 2014 paper, company-specific "operating data" was provided below the P&L: weaker candidates concentrated too much on the P&L as this was more familiar territory. Familiar/typical information is of course at the other end of the spectrum to scenario-specific points so you will not be getting as much credit for generic points.

Financial Performance Review in SBM – Audit Procedures

Obtain a split of overheads into fixed and variable overheads and investigate changes

Ascertain whether sales revenue changes are due to volume or price, based on production records and pricing lists

Ascertain reasons for changes in variables and confirm changes to documentation

Review the assumptions on which budgets were prepared

Seek explanations from management for changes in figures that cannot be verified independently: consider additional audit procedures

See also   Q1 – Technique Reminders   231

Financial Reconstruction

Key impact is on cost of capital, as a result of changes in the cost of equity and cost of debt

Impact is hard to judge and will depend on scenario-specific factors – may also not be possible to assess given the figures provided

Change in debt profile (amount, interest rate, period) will have an impact e.g. on gearing and earnings

Consider existing versus new debenture holders: value, amount held, covenants, effective amount of interest they receive, rights to conversion if any, reduction in income

Financial Reconstruction – possible calculation pro-forma

The funds generated may need to be calculated based on the following pro forma, probably involving PPE, inventories and trade receivables. The liquidator's fee should then be deducted, together with any **fixed** charge due.

Once the remaining net amount after the liquidator's fee and fixed charge(s) ("Remaining funds") is known then we can estimate what we can potentially repay to any creditors with a **floating** charge – this is found by dividing the Remaining funds by the floating charges due to find how much per £1 of floating charge will actually be repaid (it will probably be less than £1 due to the difficulties the company is facing).

(A fixed charge is a charge over a specified asset of the entity: the entity loses the freedom to dispose of this asset without the permission of the owner – a floating charge is a charge over the assets in general of the entity: the entity retains the freedom to dispose of assets unless a default has occurred as the charge is not in connection with any specified asset.)

Overall the proforma might look like that below:

Funds generated
- PPE
- Inventories
- Trade receivables
- Total proceeds

Less liquidator's fee
Less paid to holder's of a fixed charge
Remaining funds   R

Floating charges
- Loans
- Overdraft

                                                         F

Amount paid to holders of a floating charge (per £1 of floating charge) = R/F

For example, if the company has been lent amounts subject to floating charges of £10m but the R figure is only £5m then holders of floating charges will only receive back 50% (5/10) of their original investment.

Financial Reconstruction

After this, you should make some standard narrative points (see below).

Note that if the result of the fraction R/F is less than 1, then this means that floating chargeholders will not receive back the full amount of their investment – it follows that unsecured creditors and shareholders (neither of whom have any charges at all) will not receive anything back at all.

The calculation steps to follow again are:

Step 1	Calculate proceeds received based on assets
Step 2	Deduct liquidator's fee and fixed charges
Step 3	Arrive at Remaining funds (R)
Step 4	Calculate Floating charges (F)
Step 5	Find amount repayable per £1 of Floating charge (R/F) (probably to a bank)
Step 6	Make standard narrative points (see below)

Based on the November 2014 real exam, you can ignore the "prescribed part" in your calculation but should comment that this would be reserved for unsecured creditors by law: effectively, this preserves a small amount for the unsecured creditors.

Will the reconstruction succeed?

Generally the equity holders should suffer a greater loss – this is the nature of equity

If the proposal puts most of the loss onto providers of debt capital then the debt holders are more likely to benefit from a liquidation of the company's assets or take over by an asset stripper, rather than from the reconstruction (particularly if they have covenants in place)

Such a loss would prevent new debenture holders apply to fund the capital – alternatively equity holders will have to suffer dilution by offering an equity element to attract debenture holders

Consider information on likely turnaround and amounts – earnings and dividends need to be considered

Exercise scepticism of what the board of directors say

Estimate the amount by which the reconstruction will leave the company short of capital (or, less likely in an exam question, have an excess of capital)

Debentures

Consider lifetime and coupon rate – distinguish cash payments from effective interest rate for accounting purposes

Financial Reconstruction

Consider difference from the coupon rate and the market rate (i.e. the running yield: if a 5% coupon bond is sold at a price that has a running yield of 10% (i.e. a bond with a face value of £100 costs £50) then consider why this may be

Will the issue achieve the funds needed, based on the issue price estimated (see below)?

Expected market issue price of debentures

Perform an IRR calculation using the required return as the discount rate i.e. discount the coupon amounts and redemption amount in a tabular form (as done in FM or for the liability element of a convertible bond)

The PV which results will be the estimated market price

Use this to determine whether the issue will raise the funds needed

Equity

State the increase in number of shares (physical number of shares) and increase in net assets (£)

Discuss any differences compared to issue/cancellation of debentures

Calculate net asset value per share before and after the equity issue

The share price should move based on perceptions by the market/shareholders of the impact of the financial reconstruction

Issue of shares will increase the number of shares and decrease the price per share in most cases (unless there is another impact on expectations)

Consider how EPS may be affected – remember that if the equity is used to redeem debentures then there will be an impact on interest costs and therefore earnings

Corporate Governance issues

Consider if investor engagement by the board of directors is satisfactory – need to be informed and given information about the impact if there is no reconstruction and if there is a reconstruction

Ending in a position where a reconstruction is needed raises questions about the board's position and approach to risk – has it been taking excessive risk?

Is the board showing enough concern for all stakeholders? Is the board promoting a fair approach or is it favouring one set of stakeholders (such as equity stakeholders) over another?

Has the board failed in terms of providing leadership for the company? Perhaps investors should seek a significant change to the senior executive team and composition of the board.

Essential requirement for a successful restructuring deal must be the ability to improve operational performance – important that the right stakeholders (e.g. a purchaser) have control over this

Consider whether there is a stakeholder that should insist on appointment of an NED to represent its interests (e.g. a purchaser investing for a minority stake may insist on board representation)

Share schemes – amendments

Consider the terms of the agreement to establish the altered entitlements that scheme holders may have

May consider buying out existing options and cancelling these – offer a price based on expected future increase in value

Tougher approach – insist that cancelled for the reconstruction to take place – either go through with this or use it as a negotiating tactic

Estimate the likely impact on annual profits

Financial reconstruction and liquidation: Narrative points

Unsecured creditors and shareholders will receive nothing if the ratio of R/F (remaining funds to floating charges) is less than 1 – if the ratio is less than one, then we are saying that floating chargeholders are not receiving all of their money back so there is clearly nothing further available to those without any charges recorded at all (unsecured creditors and shareholders).

In some cases, it may be that you need to **compare a liquidation against an alternative option** (such as keeping the business going, but on revised terms – this would be a financial reconstruction). Again, try to consider the matter from the perspective of different **stakeholders** such as the funding bank, shareholders and creditors.

Points to consider could include:

Bank

The bank receives **certain cash back under a liquidation** but could be subject to **further risk if the money is left invested under a financial reconstruction**.

Consider the **interest rates** under the financial reconstruction – these will probably be higher than before in order to give the bank an incentive to continue to invest.

Consider **whether other stakeholders would invest** under the financial reconstruction or **will the bank remain the main funder** and therefore subject to the most risk?

Consider the **potential return** under the financial reconstruction – is this probable and/or attractive to the bank?

Shareholders

The shareholders **may get nothing back under a liquidation** but at least have some **voting power** to determine what happens.

You may wish to comment on what **shareholders are being asked to do** under the financial reconstruction option.

The amount invested in the original shares could be considered to be a sunk cost if liquidation is an active option: in other words, if the financial reconstruction does not happen then that money is lost anyway so the cost of the original investment is not a relevant or incremental cost – only the new capital injected under the financial reconstruction is a relevant cost.

Financial Reconstruction

Use the **forecast returns** for calculation purposes but **apply professional scepticism** as the projections may be optimistic in order to keep the company going (look at the position of the Board of Directors here).

Suppliers

Suppliers **may get nothing back under a liquidation** and, unlike shareholders, have no **voting power** to determine what happens.

Unsecured creditors would only get a small "**prescribed part**" back in a liquidation whereas if a financial reconstruction works then, over time, they may receive the **full** amount back.

As **suppliers are in a weak position**, it may be possible for the client company to negotiate hard and improve its position.

Resorting to court action would be a waste of time if there are other creditors which rank ahead of the suppliers (fixed and floating charge holders).

Financial reporting points

Although it remains outside the scope of this book to discuss financial reporting issues in detail, any discussion of liquidation and financial reconstruction is likely to be paired up with some financial reporting marks for points such as:

- IAS 1 and going concern presentation (valuation and also classification of liabilities and assets as current or non-current)

- ISA 570 *Going Concern* issues and the position of the auditor

- IAS 10 *Events after the reporting period*

See also		
	CAPM	69
	Change – Definition & Models	73
	Change – Management & Implementation	75
	Disposals and Assets Held for Sale (IFRS 5)	125
	Liquidation	198
	Valuations topics	

Forensic Audits

Defined as "the process of gathering, analysing and reporting on data for the purpose of finding facts and evidence in the context of financial or legal disputes and giving preventative advice in this area".

A key aspect of forensic auditing is therefore that the issue must arise in the context of a financial or legal **dispute**.

Applications of forensic auditing include:

- Fraud
- Negligence
- Insurance claims
- Shareholder and partnership disputes
- Contract disputes
- Business sales and purchase disputes
- Matrimonial disputes
- Investigation of terrorist financing
- Expert witness services

When providing expert witness services, the duties of the witness are set out in the Civil Procedure Rules (CPR):

- experts owe a duty to exercise reasonable skill and care to those instructing them but their overriding duty is to the court to help the court judge the matter justly
- experts should provide opinions which are independent
- experts should confine their opinions to matters which are material to the dispute between the parties
- experts should only offer opinions on matters which lie within their expertise

Planning a Forensic Audit

As with a statutory audit, there should be a planning stage, an evidence-gathering stage, a review process and a report to the client provided at the final stage. There are some differences to a statutory audit:

- there will be no materiality threshold

Forensic Audits

- the timing of the report will be more variable – there will not be a standardised reporting date
- documentation needs to be reviewed more critically than on a standard audit
- interviews may be required, and these will need a high level of experience and skill
- there may be greater use of sophisticated data mining techniques
- the environment could be one defined by conflict such as in a fraud of matrimonial dispute

Example procedures for a Fraud investigation could include[7]:

- developing a profile of the entity/individual under investigation
- identifying weaknesses in internal control procedures and record-keeping
- performing trend analysis and analytical procedures to identify significant transactions and variations
- identifying changes in patterns of purchases/sales
- identifying significant variations in consumption of raw materials and consumables
- identifying unusual accounts and account balances
- reviewing transaction documentation for discrepancies and inconsistencies
- tracing the individual responsible for fraudulent transactions
- obtaining information regarding all responsibilities of the individual involved
- inspecting and reviewing other transactions of a similar nature conducted by the individual
- considering all other aspects of the business which the individual is involved with and performing further analytical procedures

See also   Internal Audit topics

---

[7] As forensic audits/investigations vary considerably in nature, always ensure that you include points which are relevant to the scenario set.

Franchising

Risks

Limited control over the actions of franchisees – could damage brand quality

Financial failure of franchisee may lead to non-payment of the franchise fees (unless collected up front) – impact on cash and profits

Risk of understatement of franchise fees through understatement of sales by franchisee

Insufficient franchisees to grow the business

Risk that franchisees will not renew their agreements if they are unsuccessful

Operational and contractual disputes with franchisees

Increased monitoring costs

Franchisees may request a lower fee to allow prices to be cut but will volume respond?

Controls over understatement of fees by franchisees

Establish clear link between goods purchased and sales

Link sales with purchases within systems

Regular reconciliations of till control totals with amounts banked

Banking of all cash receipts intact (do not allow payments being made in cash from cash receipts)

Review bank reconciliations as regularly as is feasible and include a requirement for regular reconciliation in franchise agreements

Reconcile revenues reported with the financial statements and tax returns of franchisees

Require franchisees to provide management accounting records on a regular basis

Review management accounting information comparing monthly sales over time and between outlets for evidence of understatement – e.g unusual fall in sales or unusual movements in gross profit margins

Review of staff physically in the branches against payroll records

Random unannounced visits and cash accounts

Overall, ensure that the franchise agreement reflects the above points so that both parties understand the controls and requirements

See also	Joint Arrangements – Assurance	189
	Organic Growth	209
	Outsourcing	211

FRC Risk Guidance

The FRC publication *Guidance on Risk Management, Internal Control and Related Financial and Business Reporting* was published in September 2014 – this is known as the Risk Guidance

It revises, integrates and replaces existing FRC guidance on internal control and going concern and reflects changes made to the UK Corporate Governance Code

Objectives

To encourage companies to adopt a risk-based approach to establishing a system of internal control i.e. to manage and control risk appropriately rather than eliminate it – the company must:

Establish business objectives

Identify the key risks associated with these objectives

Agree the controls to address the risks

Set up a system to implement the decision, including regular feedback

Responsibilities of Directors

Ensure the design and implementation of appropriate risk management and internal control systems

Determine the nature and extent of the principal risks faced and the organisation's risk appetite

Ensure that appropriate culture and reward systems have been embedded throughout the organisation

Agree how the principal risks should be managed or mitigated

Monitor and review the risk management and internal control systems and the management's process of monitoring and reviewing

Ensure sound internal and external information and communication processes are in place and communicate with external stakeholders on risk management and internal control

Determine the company's going concern status as part of assessing how risks affect longer term sustainability

The 2014 UK Corporate Governance Code contains a new provision requiring a "viability statement" – directors should explain how they have assessed the prospects of the company, over what period they have done so and why they consider that period to be appropriate – except in rare circumstances the period covered should be significantly longer than 12 months but the longer the period considered the lower the level of certainty possible

The guidance emphasises the importance of identifying those risks that might threaten business sustainability and suggests the use of stress testing and sensitivity analysis as useful techniques for assessing both the company's overall resilience and the appropriateness of the going concern assessment

Responsibilities of management

Implement board policies on risk and control

Provide the board with timely information

FRC Risk Guidance

Establish clear internal responsibilities and accountabilities at all levels of the organisation

Responsibilities of employees

Acquire the necessary knowledge, skills and authority to establish, operate and monitor the system of internal controls

Globalisation

Globalisation can be defined as "the procurement, production, distribution and selling of products and services of a homogenous type and quality on a worldwide basis" – key aspects include:

- consumers having the same needs and attitudes and using the same products
- extended supply chains – different parts of the product (or service) originate in different countries
- global human resource management – pan-national recruitment and development of human resources

Requires an effective IT infrastructure to allow work and collaboration anywhere in the world – needs to allowing sharing of ideas and best practice and create and maintain relationships with supply chain partners

Improved digital technologies have made it easier for entrepreneurs and start-ups to enter markets – equally, competition from foreign competitors is likely to become more pervasive

There should be greater opportunity for small businesses who specialise in one activity to collaborate with other best-in-class organisations to compete internationally or globally

Impact on business management

Managers will need to change the way they think about their industry because of the fast pace of innovation and change

Managers will need to change the way they think about their firms and management tasks

Significant diversity in enterprise structures and management styles is expected

Multinational companies and taxation

Transfer pricing is likely to be very important here – high profile media stories have emerged suggesting that some large companies have used transfer pricing to reduce the amount of tax that they pay in the UK

The OECD Base erosion and profit shifting (BEPS) programme addresses tax planning strategies and exploits gaps and mismatches in tax rules to artificially shift profits – developing countries are particularly dependent on corporate income tax from multinational companies

The UK government has begun to offer low corporation tax rates with a proposal to reduce rates to 18% to bring the UK into competition with the statutory rates in Switzerland, Singapore and Hong Kong – this could be helpful in attracting overseas business in the UK and dissuading businesses from relocating operations away from the UK

Hedging – Audit and Financial Reporting Points

Audit Points

Exam tip – always check whether these are really needed – is there an assurance aspect to the question? If not, just leave out the below and do something else

Check whether the following documentation is available:

- Details of the risk management objectives and strategy for undertaking the hedge
- Identification and description of the hedging instrument
- Details of the hedged item or transaction
- Nature of the risk being hedged
- Description of how the entity will assess the instrument's effectiveness

Financial Reporting Points

Hedge Accounting

Discuss IAS 39 criteria briefly: risk being hedged is clearly defined, hedge is effective (80-125% rule), measurability

Discuss whether cash flow or fair value (or choice of these – rare)

Strict requirements for designation as a hedge

1. Formal designation and documentation of the hedging relationship and risk management objective and strategy
2. Must be a highly effective hedge (80-125% rule)
3. Must be possible to reliably measure effectiveness
4. Effectiveness must be checked on an ongoing basis to ensure that it has been highly effective post designation as a hedge

Cash flow hedge – movements **stored up in Equity (and through OCI, not P&L)** and released later

Fair value hedge – movements **straight into P&L**

Disclosures under IFRS 7 will be needed

Hedging – Audit and Financial Reporting Points

Matching assets and liabilities

Minimal impact prior to a loan being drawn down (costs likely to be rolled up into the borrowings (assuming that we are matching against a liability)) – if are matching against a liability by taking on an asset/investment then may be some interest earned as income

Consider commenting on whether the hedged item is monetary or non-monetary and therefore whether there are year end implications when updating for a new exchange rate

Money market hedge

Requires accounting entries right now as the relevant loan is taken out

This creates a monetary asset which will be translated at spot value on inception and then retranslated

Forward contract

A derivative and hence accounted in accordance with IAS 39

Shown at fair value with differences being recorded in profit or loss

No accounting on inception (unless there are some transaction fees)

Adjust at year end (and maturity date) for the current spot rate and recognise changes in P&L

Likely to be settled **net** (i.e. only the difference is paid to or from the bank – the party and bank do not pay each other separate currency amounts for the full amount hedged) – this reduces the cash impact

See also   Hedging – Choices, Methods and Risks   148
              Overseas Operations topics

Hedging – Choices, Methods and Risks

For advice on derivatives calculations, see our various topics starting on page 99.

Exam warning for this topic – do not just list out hedging strategies – the examiners have stated they are tired of this – ensure you select appropriate strategies only and look out for any examiner "twists" which mean that the technique will not work as it normally would in the Financial Management examination (e.g. company is paid in advance of delivery of goods or has large costs in the foreign currency and may therefore not need any hedging)

Methods

Forward contracts

Futures

Money market hedge

Forward Rate Agreement (FRA)

Currency swaps – explanation

A currency swap is an interest rate swap with cash flows in different currencies – the entity first takes out a domestic currency loan and immediately swaps this into foreign currency to set up the project – the entity then takes out a currency swap with a bank: this involves the entity taking out a foreign currency loan and paying interest on this amount and the bank taking out a loan in the domestic currency of the client, paying interest to the entity on this amount

The entity pays interest on the foreign currency amount and receives interest on an amount in its domestic currency: at the end of the term, the entity pays the foreign currency loan back and receives payment from the bank to cancel the domestic currency loan extended by the entity to the bank – the interest received during the loan on its domestic currency loan to the bank could be used to pay interest on the initial domestic currency loan taken out at the start of the project to fund the project (after being instantly swapped into foreign currency) – the swap interest in a foreign currency that the entity needs to pay could be repaid from cash flows from the foreign investment, **without the need for any currency exchange**

At the end of the project, the repayment of the foreign currency leg of the swap could be made from proceeds realised on disposal of project assets – the domestic currency amount received from the swap bank could be used to make an instant repayment of the underlying domestic currency loan.

(See November 2015 Mock Q2 for an example.)

FX swap – spot transaction with agreement to reverse at a pre-set date by an offsetting forward transaction

Example of currency swap
Parent and subsidiary in different countries but need each other's currency

Example of FX swap
Overseas investment to set up a factory but borrowing done in domestic currency – spot swap to get the forex needed now and loan in domestic currency starts; use the forex to set up production and then convert back into domestic when the domestic currency loan needs repaying

*Do not forget to take into account the interest accruing on the domestic currency loan between the date of the spot deal and the date of reversal at a later time

Points to make

Can be expensive and unnecessary

Removes upside risk

Look at macro hedging – i.e. hedging total amounts rather than looking at each contract individually
If the transaction is uncertain and does not happen then actually hedging worsens the risk

The 3 currency risks

Mnemonic	**TET**
Transaction risk	adverse short term movements during ordinary progress of business
Economic risk	effect of exchange rates over the longer term on international competitiveness of a company
Translation risk	risk of exchange losses when translating foreign branches/subsidiaries into home currency

Managing economic risk

Diversification of operations worldwide

Market and promotional management to promote the diversification

Product management

Pricing

Production management – set up production in countries with lower relative production costs

Reasons not to hedge

Costs may be too high

May not be a material amount

Company may want to leave opportunity for upside risk

Portfolio effect – company may have products/shareholdings which reduce risk

Hedging – Choices, Methods and Risks

If shareholders are already fully diversified then no need to hedge

Key risk identified in QB questions – removes upside risk and ability to benefit from improvements

Risks of using derivatives

- Legal
- Market
- Currency
- Credit
- Settlement
- Solvency
- Interest rate
- Accounting – complexity of the accounting, impact on financial statements (if not a hedging instrument, accounted for in the income statement at FV so introduces volatility)
- Business may lack necessary expertise

Forwards versus futures versus options

Forwards

- Fix amount due in advance
- Binding contract – trade must take place even if foreign currency is no longer received/needed
- Customised to user's needs
- Bank may default (if using an OTC contract)
- Administrative convenience – agreed with the bank and nothing required until the settlement date

Futures

- Binding contract
- Standardised amounts which may not match requirements precisely
- Lower transaction costs due to standardisation
- Deposit is smaller than a forward or option
- Ready market – not a contract which a specific counterparty (bank) which could default
- Basis risk
- Only a limited number of currencies are available
- Administrative complexity – system of regular margin payments to cover potential and actual losses on futures positions
- Can be closed at any time (unlike forwards)

Options

- Not binding – can be left to lapse if no longer desirable outcome
- Can be tailor made or bought on market
- Cost generally 5% of total foreign currency covered
- Not available for all currencies

Using interest rate options – considerations

Premium may be high

If using OTC options:

- Can be tailored
- Used over a long period
- May only be exercisable at a particular time
- Not transferrable

If using traded options:

- Exercisable at any time
- Straightforward to use
- Could be sold on if an early exit is needed

Reasons to use an interest rate swap

- Gain lower interest rate for preferred type by exploiting quality spread difference
- Better match of assets and liabilities
- Access to market rates that may not be possible otherwise
- Swap from floating to fixed or vice versa
- Restructure debts without incurring new loans/fees
- Speculate on future course of interest rates
- Available for longer period than other methods

Risks of interest rate swaps

Mnemonic   DUT

- Default – other party may default and not pay its side

- Unfavourable movements – one side will lose out when things change

- Transparency – may undermine the clarity and transparency of financial statements

Hedging without use of derivatives

Change invoice currency

Use money market hedging

Matching payments and receipts

Matching assets and liabilities

Leading and lagging
Netting

Hedging – Choices, Methods and Risks

Hedge the net investment in a foreign subsidiary by borrowing in a foreign currency

Note that most hedging methods are relatively short term in nature and unlikely to protect against economic exposure of long-term shifts in exchange rates

See also Derivatives Calculations topics
Hedging – Audit and Financial Reporting Points 146
Interest Rate Calculations 169
Overseas Operations topics

IFRS 9 – classification and measurement

The **IAS 39** classification of financial assets has been criticised as a **complex** and **inflexible rule-based** approach so the IAS 39 approach will be replaced by a **principles-based** approach under **IFRS 9**

IFRS 9 is **mandatory** for accounting periods beginning **on or after 1 January 2018**

Impact of IFRS 9 on financial statements

IFRS 9 classification-based measurement categories may lead to **different accounting treatment** compared with IAS 39.

On transition to IFRS 9, some instruments **may no longer be eligible** for **amortised cost** classification.

Other instruments, like those that are not held within the business model to collect contractual cash flows or hybrid contracts with a financial host, will have to be measured **at fair value** under IFRS 9.

If a financial liability is classified at FVtPL, **fair value movements due to changes in credit risk** are recognised in **OCI** under IFRS 9 – this will reduce the **volatility** arising in profit or loss as a result of the "**own credit**" problem (see below) in IAS 39.

Aspects with no significant changes under IFRS 9

The basic **scope** of IFRS 9 is the same as that of IAS 39

Recognition and derecognition criteria are unchanged from IAS 39 – however, improved **disclosure** requirements have been added to **IFRS 7**, *Financial Instruments: Disclosures* in relation to transfers of financial assets

New rules under IFRS 9

Classifications of financial assets on initial recognition

On initial recognition, financial assets will have to be classified as at **amortised cost**, fair value through other comprehensive income (**FVtOCI**) or fair value through profit or loss (**FVtPL**)

Subsequent measurement of financial assets

Subsequent measurement is based on the entity's **business model** for managing the financial assets and the **contractual cash flow characteristics** of the financial assets

Assets held at **amortised cost** are **not revalued** to fair value at each year end – **interest** measured at the effective interest rate (**EIR**) is recognised in **profit or loss** – **gains and losses** on disposals are recognised in **profit or loss**

IFRS 9 – classification and measurement

Assets held at **FVtOCI are remeasured** to fair value at each reporting date – gains or losses are recognised in **OCI** and are **reclassified** to profit or loss on disposal – **interest** measured at the **EIR** is recognised in profit or loss – **foreign exchange gains or losses** and **impairment** are recognised in profit or loss

Assets held at **FVtPL are remeasured** to fair value at each reporting date – **gains or losses** (whether at a year-end remeasurement or on disposal) are recognised in **profit or loss** – interest measured at the **EIR** is recognised in **profit or loss**

Reclassification of financial assets

If an entity **changes** its business model for managing financial assets, it should **reclassify** all **affected** financial assets – however, this is expected to be a **rare** event which would only occur when an entity **begins** or **ceases to perform** an **activity** that is **significant** to its operations such as **acquiring**, **disposing of**, or **terminating** a business line

The following are **not** changes in business model: a change in **intention** related to particular financial assets even in circumstances of significant changes in market conditions, the **temporary disappearance** of a particular market for the financial assets or a **transfer** of financial assets between **parts** of the **entity with different business models**

Any **reclassification** is applied **prospectively** from the reclassification date – a **reclassification** requires **disclosures** under **IFRS 7**

If an asset at **amortised cost** or at **FVtOCI** is reclassified, the **recognition** of **interest revenue** will **not** change and the **same EIR** applies in future

If an asset at **FVtPL** is reclassified, the EIR is determined on the basis of the **fair value** of the asset at the **reclassification date**

Classifications of financial liabilities on initial recognition

The classification rules are **unchanged** from those previously contained within IAS 39.

Initial recognition should always be at **fair value**, which is normally the transaction price.

Financial liabilities can be measured either at **FVtPL** or at **amortised cost** – **transaction costs are deducted** from the amount of any financial liability classified at amortised cost.

Subsequent measurement

Measurement at FVtPL or amortised cost continues

Derivatives are **always** measured at **FVtPL except** for **effective hedging instruments** in certain types of hedge

"Own credit" liabilities (liabilities for instruments issued by the entity itself)

IFRS 9 **improves** on IAS 39 rules here – under IAS 39, **all gains or losses on financial liabilities held at FVtPL are recognised in profit or loss** – this is **counterintuitive** because a **gain** would be recognised in profit or loss when the **creditworthiness** of the issuer (the issuer's "own credit")

deteriorates – in other words, if an entity **issues** a bond and so has a financial liability, under IAS 39 it would record a **gain** in profit or loss if its **own creditworthiness suffers** and the bond loses fair value, meaning that the entity **records a profit when its performance is weak**

To **correct** for this problem, **IFRS 9** requires a gain or loss in the period on a FVtPL financial liability to be **split** into (1) the gain or loss resulting from **credit risk** and (2) any **other** gain or loss

The gain or loss as a result of **credit risk** is recognised in **OCI** unless it creates or enlarges an accounting mismatch, in which case it is recognised in profit or loss

The **other** element of any gain or loss is recognised in **profit or loss**

On **derecognition**, any gains or losses recognised in OCI are **not** transferred to **profit or loss**, although the cumulative gain or loss **may** be transferred within **equity**

Reclassification of financial liabilities

Reclassification of financial liabilities is **not** permitted under IFRS 9

IFRS 9 – embedded derivatives

Financial asset host contracts

IFRS 9 simplifies the IAS 39 rules by applying its rules to the **entire** hybrid contract – hybrid contracts with an IFRS 9 financial host such as convertible bonds are simply measured at FVtPL

Under IAS 39, embedded derivatives are required to be **separated** out from their host contract and accounted for as derivatives when certain conditions are fulfilled

Other host contracts

If the host contract is **not** a financial asset, IFRS 9 requires an embedded derivative to be **separated** out from its host contract when **all** the following conditions are met:

1. the **economic characteristics** and risks of the embedded derivatives are **not closely related** to the economic characteristics and risks of the host contract

2. a **separate instrument** with the same terms as the **embedded derivative** would meet the definition of a derivative

3. the **hybrid** (combined) instrument is **not already measured** at **FVtPL** (in other words, if the instrument is already held at FVtPL then there is no need to go through the trouble of splitting out the derivative simply to ensure that the derivative is correctly recorded in the P&L – the instrument as a whole is **already** at FVtPL so the derivative element is already in the P&L, just like the rest of the instrument)

IFRS 9 – hedge accounting

Problems with IAS 39 hedge accounting rules

Considered to be **complex** and not reflective of the way in which an entity normally **manages** its risks

Often **prevents entities applying hedge accounting** to transactions which have **genuinely** been entered into for hedging purposes and which do involve a **hedging effect in practice**

IFRS 9 – impact on the entity and auditors

IFRS 9 is effective for reporting periods commencing on or after **1 January 2018**

Adoption of IFRS 9 rules on hedge accounting will require the **entity** to have appropriate processes in place to identify **new hedging opportunities** and to ensure that the extensive new disclosure requirements of IFRS 9 are met

Auditors will need to test management's judgements with regard to the hedge effectiveness criteria (the "**economic relationship**" test – see below) and will also need to obtain comfort over the fair value measurement of the components of non-financial hedged items, purchased options, forward contracts and cross currency swaps

IFRS 9 approach – basics

Applies a **principles-based** approach (compared to the **rules-based** approach of IAS 39)

Use of a principles-based approach will require **judgement** in relation to the determination of whether a hedging relationship meets the **hedge effectiveness criteria** (the "**economic relationship**" test – see below) and the determination of when "**rebalancing**" will be required (see below)

Aims at **better alignment** with the risk management practices actually used by **management**, allowing transactions which are **genuinely intended to be hedges** to **apply hedge accounting** in situations where **IAS 39 rules may preclude this**

Allows **both** derivatives and non-derivative financial assets or liabilities to be hedging instruments, provided that they are measured at Fair Value through Profit or Loss – IAS 39 requires hedging instruments to be **derivatives** except for the hedge of foreign currency

Replaces the **IAS 39 "bright line" 80% - 125% test** with an "**objective-based assessment**", designed to create an assessment more closely aligned with the actual practices of companies in managing their risks

Requires an "**economic relationship**" between the hedged item and hedging instrument – in other words, the hedging instrument and the hedged item must have values that generally move in opposite directions because of the same risk (which is the hedged risk)

Allows **changes to the hedging relationship** if the risk management objective for that designated hedging relationship remains the same – this is known as "**rebalancing**" – IAS 39 generally requires discontinuation of hedge accounting if there is a change in the hedging relationship

IFRS 9 – hedge accounting

IFRS 9 approach – discontinuation of hedge accounting

Voluntary discontinuation of hedge accounting is **not permitted** when the risk management objective for the hedging relationship has not changed

This is a notable **contrast** with IAS 39 rules which allow an entity to **revoke hedge accounting at any time**

As such, **discontinuation** of hedge accounting is a **rare instance** where the **IFRS 9** rules are **less flexible** than the **IAS 39** rules

IFRS 9 and IAS 39 – shared rules

The following 4 points have not changed under the IFRS 9 approach

- the **terminology** of the standards is generally the same

- the **3 types** of hedge (fair value hedge, cash flow hedge and hedge of a net investment) are the same

- hedge **ineffectiveness** is recognised in **profit or loss** (except for the Other Comprehensive Income option for equity investments, which is a category only available under IFRS 9)

- hedge accounting with **written options is prohibited**

IFRS 9 approach – more complex points

Allows the **time value** of purchased options and the **forward element** of forward contracts and foreign currency basis spreads to be **excluded** from the hedging relationship, which should decrease volatility in profit or loss – under IFRS 9 the time component of an option is a cost of hedging presented through **OCI** (rather than in the P&L) and the forward element of forward contracts may also be presented in **OCI** (rather than in the P&L)

Allows **more items** to be designated as **hedged items** than under IAS 39 – examples include risk components of non-financial items, groups of items and net positions even if the change in value attributable to the hedged risk is not proportional to that of the designated items within the group (unlike under IAS 39) and equity investments at Fair Value through Other Comprehensive Income (this category does not exist under IAS 39)

May be beneficial to **banks** – under IAS 39, banks do not often achieve hedge accounting on the **credit risk of exposures** due to certain complications with the rules – IFRS 9 will make it easier to achieve hedge accounting on this type of risk

Does **not permit** hedge accounting to apply when **credit risk dominates the value changes** that result from an otherwise qualifying "economic relationship"

IFRS 9 – impairment

IAS 39 uses an "**incurred loss**" model for the impairment of financial assets – impairment only occurs once a specific **event actually happens** (even if, earlier in time, it was almost certain that this event would occur)

IFRS 9 instead uses an "**expected losses**" model in which the financial statements reflect the general pattern of deterioration or improvement in the credit quality of financial instruments – there is **no need to wait for a specific event** to **actually happen** before impairment is recognised

Impairment on initial recognition under IFRS 9

The entity creates a credit loss allowance/provision equal to 12 months' expected credit losses

This amount is calculated by multiplying the probability of a default occurring in the next 12 months by the total lifetime expected credit losses that would result from such a default (which is not the same thing as the expected cash shortfalls over the next 12 months)

Subsequent years under IFRS 9

If credit risk increases significantly after initial recognition, the 12 months' expected credit losses figure per the above is replaced by lifetime expected credit losses – this is calculated as the present value of expected credit shortfalls over the remaining life of the asset

If credit quality subsequently improves and the lifetime expected credit losses criterion is no longer met, the 12 months' expected credit loss basis can be reinstated

Amount of impairment under IFRS 9

The amount of impairment to be recognised depends on the IFRS 9 Stage of impairment:

Stage 1 – financial instruments whose credit quality has **not significantly deteriorated** since their initial recognition

In this case, the **12 months' expected credit losses** figure is used and **interest revenue** continues to be recognised based on the **gross** value of the assets (i.e. **before** deducting expected credit losses from the carrying amount)

Stage 2 – financial instruments whose credit quality **has significantly deteriorated** since their initial recognition

In this case, the **lifetime expected credit losses** figure is used and **interest revenue** continues to be recognised based on the **gross** value of the assets (i.e. **before** deducting expected credit losses from the carrying amount)

Stage 3 – financial instruments for which there is **objective evidence of impairment** as at the reporting date

This case is the same as Stage 2 except that **interest revenue** would be recognised based on the **net** value of the assets (i.e. after deducting expected credit losses from the carrying amount)

In both Stage 2 and Stage 3, entities are required to reduce the gross carrying amount of financial assets in the period in which they no longer have a reasonable expectation of recovery.

IFRS 13 and Valuation of Intangibles

Valuation under IFRS 13

Some intangibles such as brands are not recognised separately in the SFP but there may be a need to value before an acquisition or disposal

IFRS 13, paragraph 9: fair value is "the price that would be received to sell an asset or paid to transfer a liability in an orderly transaction between market participants at the measurement date"

IFRS 13 requires us to determine FV based on "highest and best use" from a market participant's perspective – acquirer permitted to assume that current use is highest and best use without searching for alternatives unless market or other factors suggest otherwise

Level 1 inputs – quoted prices in an active market – not normally relevant as a brand is unique

Level 2 inputs – other observable prices e.g. in non-active markets such as a recent bid

Level 3 inputs – unobservable inputs, including internal company data

Methods set out in IFRS 13:

Market basis – market price and other market transactions – difficult if intangible is unique

Income basis – present value of **incremental** income generated by the intangible, considering value including any possible price premium effect and additional sales

Cost basis – current replacement cost of the intangible, which might be estimated as the present value of the expenditure needed to set up an equivalent intangible, including an allowance for risk and how expenditure could replicate the intangible in varying market conditions (this requires a large amount of judgement and estimation, hence apply **professional scepticism** – see page 224)

See also	Branding and Rebranding (IFRS 13)	62
	Valuations topics	

IFRS 16

IFRS 16 adopts a single model for all types of lease but **retains** the IAS 17 classification of a lease as a finance lease or an operating lease for **lessors** – for **lessees**, there is **no requirement to distinguish** between operating and finance leases

A **lease** is defined as a contract, or part of the contract, that conveys the **right to use an asset** (an "**underlying asset**") for a period of time in exchange for consideration.

> A lease does **not** arise if the **lessor** can **substitute** the underlying asset for another asset during the lease term and the **lessor** would **benefit economically from doing so** (for example, the lessor might benefit from the **convenience** of being able to select which particular asset (e.g. which particular machine) to provide to the lessee)

An **underlying asset** is defined as an asset that is the subject of a lease, for which the right to use that asset has been provided by a lessor to a lessee.

The "**right to control**" the use the of asset requires the right to **obtain substantially all of the economic benefits from use** of the identified asset, and the **right to direct the use** of the identified asset

In cases where the contract includes a **lease element** and also an **element which is not a lease** (such as a service contract), the element which is not a lease must be **separated out** from the lease and **accounted for separately**.

Where a lease exists, a lessee will recognise a "right of use asset" initially measured at cost (plus lease payments made before the commencement date, less lease incentives, plus initial direct costs incurred plus dismantling and restoration costs that a lessee is obliged to pay at the end of the lease term)

The asset is then measured at cost less depreciation and impairment unless the revaluation model is used or the item is an investment property and the lessee applies the fair value model

The asset is depreciated over the shorter of the useful life of the underlying asset and the lease term

An election to apply simplified accounting can be used for a lease with a term of 12 months or less or for a lease for a low value asset

IFRS 15 (revenue) guidance will be applied to **sale and leaseback** transactions to determine if a sale has taken place

If a sale has taken place, a gain or loss is recognised based on the value of the rights transferred to the buyer

If no sale has taken place, there is no derecognition and proceeds are treated as a financial liability under IFRS 9

IFRS 16

IFRS 16 – illustration of concept of substitution and economic benefit to the lessor

User Ltd has entered into an arrangement with Provider Ltd regarding the use of certain machinery which will be used to produce car engine parts. Provider Ltd has agreed to provide User Ltd with any one of a selection of 10 similar machines on a weekly basis and has also agreed that the relevant machine must be able to produce 5,000 car parts per day. Provider Ltd can provide User Ltd with any of its 10 similar machines as required at its absolute discretion.

A lease **does not arise** because there is **no identifiable asset** and Provider Ltd (**the lessor**) can **substitute** the machine as it wishes, deriving **economic benefits** from doing so in terms of **convenience**.

User Ltd should account for the rental payments as **a normal expense** in the P&L rather than applying IFRS 16.

IFRS 16 sale and leaseback numerical example – calculation of gain

On 1 July 2016, First Ltd bought a specialised printing machine for £1.2m. The carrying amount on 30 June 2017 was £1.0m.

On 1 July 2017, First Ltd sold the machine to Second Ltd for £1.48m, which was the fair value of the machine. First Ltd immediately leased the machine back for 5 years (the remainder of its useful life) at £320,000 per annum payable in arrears.

The present value of the annual lease payments is £1.4m and the transaction satisfies the IFRS 15 criteria to be recognised as a sale.

Step 1 – calculate the accounting profit on disposal: 1.48m - 1m = 480,000

Step 2 – apply fraction of (PV of leaseback payments / FV of asset): 1.4/1.48 x 480,000 = 454,054

Step 3 – deduct amount found in step 2 from the amount found in Step 1: 480,000 - 454,054 = 25,946

Treat the amount from Step 3 as the gain to recognise immediately.

Note – a shortcut can be applied – the gain to recognise can be calculated simply as 0.08/1.48 x 480,000 = 25,946 – in other words, place the difference between the FV of the asset and the PV of leaseback payments (0.08 in this example) over the FV of the asset and apply this to the accounting profit on disposal – this will be slightly quicker to calculate

Impairment (IAS 36)

Impairment testing is designed to ensure that assets and cash-generated units (CGUs) are stated at no more than their **recoverable amount**

Recoverable amount is the **higher** of

>FV less costs to sell, and

>Value in use (the present value of net cash inflows relating to the asset)

Recoverable amount therefore effectively measures the best return the entity could generate (either by selling or continuing to use the asset)

IAS 36 requires an entity to discount future cash flows at a rate that reflects the current market assessments of (a) the time value of money, and (b) the risks specific to the asset for which future cash flow estimates have not been adjusted

The discount rate should also be a before tax interest rate

Tax and interest should be excluded from cash flows from the asset or cash generating unit

The FV less costs to sell should be estimated following IFRS 13 – this should represent the market value of the assets at a point in time

If the asset is impaired, remember to mention that this will reduce the asset value on the SFP but would also reduce the future amortisation charge in profit or loss

Goodwill

Remember that goodwill is not amortised under IFRS but is tested annually for impairment

See also   IFRS 13 and Valuation of Intangibles   160

Insurance

Arguments in favour of using insurance

- Scale of risk
- May be a higher incidence of unfavourable events than expected
- Potential going concern issues in some cases
- Shows that the company has taken financially reasonable steps
- Ensures that can pay third parties following impact – beneficial from a public interest perspective
- Demonstrates corporate responsibility

Arguments against using insurance

- Cost – may exceed cost of the negative event
- Liquidity – needs to be paid upfront whereas the events may occur sometime in the future
- Does not offset all costs such as reputational damage
- May lead to higher claims – the claimant may know that the insurance company has a lot of money available to make the payment

Integrated Reporting

Summary of Question Bank Content

Integrated Reporting (IR) aims to combine the different strands of reporting (financial, management commentary, governance and remuneration and sustainability reporting) into a coherent whole

Looks at the short, medium and long term – highlights the importance of long-term business sustainability

Helps to make decisions more sustainable and allocate scarce resources effectively

Entity will report on financial and operational performance as normal but also social and environmental aspects

This may include controls over environmental risks, for example

"What gets measured, gets done" – should force more attention onto key issues

6 different types of capital: (1) financial, (2) manufactured, (3) intellectual, (4) human, (5) social and relationship, and (6) natural – this gives a much broader framework for analysis than just financial performance

"Integrated" means highlighting the **interrelatedness and dependencies** between various factors – helping to understand how to generate value

Greater focus on future strategy and outlook than traditional reporting which is backward-looking – IR emphasises the importance of planning and looking forward, considering strategy, governance and performance

Performance measurement – (1) to what extent has a company achieved its strategic objectives? (2) what are the outcomes of its performance in terms of the 6 capitals? Assumed that you need all 6 types of capital (but obviously with varying significance)

So performance measures needed for all 6 capitals with related targets

Probably the case that existing targets will be financial in nature so will need to look at the other capitals – important to consider properly how these will really add to long-term value and then measure accordingly

Social capital – includes company reputation, brand reputation and relationships with stakeholders – reputation for fair dealing and compliance with regulations – hard to have KPIs for this aspect

# Summary of Study Manual Content

Benefits of Integrated Reporting

Streamlined performance reporting with efficiencies found within the organisation

Reduction in duplication of information and consistency of messaging

Aligns and simplifies internal and external reporting for consistency and efficiency

Greater focus on what is material to the organisation and helps identify what is not material

Less time and effort is wasted on reporting unimportant issues

The 6 Capitals

There has been increasing interest in Integrated Reporting (IR) due to a belief that traditional corporate reporting does not "tell the whole story".

The International Integrated Reporting Council (IIRC) introduced the integrated reporting framework in 2013. This framework is based around the concept of 6 different "types of capital":

Financial capital – funds available and obtained from operations, debt, equity or grants

Manufacturing capital – manufactured physical objectives available for use

Intellectual capital – knowledge-based intangibles developed by the organisation

Human capital – competencies, capabilities and experience

Natural capital – environmental resources and processes

Social and relationship capital – relationships with stakeholders and networks

These types of capital will interact in positive and negative ways.

Integrated reporting should look at the long-term impact and value creation, where value creation is not understood simply in monetary terms.

Some implications of introducing integrated reporting into an entity include:

- IT costs
- Time and staff costs
- Consultancy costs

- Disclosure risk – the entity may disclose more information about its operational performance than intended

The Corporate Reporting Study Manual provides ICAEW's own integrated report as an example of integrated reporting: the following sections were included:

- Organisational overview of aims, people, relationships and thinking.

- Performance: student and membership numbers, year on year changes and commentary

Guiding Principles of Integrated Reporting

Strategic focus and future orientation – insight into strategy

Connectivity – holistic and relates to the connections between different elements

Stakeholder relationships

Materiality

Reliability and completeness

Conciseness

Consistency and comparability

Elements of an integrated report

Organisational overview and external environment

Governance

Business model

Risks and opportunities

Strategy and resource allocation

Performance

Future outlook

Implications of an integrated report

Need to be careful what forward-looking information is disclosed – do we want to reveal our strategy?

Should force the business to take a long-term perspective and think about the 6 capitals

Increased use of non-financial information

Report must give insight into strategy

Significantly increased information requirements: need to consider whether systems can provide this, whether non-financial issues can be embedded and any necessary improvements to reporting

Auditing Integrated Reports

Performance will depend on a variety of factors rather than separate independent variables. Therefore, the auditor may have to adjust for background factors that have changed in the meantime to assess performance correctly. However, this will require substantial professional judgement.

Additionally, look out for any incentive to manipulate the figures, particularly if there is any performance-related element.

The auditor should also look out for any perverse incentives where motivations are not appropriate for the organisation as a whole: if the performance metric for a call centre is "number of calls answered", will this result in good quality responses from operators or will it just result in a lot of short and unhelpful calls, just to meet targets?

Conducting an audit of performance information

- Identify the objectives against which the organisation is to be evaluated

- Plan procedures to determine whether objectives are being achieved: these procedures could include social-scientific research methods as well as more traditional audit-type approaches.

- Express a conclusion in the form of a report, either separately or within another document. Ideally, both the performance statistics and the auditor's view will be presented alongside each other within the same document

See also	Balanced Scorecard	48
	Critical Success Factors	92
	Key Performance Indicators	194

Interest Rate Calculations

Importance of Annuity Factors

Most calculations will be "rough and ready" or simple calculations – the easiest way for the examiner to set this style of question is to use an Annuity Factor approach (so that you do not need to do separate calculations for each year of the analysis). So ensure that you are comfortable with using Annuity Tables!

Zero Coupon Bond with a Premium – Effective Interest Rate

Example: a £1m bond is redeemable at a premium of 15% in 4 years

Find a rate which fairly allocates the 15% (or £150,000) over each of the 4 years, but which also takes into account the effect of compound interest

The correct formula to use is to apply the nth root (where n is the number of years) to a fraction of 100 + interest rate/100, and then deducting 1 to find the interest rate.

So for the example bond above the calculation would be $[(115/100)^{0.25 \text{ or } 1/4}] - 1$ or **3.6%**

Exam Tip – this is an excellent opportunity to comment on cash versus accounting principles – no cash flow until the final year (with a large outflow) but finance charges each year under accounting rules

Exam Tip – check whether the loan is in a foreign currency – this further increases risk due to uncertainty regarding the future exchange rate

Standard Bond with Transaction Fees – Effective Interest Rate

Example: issue of a £20m bond with fees of 2% and a 5% coupon payment for 4 years

Exam tip – the EIR should be just slightly higher than 5% because we are going to set up a liability just below £20m as transaction fees are always a debit entry

Coupon will be £1m or £20m x 5% and final cash flow can be done in one go as £20m plus £1m

$(£20m \times 0.98) = £1m/(1 + i) + £1m/(1 + i)^2 + £1m/(1 + i)^3 + £21m/(1 + i)^4$

Implicit Interest Rate on a Sale and Leaseback

Example

The business sells an asset for £150,000 receivable immediately and in return has to pay rentals of £70,000 for 3 years

The entity thus gains £150,000 now in return for paying £70,000 for 3 years.

Solution

The internal rate of return of the transaction is given by finding the Annuity Factor A such that

150,000 – (70,000 x A) = 0

Therefore **A = 2.1429.** Using Annuity Tables, this implies an interest rate of around **19%** (quite a high rate)

Bond transaction fees – always a Debit entry

Since the cash paid on the intermediary or lawyer's fee must result in a Credit entry to cash then it follows that the Debit must be to the financial instrument.

In the case of an issued bond (liability), this will **reduce** the first liability entry in the bond working.

In the case of a purchased bond (asset), this will **increase** the first asset entry in the bond working.

See also	Acquisitions – Financing	29
	Bank Loans	49
	Bonds (Loan Notes) v Bank Loans – Comparisons	60
	Option valuation	207

Internal Audit – Objectives, Contribution and Comparison to Statutory Audit

Objectives of Internal Audit

The objectives of internal audit include:

- review of accounting and internal control systems
- examination of financial and operating information
- review of the economy, efficiency and effectiveness of operations
- review of the safeguarding of assets
- review of the implementation of corporate objectives
- identification of significant business and financial risks
- special investigations such as fraud investigations

Differences to Statutory Audit

The following table provides some useful reminders of the key differences on which you may be tested:

	Internal audit	External audit
Purpose	Add value to operations	Express an opinion on the financial statements
Reporting to	Board of Directors or Audit Committee	Shareholders
Relating to	Operations of the organisation	Financial statements
Relationship with the company	Often employees of the entity – can be outsourced	Independent of the company and its management

Therefore, internal audit has a much wider scope than statutory audit as internal audit considers all the operations and objectives of the entity and is not limited just to the financial statements.

Does an Entity Need an Internal Audit Function?

Per the Study Manual, several factors should be considered:

- scale, diversity and complexity of the company's activities

- number of employees
- cost-benefit considerations
- changes in organisational structure
- changes in key risks
- problems with internal control systems
- an increased number of unexplained or unacceptable events

These factors could be relevant if you have a particularly small client in your scenario and the company does not yet have an internal audit function: it may perhaps be too early for the smaller client to implement internal auditing formally.

How Does the Internal Audit Function Assist the Board?

The internal audit department can act as auditors for Board reports which are not audited by the external auditors.

Internal auditors may be experts in fields such as auditing and accounting standards and can assist in implementing new standards.

Internal auditors can liaise with external auditors to reduce the time and therefore cost of the external audit.

Internal auditors can check that external auditors are performing their job properly and reporting all relevant facts back to the Board.

Internal auditors also have a two-fold role in relation to risk management:

- Monitoring the overall risk management policy to ensure that it operates effectively
- Monitoring the strategies implemented to ensure that they continue to operate effectively

See also   Internal Audit topics

Internal Audit – Types of Assignment

Value for Money (VFM) Audits

A VFM audit tests for the 3 Es: **economy**, **efficiency** and **effectiveness** where these concepts are defined as follows:

Economy – obtaining the appropriate quantity and quality of resources at minimum cost

Efficiency – maximising the output from a given set of inputs or minimising the inputs used to produce a given output

Effectiveness – how well an activity achieves its policy objectives or other intended effects

We strongly recommend you to learn the difference between the 3 Es above. Remember to relate them to the scenario by quoting back information in the extracts.

Information Technology Audits

An IT Audit tests the computer systems of a business. Effective IT systems are vital to the functioning of most modern businesses. The internal auditors would look at issues such as:

- the operating system
- e-business
- the database management system
- system development processes
- problem management
- change management
- asset management
- desktop audits
- capacity management
- access controls

Financial Audits

A financial audit involves reviewing all the available evidence (usually the company's records) to substantiate information in management and financial reporting. As such, this role is quite like that of external or statutory audit and therefore the Study Manual indicates that it is a minor part of the function of internal audit and one which does not add huge value to the business.

Operational (or Management and Efficiency) Audits

This type of audit involves examination of the operational processes of the organisation. The primary objective is to monitor management performance to ensure that company policy is adhered to.

The internal auditor will ensure that the policies in place are adequate for the purpose and will then also ensure that the policy works effectively in practice.

Examples of operational audits given in the Study Manual include:

Procurement – checks to ensure that the process of purchasing for the business achieves its key objectives and that it operates per company guidelines

Marketing – checks to ensure that the process of assessing and enhancing demand for the company's products is managed effectively. This will require that information is freely available to manage demand and to ensure that risks are being managed correctly.

Treasury – checks to ensure that the risks involved (such as interest rate and foreign exchange risk) are managed effectively and in accordance with company procedures. As with marketing, this will require that information is freely available to the treasury department so that they can ensure funds are available when required.

Human resources – checks to ensure that processes are in place to ensure that people are available to work for the business and that there is appropriate planning and control of the business. Once again, this will involve ensuring that company polices are maintained and that information is freely available on key risk factors.

See also   Internal Audit topics

Internal Audit – Process and Reporting

The standard steps in an Internal Audit assignment are:

- setting the process objective
- determining the audit terms of reference
- reviewing current processes and controls
- analysing risks
- testing and results
- reporting
- management actions and monitoring

The Standard Internal Audit Report

There are no formal requirements for internal audit reports (unlike with statutory audit): the document can be adapted to suit the relevant purposes. A suggested outline would include:

- Executive Summary – objectives, outcomes, key action points and further work to complete
- audit tests carried out and their findings
- list of action points
- future time-scale and costs
- summary of existing culture of control
- overall opinion on the managers' willingness to address risks and improve
- implications of outstanding risks
- results of control evaluations
- causes of basic problems detected

The Qualities of Good Internal Audit Recommendations

Internal audit recommendations should consider:

- the available options, emphasising the internal auditor's preferred solution

- the removal of obstacles to control such as poor communication or lack of management willingness to enforce controls

- resource issues: how much will recommendations cost and what are the costs of poor control?

- the terms of reference of the internal audit report, the work performed and the results

See also   Internal Audit topics

Internal Controls

Responsibilities

Duty of management to implement and monitor the effectiveness of risk management procedures to manage the risk for investors and other stakeholders – therefore the responsibility of the Board – if a listed company then needs to comply with the disclosure requirements of the UK Corporate Governance Code

Assurance assignments

ISAE 3410 identifies varied procedures depending on the nature and purposes of the assurance to be provided

This assignment should review the assertions about risk management made by the Board if an annual report is produced

Important to have clarity over the desired purpose of the assurance report: is the scope the design of risk management procedures and internal controls and/or the operation of those controls? The nature and scope of each of these engagements would be different and therefore the benefits would also differ

Sufficient appropriate evidence that internal controls have operated as designed

Judgement needed to assess the likelihood and potential impact of risk

Impossible to determine whether all significant risks have been identified and properly evaluated and managed

Limited assurance in the form of a negatively expressed conclusion

Benefits of assurance on internal controls

If carried out by a professional accountant with the relevant experience applying the highest standards to examine data, processes or information and expressing an assurance conclusion which provides a strong signal of reliability and offers attestation to stakeholders

Identifying deficiencies in internal control and risk management procedures helps LL's management to enhance the quality of its internal systems and controls

Assurance conclusion and any related recommendations resulting from the work of the assurance provider can be used by management to improve the quality of systems and controls and the information derived from them

See also Internal Audit topics

Investment Appraisal Methods

Use round thousands in your calculations to save time – you do not have to be exact

General Narrative Points

State the highest outcome, the next highest and so on – not hard but needs to be done

Examine the project with the best result very carefully – is there some kind of downside?

Consider operational and strategic issues, thinking of scenario-specific points

Pros and Cons of Different Standard Methods

	Positive	Negative	Overall rank
Payback period	-simple -quick -considers risk to certain extent	-too simple -does not consider time value of money -ignores flows after payback achieved (i.e. total returns)	Useful for initial filtering
ARR	-uses profit, so consistent with ROCE -uses balance sheet values -easy to understand	-does not consider time value of money -does not maximise wealth -profits can be manipulated -higher % ARR is not necessarily best in absolute terms	Not very useful
NPV	-considers time value of money -absolute measure -considers all cash flows	-hard to estimate discount rate -difficult to be accurate about all costs/benefits -assumes flows occur at year ends	Technically strong technique
IRR	-considers time value of money -not dependent on discount rate chosen -considers all cash flows	-may conflict with NPV -assumes cash reinvested at IRR – is this possible?	Easier to use and communicate practically

Also consider our notes on the **APV**, **EVA®** and **Free Cash Flow** models.

Exam tips

Flex some of the figures and retest the results – what difference is made? How likely is this in practice? (There are no right answers here, just try to make some suggestions.)

If a foreign currency is involved, try to do as much as possible in that currency and then only do one translation into sterling at the end

Standard scepticism points for any model

Length of model time horizon – too long or too short

How have revenue and cost figures been arrived at

Query the exchange rate assumptions

What happens after the end of the time horizon?

Query the discount rate applied

Calculating the breakeven exchange rate (sensitivity analysis)

We need to find how much the present value of a particular flow can change before the project realises an NPV of 0.

Example

PV of revenues	$100,000
NPV of project	$7,000
Current exchange rate	$2:£1
Breakeven exchange rate	100,000/(100,000 – 7,000) x 2 = 2.15

Provided that the dollar does not depreciate to $2.15:£1 then the project will continue to break even. This would be a change in the rate of 0.15/2 or 7.5%

See the model answer to the July 2015 past paper Q1 for further explanation.

See also Investment Appraisal Methods – APV   180
Investment Appraisal Methods – Free Cash Flow Model   181

Investment Appraisal Methods – APV

Adjusted Present Value approach

Based in NPV methodology but adding in the present value of the tax shield (i.e. interest savings from using loans as a financing method)

Cash flows are discounted at the ungeared cost of equity

Tax savings (tax shield) are discounted at the interest rate of the debt used to finance the activity

Therefore you must use 2 different discount rates and allocate these to the correct parts

Step 1   **Calculate free cash flows and discount at an ungeared cost of equity**

Calculate cash flows after CAPEX and discount using a cost of equity which does not take into account any loan financing (loan financing and its tax impact are considered in Step 2 below)

To obtain the ungeared cost of equity you may need to use the CAPM formula

$k_{eu} = r_f + \beta_a (r_m - r_f)$

where

r_f risk free interest rate
r_m expected market return
β_a asset beta

Do not forget to value the terminal value (i.e. cash flows into perpetuity from the final year of detailed data: see question and reference to flows for the "foreseeable future") and then discount this terminal value and note that the discount factor should be the same as the final year for which non-perpetuity figures are given – see page 182 on this principle.

Step 2   **Calculate interest tax savings and discount at the (risk-free) cost of debt**

Find the annual tax savings (interest x tax rate) and discount at the same interest rate as the debt

This should be at a lower discount rate than in step 2

If the tax saving is to **perpetuity** rather than for a fixed number of years, then simply find (tax rate x debt principal) – due to interest rates cancelling, this will quickly find the present value.

Step 3   **Add up the present value of step 1 and 2**

This will give the total present value of the undertaking/acquisition so compare this to the cost to find the APV

If the APV is positive, **proceed**

See also	Investment Appraisal Methods	178
	Investment Appraisal Methods – Free Cash Flow Model	181

Investment Appraisal Methods – Free Cash Flow Model

Exam tip – do not forget to **knock off the value of debt** at the final stage of the calculation to obtain the **equity value of shares only** (students always seem to forget to do this!).

For some important narrative points, see next page.

Step 1 Find Free Cash Flows (based on precise estimates given)

Earnings before interest and tax (EBIT)

Less	tax
Plus	non-cash charges such as depreciation
Less	CAPEX
Plus/Less	net change in working capital
Plus	sales proceeds from PPE sales

Step 2 Find Terminal Value (TV) (to cover the period after the end of the estimates)

Find value of perpetuity flows using formulae below:

If no growth   TV = annual flow / discount rate

If growth of g assumed $TV = \dfrac{cash\ flow \times (1+g)}{(discount\ rate - g)}$

Do not forget to discount the TV using the same discount factor as for the final specific Free Cash Flow figure estimated above (see below) – e.g. if you have 3 years of specific figures and the TV applies from year 4 onwards, then discount the TV using the **year 3 discount rate**

Step 3 Discount at the WACC

Find the discounted value of the cash flows, using WACC as the discount factor.

You may have to calculate the WACC, given the cost of equity, cost of debt and market values of equity and debt:

WACC = k_e x (E / E + D) + k_d x (D / E + D)

Step 4 Remember to deduct the market value of debt

This transforms the cash flows into an equity value (the value of the shares of the company)

Investment Appraisal Methods – Free Cash Flow Model

Future Flows into Perpetuity – Same Discount Factor in Final 2 Columns

It will be common to be given 3 years (for example) of specific figures and then a statement that "from year 4 into the foreseeable future" cash flows will be at a particular level

Use the formula cash flow / discount factor to find this terminal value

e.g. £1m into perpetuity at a discount factor of 10% is £1m / 0.10 = £10m terminal value

Note that this terminal value should be discounted at **the same discount factor as the previous year of figures for which a specific estimate is possible** (year 3 in our example) – this is because (for mathematical reasons) the formula provides the PV of the perpetuity **one year before the perpetuity flows start**

	Year 1	Year 2	Year 3	Year 4+
	Precise estimate	Precise estimate	Precise estimate	*Perpetuity formula*
Discount factor at 10%	0.909	0.826	**0.751**	**0.751**
			\multicolumn{2}{c}{**Identical discount factors for final 2 columns**}

In this example, the perpetuity formula applied for Year 4+ gives the PV of Year 4+ flows but **in terms of Year 3 values**. Therefore discount at the Year 3 discount rate.

Advantages of the FCF approach

Model is flexible to allow for specific data and details, including a period of temporary growth followed by a perpetuity (with or without growth)

Depreciation and CAPEX

Add back depreciation and deduct CAPEX

If no data given, perhaps the best you can do is assume that these are approximately equal but make sure you state this and then criticise this assumption (as it is not realistic)

Perpetuity cash flows – the correct discount factor

Example: exam paper gives detailed specific cash flows for years 1 to 4 followed by a perpetuity from year 5 onwards

Remember that the correct discount factor to apply to the perpetuity is the **year 4** value (not the year 5 value) – this is because the perpetuity formula provides the present value of flows starting with **1 year of delay** – so applying the formula to the flows from **year 5** onwards gives the present value in **year 4** and therefore needs to be discounted by the **year 4 discount factor**

Investment Appraisal Methods – Free Cash Flow Model

Professional scepticism points

Perpetuity assumption may be simplistic and unsustainable – requires forecasts to be reliable and the discount rate to be correct – future cash flows are just estimates

Query whether there is enough information on capital cash flows, CAPEX outlays and taxation

Determine whether depreciation assumptions/add backs are reasonable

Query validity of the discount rate (risk, changes in business, size, nature of business (private?))

Possible adjustments

Consider all incremental costs and revenues that may result

Will director salaries and remuneration change if the Board of Directors is changed?

Eliminate one off items

Adjustments for inflation and other similar changes?

Deduct earnings from opportunities now foregone?

CAPEX

See also	Investment Appraisal Methods	178
	Investment Appraisal Methods – APV	180

ISAE 3402 – example answer points

Note – ISAE 3402 is potentially more relevant than ever as **cloud computing** and other technological services grow – organisations will increasingly be relying on **third parties for the provision of services** and may therefore require **assurance** over those services – ISAE 3402 may then apply

[Useful points taken from SBM November 2017 Mock 1 Q2]

ISAE 3402 may be applicable when the assurance provider needs to review the controls of a "service organisation" – example from SBM November 2017 Mock 1: the adviser's client was a manufacturer of paints which offered an online system for its regular customers to place orders – a new customer was interested in a contract but required assurance over the online ordering system as a pre-condition of signing the contract: the paint manufacturer would be acting as a "service organisation" for the new customer

Benefits of assurance under ISAE 3402

Provides an **independent**, **expert** opinion on the effectiveness of controls at a third-party organisation

The assurance conclusion and any related recommendations resulting from the assurance provider's work can be used by the client to provide assurance over the **integrity** and **quality** of systems which ensure the complete, accurate and timely processing of transactions – assurance could also be provided that the systems are **available for use as required**, **protected** from unauthorised access and that **confidential information is protected**

If the system has an online element, there could be concerns about **cyber-security** – assurance could be provided regarding firewalls and also virus and ransomware protection

The assurance conclusion and any related recommendations resulting from the assurance provider's work can be used by the **service organisation's management to improve the quality of systems** and controls if this is deemed necessary

Exam tip – ensure that you develop the above benefits by referring to scenario-specific details

Requirements for an ISAE 3402 report to be possible

Disclosure regarding the system of controls and processes must be **sufficiently detailed**

Sufficient appropriate evidence must be gathered by the assurance provider

Type of assurance offered under ISAE 3402

Limited assurance in the form of a **negatively expressed** conclusion is all that is likely to be possible

Judgement is needed and it is likely to be impossible for the assurance provider to be able to determine, with any degree of certainty, that all risks have been identified and properly evaluated

ISAE 3402 – example answer points

Objectives of the service auditor under ISAE 3402

To obtain assurance whether, in all material respects, and based on suitable criteria:

- the service organisation's **description** of its systems fairly presents the systems as designed and implemented (assurance provided by both Type 1 and Type 2 reports)

- the controls related to the control objectives stated in the service organisation's description of its system are **suitably designed** (assurance provided by both Type 1 and Type 2 reports)

- the controls **operated effectively** to provide reasonable assurance that the control objectives stated in the service organisation's description of the system are achieved (assurance provided by a Type 2 report only)

Types of report under ISAE 3402

Type 1 report – provides an opinion on the **design** and **existence** of the control measures in place

Type 2 report – provides an opinion on the same matters as a Type 1 report but also on the **operating effectiveness of the controls in practice**

Ethical implications if the ISAE 3402 assurance provider is also an auditor

If the auditor's client implements **new** procedures **based on assurance work carried out by the auditor** then it would be more difficult to be **critical** of the client's systems during the audit

Safeguards would be required:

- **separate staff** on the audit engagement and the assurance engagement
- **inform the client** that internal controls remain the **responsibility of its management**
- consider **not accepting** the assurance work, if the above safeguards are deemed insufficient

See also   Assurance Reports on Controls at a Service Organisation   46

IT Due Diligence

Assesses the suitability and risks arising from IT factors in the target company – for example, any issues surrounding IT security or integrating IT systems post-acquisition

Given the increasing importance of IT systems to modern businesses and increased cyber-risks, IT due diligence has become more important

The ICAEW (2014) publication Cyber-Security in Corporate Finance provides an example of a larger company purchasing a smaller company and therefore inheriting the weaknesses of the smaller company's security – a cyberattack on the smaller company then allowed access to the whole network, resulting in theft of data relating to a new technology used by the larger company

Key questions to ask on cyber-security as part of a due diligence exercise:

> When did the board last consider cyber-security? Who is responsible for managing cyber-security?
>
> Has the company audited its cyber-security?
>
> Is the company confident that its most valuable information is properly managed and protected from cyber-threats?
>
> Has the company experienced a cyber- or information-security breach? What steps were taken to mitigate the impact of the breach?

See also	Big Data topics	
	Cloud computing	76
	Cyber security	95
	Digital Strategies	120
	Digital Transformation	123

IT – Strategic Information Systems

Benefits

Facilities improved decision-making – summarises key information whilst also allowing drill down into operational records

Amount of information available – increases the amount of information that will be available to managers and the speed with which it becomes available to them – may provide real time information

Consistency – collates information into a single database and should use the same principles and processes – less time required to reconcile and convert

Tactical information – provides access to tactical information such as budgets and comparisons to budget

External information – allows access to external sources as well as internal information

Problems and issues

Information overload – could lead to too much time reviewing and studying data, particularly detailed data, rather than looking at strategic issues and overall performance against KPIs

Training – managers will need to be trained to get the best use from the system – this will take time and money

Extent of data captured – may not be clear how much non-financial information the system will collect or provide to management – if important information is not recorded, then it will still not be possible to monitor performance in some of the key areas of the business

Specific Types

Do not discuss these in too much detail unless the question appears to need it

Executive Information Systems
A system that pools data from internal and external sources and makes information available to senior managers in an easy to use form. Assists in the making of strategic, unstructured decisions.

Management Information Systems
A system that that converts data from mainly internal sources into information such as summary reports and exception reports. Allows managers to make timely and effective decisions for planning, directing and controlling the activities for which they are responsible.

Decision Support Systems
A system that combines data and analytical models or data analysis tools to support semi-structured and unstructured decision-making.

Value added networks (VANs)
Networks that facilitate the adding of value to products and particularly to services by the strategic use of information – often the VAN will link separate organisations together through electronic data interchanges (EDIs), contributing to the development of business networks

See also	Balanced Scorecard	48
	Big Data topics	
	Cloud computing	76
	Critical Success Factors	92
	Cyber security	95
	Digital Strategies	120
	Digital Transformation	123
	Key Performance Indicators	194

Joint Arrangements – Assurance

Benefits of Assurance

If profits are to be shared equally between 2 parties, it could be valuable for both of the parties to have assurance that those profits have been calculated correctly in accordance with the terms of their agreement

Although the percentage split of profits in the joint arrangement may be clear, the profit allocation/determination may still need clarification between the 2 parties – both parties will benefit from assurance that the profit allocation has been calculated properly and that full disclosures have been made

This is likely to require initial Due Diligence and ongoing monitoring of the arrangement to sustain assurance

Nature of the Assurance work

Determine the scope of the engagement by establishing the rights and access to information noted in the contract

Level of assurance needs to be determined (reasonable or limited)

Procedures prior to commencement of operations

Review the agreement in combination with legal advisers for onerous, ambiguous or omitted clauses

Ensure that the purpose of the arrangement is clear and that the respective rights of the parties are established in the initial contractual arrangements

Ensure that there is clear separation from the other operations of each company which is a party to the joint arrangements

Review the tax status of the joint arrangement entity (if applicable)

Review the governance procedures involved in the arrangement including shared management, control, rights over assets, key decision-making processes

Establish that any initial capital has been contributed in accordance with the agreement and that legal rights over assets have been established

Establish the creditworthiness, going concern and reputation of the other party based on local enquiries from stakeholders and a review of internal documentation as well as that in the public domain

Ensure that the terms of disengagement and residual rights at the end of the arrangement are clear so that there is a transparent and legitimate exit route

Establish the fair value of any assets to be transferred into the joint arrangement

Clarify the revenue sharing agreement with respect to existing sales in progress or orders contracted for but not yet commenced

Investigate health and safety responsibility and establish how liability will be shared

Procedures – ongoing assurance

Determine rights and access to information as this will affect the scope of the assurance work

Level of assurance needs to be determined (reasonable or limited)

Ensure that operations are within the terms of the joint arrangement agreement and that there have been no violations of the contractual agreement

Ensure that internal controls and accounting systems are being applied and are effective

Ensure that the accounting systems for any joint arrangement entity are capable of recording time accurately and completely

If permitted within the terms of the contract, access to the accounting records of the other party would provide additional assurance – this could mean, however, that a reciprocal arrangement may need to be made available so that information can be transferred to (and not just from) the other party

Consider the additional assurance problems relating to the eventual dissolution of the agreements – terms of disengagement, return/sale of assets, intellectual property rights, rights to future customer access

Audit-specific points

If a separate joint arrangement entity is established then this may mean that our firm is a component auditor in the context of IAS 600 and will need to report to the principal auditors – question over independence of advisory work being done?

May be a requirement for a separate audit/assurance for a joint arrangement entity

Joint Arrangements – Strategy and Financial Reporting

Strategy – benefits

Likely to lead to **diversification** (geographical, product)

May involve **less financial risk** than setting up a new subsidiary if a **lower level of borrowing** is required

Costs are **shared** – particularly beneficial for **risk-averse** firms or where **expensive new technologies** are being established

Lower setup costs **reduce exit costs** if the venture fails

Could allow **economies of scale** and **economies of scope**, subject to what the other party offers

Shares the **risk** of the project if it fails but the **benefits** must also be **shared**

Allows the party to capitalise on **reputational enhancement** by making use of **existing** brand recognition and/or experience (making the most of the more recognised/more experienced party in the arrangement)

Synergies – one firm's production expertise can be **supplemented** by the other's marketing and distribution expertise, for example

Joint arrangement partner may have **better local knowledge** of foreign markets allowing a quicker expansion

Joint arrangement partner may have an **existing supply chain** in operation

Strategy – disadvantages

Shares the **risk** of the project if it fails but the **benefits** must also be **shared**

May be **conflicts of interest** between the parties in terms of prioritisation of the short-term use of resources as well as longer-term objectives (one party may be looking for short-term profits whilst the other wants to invest over the longer term)

Disagreements may arise over profit shares, amounts invested, the management of the joint arrangement and marketing strategy, amongst other areas

Requires a degree of **business trust** between the parties to promote openness and access to information

Project could be **cut short** if one of the parties decides to **terminate** the arrangement earlier than the other party would wish – a **wholly-owned subsidiary** would prevent this possibility

Financial Reporting – Joint Ventures versus Joint Arrangements

The terms of the contractual arrangement between the parties to a joint arrangement are key to determining whether the arrangement is a "joint venture" or a "joint operation" – if the parties have **rights to the net assets** of the arrangement, then a "joint venture" occurs whereas if the parties have **rights to the assets, and obligations for the liabilities, of the arrangement**, then a "joint operation" occurs

An arrangement **not** structured through a **separate** entity is always a **joint** operation

Financial Reporting – Joint Operation

A joint operation should be recognised **line by line** in each of the party's own financial statements in relation to its interest in the joint operation's:

- **assets**, including a share of any jointly-held assets
- **liabilities**, including a share of any jointly-incurred liabilities
- **revenue** from the sale of its share of the output arising from the joint operation
- **expenses**, including a share of any expenses incurred jointly

Where the operations are in a foreign currency, each of the amounts relating to items in the statement of profit or loss will be translated into the functional currency of the entity, normally using the average exchange rate.

Where the operations are in a foreign currency, in respect of assets and liabilities, **monetary items should be translated** and then reported using the **closing rate** – **non-monetary** items carried at historical cost are translated using the exchange rate **at the date of the transaction** when the asset or liability arose

Financial Reporting – Joint Venture

Joint control of an entity is split between different parties – **usually** there will be a **separate entity** set up (but activity involving a separate entity could also potentially be a **joint operation**)

There is a **contractual arrangement** to share profits and losses and the parties have rights to the **net assets** of the arrangement

Apply the **equity method** – recognise the investment at cost and then add the **share of the joint venture's post-acquisition change in net assets** (**generally** the change in net assets will be equivalent to the **profits and losses** of the venture) – look out for time apportionment here

The **share** of the joint venture's post-acquisition change in net assets will be recognised in the **P&L**

The investment will be shown as a **non-current asset** in the SFP

An **investor** in a joint venture is a party to the joint venture which does not have **joint control** over the joint venture – if there is **significant influence** then an Associate exists: if there is no **significant influence** then the accounting should be as for a financial asset

Financial Reporting – comparison to the establishment of a separate foreign subsidiary

If the subsidiary operates in a foreign currency, it would have a **different functional currency to the parent** – the subsidiary's financial statements would therefore be **consolidated in accordance with IAS 21** into the consolidated financial statements of the parent, translated into the parent's presentation currency

Translate all **assets** and **liabilities** (both monetary and non-monetary) in the SFP using the **closing rate** at the reporting date

Translate **income** and **expenditure** in the current statement of profit or loss and OCI using exchange rates applicable at the transaction dates (in practice, an **average rate** for the year may be used)

Report the exchange differences which arise on translation as **Other Comprehensive Income**

Any loan from the parent to the subsidiary would be a "**net investment in a foreign operation**" – exchange differences will be recognised in profit or loss for the company which has a different functional currency to the currency of the loan itself (for example, if the **parent** has loaned money in the **parent's** functional currency to the subsidiary, then any exchange differences will be recognised in the **subsidiary's** profit or loss)

Key Performance Indicators

Quantifiable measures that can be used for setting strategic targets and monitoring actual performance by comparing performance against targets

Does depend on having an appropriate strategy first before designing the KPIs

Need an indicator and then also a way of measuring this easily and objectively

Some examples (Question Bank question on a travel company: ensure that you amend these to your scenario!)

Strategic aim – Develop an online business

KPIs

Increase in volume of online bookings (percentage annual revenue growth) – target relating to volume

Increase in online sales as a percentage of total annual sales revenue – target relating to diversification

Strategic aim – Sell a tailored product

KPIs

Percentage annual growth in sales revenue from the tailored product

Average operating profit margin on tailored holidays

Strategic aim – Develop a new brand and ensure good awareness

KPIs

Percentage annual growth in sales of the brand

Operating profit margin

Annual market survey responses to the brand

Key Performance Indicators

Strategic aim – Exploit technology and Big Data

KPIs

Growth in the number of visits to the website

Average time for visitors to remain on the web site (length of time browsing)

Strategic aim – Geographical expansion

KPIs

Growth in annual sales in the specific geographical area

Total sales growth in geographical areas where the company has established new operations within the previous 3 to 5 years

Strategic aim – Developing the company's people

KPIs

Minimum retention rates for employees including strategically important employees

Training provided to employees measured by average training days or expenditure per employee

Other examples – retail example

Customer satisfaction rating per outlet

% of staff who have been trained

Employee satisfaction scores

Staff retention rates per outlet

See also		
	Balanced Scorecard	48
	Critical Success Factors	92
	IT – Strategic Information Systems	187

Lease or buy?

Use an after-tax cost of borrowing as the cost of capital

Lease

Determine whether the lease is a finance lease or an operating lease under IAS 17 – if the lease is for the major part of the economic life of the asset and the PV of the minimum lease payments is substantially all of the fair value of the leased asset then a finance lease occurs

Set up a normal NPV calculation – remember that tax benefits will arise from interest payments on the lease – if the lease is for an intangible asset then there may also be a tax benefit from amortisation (if the item is a tangible asset then it is possible that depreciation will not be allowable for tax purposes: you may have to raise a scepticism point here if the information is not available)

Make the point that a lease approach is more flexible, especially in a market where technologies are changing quickly – rather than purchasing the item outright, a lease means that the company only has to pay for the asset for a certain period of time and can make a decision at the end of that period whether to continue using the same asset or upgrade to a better option

Types of lease

Finance lease – substantially all the risks and rewards of ownership are transferred to the lessee and the asset is recognised as a resource from which future economic benefits will flow – the asset acquired and the obligation to make lease payments are recognised in the SFP and an interest expense based on the effective interest rate is recognised in the P&L

Operating lease – leases other than finance leases i.e. where the transfer of risks and rewards does not take place – lease payments are recognised in the P&L and the lessee does not recognise the asset or obligation in the SFP

Buy

Set up a normal NPV calculation – look out for an opportunity to apply an annuity formula approach to save time i.e. if the annual flows are the same the several years (this is quite likely in SBM)

Remember to consider whether tax savings on capital allowances are possible

Consider the company's existing overall borrowing position (or raise a scepticism point if there is no information) – consider how additional borrowing could affect earnings and gearing as well as the ability to raise debt for other purposes

Consider whether there are other better uses of the substantial upfront cash requirement under a "buy" decision

A "buy" decision means more of a commitment to a particular asset/technology (unless this can be re-sold easily at a future date) – on the other hand, a lease is only for a certain period of time and there is less risk of being stuck with an obsolete technology (which is then hard to sell in future)

Lease or buy?

Decision

Consider a comparison in relation to

    Lease term and useful life

    Results of NPV but also other factors

    Liquidity – buying requires an initial payment which could use up cash – company may be near its debt capacity

    Risk and flexibility – what happens if the business/project does not succeed as well as planned? A lease might include a break-clause (or you could recommend to include one) whereas buying the asset might involve more risk unless it can be sold off easily

    Tax implications would need to be known

    Interest rate assumed in the PV calculation is a key variable that would need to be confirmed

Do not forget to conclude and recommend on the best option – easy to forget to do!

Do not make a decision based only on the different NPV – look at some other issues surrounding the decision

Consider a mixed recommendation – lease some assets, buy other assets?

Liquidation

In a liquidation, the main stakeholders to comment on are likely to be:

- A bank or provider of funds (which probably holds a charge over property)
- Shareholders
- Suppliers and other creditors

Try to find some different points to say under 3 specific headings for these groups.

The funds generated should be based on a pro forma, probably involving PPE, inventories and trade receivables. The liquidator's fee should then be deducted, together with any **fixed** charge due.

Once this amount ("Remaining funds") is calculated we know what we can potentially repay to any creditors with a **floating** charge – this is found by dividing the Remaining funds by the floating charges due to find how much per £1 of floating charge will actually be repaid (it will probably be less than £1 due to the difficulties the company is facing).

(A fixed charge is a charge over a specified asset of the entity: the entity loses the freedom to dispose of this asset without the permission of the owner – a floating charge is a charge over the assets in general of the entity: the entity retains the freedom to dispose of assets unless a default has occurred as the charge is not in connection with any specified asset.)

Financial Reconstruction – possible calculation pro-forma

The funds generated may need to be calculated based on the following pro forma, probably involving PPE, inventories and trade receivables. The liquidator's fee should then be deducted, together with any **fixed** charge due.

Once the remaining net amount after the liquidator's fee and fixed charge(s) ("Remaining funds") is known then we can estimate what we can potentially repay to any creditors with a **floating** charge – this is found by dividing the Remaining funds by the floating charges due to find how much per £1 of floating charge will actually be repaid (it will probably be less than £1 due to the difficulties the company is facing).

(A fixed charge is a charge over a specified asset of the entity: the entity loses the freedom to dispose of this asset without the permission of the owner – a floating charge is a charge over the assets in general of the entity: the entity retains the freedom to dispose of assets unless a default has occurred as the charge is not in connection with any specified asset.)

Overall the proforma might look like that below:

Liquidation

Funds generated
    PPE
    Inventories
    Trade receivables
    Total proceeds
Less liquidator's fee
Less paid to holder's of a fixed charge
Remaining funds   R

Floating charges
    Loans
    Overdraft
                                                   F

Amount paid to holders of a floating charge (per £1 of floating charge) = R/F

For example, if the company has been lent amounts subject to floating charges of £10m but the R figure is only £5m then holders of floating charges will only receive back 50% (5/10) of their original investment.

After this, you should make some standard narrative points (see below).

Note that if the result of the fraction R/F is less than 1, then this means that floating chargeholders will not receive back the full amount of their investment – it follows that unsecured creditors and shareholders (neither of whom have any charges at all) will not receive anything back at all.

The calculation steps to follow again are:

Step 1   Calculate proceeds received based on assets

Step 2   Deduct liquidator's fee and fixed charges

Step 3   Arrive at Remaining funds (R)

Step 4   Calculate Floating charges (F)

Step 5   Find amount repayable per £1 of Floating charge (R/F) (probably to a bank)

Step 6   Make standard narrative points (see below)

Based on the November 2014 real exam, you can ignore the "prescribed part" in your calculation but should comment that this would be reserved for unsecured creditors by law: effectively, this preserves a small amount for the unsecured creditors.

Financial reconstruction and liquidation: Narrative points

Unsecured creditors and shareholders will receive nothing if the ratio of R/F is less than 1 – if the ratio is less than one, then we are saying that floating chargeholders are not receiving all of their money back so there is clearly nothing further available to those without any charges recorded at all (unsecured creditors and shareholders).

In some cases, it may be that you need to **compare a liquidation against an alternative option** (such as keeping the business going, but on revised terms – this would be a financial reconstruction). Again, try to consider the matter from the perspective of different **stakeholders** such as the funding bank, shareholders and creditors.

Bank

The bank receives **certain cash back under a liquidation** but could be subject to **further risk if the money is left invested under a financial reconstruction**.

Consider the **interest rates** under the financial reconstruction – these will probably be higher than before in order to give the bank an incentive to continue to invest.

Consider **whether other stakeholders would invest** under the financial reconstruction or **will the bank remain the main funder** and therefore subject to the most risk?

Consider the **potential return** under the financial reconstruction – is this probable and/or attractive to the bank?

Shareholders

The shareholders **may get nothing back under a liquidation** but at least have some **voting power** to determine what happens.

You may wish to comment on what **shareholders are being asked to do** under the financial reconstruction option.

The amount invested in the original shares could be considered to be a sunk cost if liquidation is an active option: in other words, if the financial reconstruction does not happen then that money is lost anyway so the cost of the original investment is not a relevant or incremental cost – only the new capital injected under the financial reconstruction is a relevant cost.

Use the **forecast returns** for calculation purposes but **apply professional scepticism** as the projections may be optimistic in order to keep the company going (look at the position of the Board of Directors here).

Suppliers

Suppliers **may get nothing back under a liquidation** and, unlike shareholders, have no **voting power** to determine what happens.

Unsecured creditors would only get a small "**prescribed part**" back in a liquidation whereas if a financial reconstruction works then, over time, they may receive the **full** amount back.

As **suppliers are in a weak position**, it may be possible for the client company to negotiate hard and improve its position.

Resorting to court action would be a waste of time if there are other creditors which rank ahead of the suppliers (fixed and floating charge holders).

Liquidation

Financial reporting points

Although it remains outside the scope of this book to discuss financial reporting issues in detail, any discussion of liquidation and financial reconstruction is likely to be paired up with some financial reporting marks for points such as:

- IAS 1 and going concern presentation (valuation and also classification of liabilities and assets as current or non-current)

- ISA 570 *Going Concern* issues and the position of the auditor

- IAS 10 *Events after the reporting period*

See also	Cash Flow Forecasts – Evaluation	72
	Change – Definition & Models	73
	Change – Management & Implementation	75
	Disposals and Assets Held for Sale (IFRS 5)	125
	Financial Reconstruction	135

Loan Decision by a Bank

The bank will consider 3 main areas:

- creditworthiness of the borrower
- term and structure of the loan
- return for the bank

Creditworthiness of the borrower

The bank will consider the financial stability of the borrower, its existing capital structure and the track record of management (including past credit behaviour and credit histories)

The bank will examine published financial statements, financial forecasts of future periods and key ratios in the areas of performance, efficiency and gearing.

Financial forecasts should cover the term of the loan.

The terms and structure of the loan

Is the loan amount appropriate for what the funds will be used for?

Is the length of time before repayment appropriate? A longer term loan will generate more interest but could present a greater risk of default for the bank.

How will the repayments be structured? Will there be gradual repayment of capital throughout the life of the loan will alone be interest only with a final "bullet" repayment of capital at the end of the term?

What security will be offered in terms of legal charges such as fixed or floating charges over assets?

The bank is likely to attach covenants which impose conditions and obligations on the borrower – these can be financial, such as meeting a specified ratio, or non-financial, such as requiring disclosure of significant events

The return for the bank

The bank will consider

- The rate of interest on the loan, and the term over which interest will be paid
- Other remuneration from the loan such as arrangement, underwriting or facility fees
- The value of other relationships within the bank – the potential borrower may have lucrative relationships with other banking operations

Marketing Strategies

The 4 Ps for a physical product

Price

Product

Place

Promotion

The additional 3 Ps for a service

People

Physical evidence

Process

| **See also** | Branding and Rebranding (IFRS 13) | 62 |
| | Organic Growth | 209 |

Modified Internal Rate of Return (MIRR)

This is similar to an IRR calculation but assuming that amounts are invested at the cost of capital

Therefore if we have a 4 year project then cash generated in year 1 will have 3 further years of growth at the cost of capital, cash generated in year 2 will have 2 years of growth at the cost of capital, and so on

We adjust the cash flows upwards by these relevant multiples to find the total amount generated after allowing for reinvestment

We then compare this to the initial investment and use this as the basis of finding the MIRR by using a compound growth formula

Worked example

Assumes a discount rate of 10%

	Year 0	Year 1	Year 2	Year 3
Cash outflows	-5,000	0	0	0
Cash inflows	0	2,000	5,000	6,000

Answer

Interest rate multipliers

Year 1   1.1 x 1.1 = 1.21 (cash received at the end of year 1 has 2 further periods to grow)

Year 2   1.1

Year 3   no multiplier for the final year

	Year 0	Year 1	Year 2	Year 3
Cash outflows	-5,000	0	0	0
Cash inflows	0	2,000	5,000	6,000
Multiplier		1.21	1.1	no multiplier
Reinvested value		2,420	5,500	6,000

Total reinvested value is 13,920

Present value of the outflows is 5,000

MIRR is $(13,920/5,000)^{1/3} - 1$ or 40.7%

Advantages of MIRR

Avoids the problem of multiple IRRs

Avoids the weakness of traditional IRR of assuming that profits are reinvested at the IRR itself (which is often not possible)

Modified Internal Rate of Return (MIRR)

Disadvantages of MIRR

May lead an investor to reject a project which has a lower rate of return but which, in terms of size, is a very good project – this is because it is based on a rate

Does not look at project life – a high return project with a short life may be preferred over a lower-return project with a longer life

See also   Investment Appraisal Methods topics

Online Sales Strategies

Data required to determine whether a worthwhile investment

Generally seems reasonable to develop a strategy as most modern companies have an online presence

Without a presence, may be a competitive disadvantage

Requires careful planning and efficient implementation

Plans needed for web site design, marketing and advertising the online service, online payment arrangements and arrangements for distributing goods/services to customers (globally)

Clear timetable needs to be designed

Clear target date set for "going live"

Exam tip

The points made here definitely not rocket science! There will be nothing wrong with making simple and obvious points

See also

Big Data topics	
Cloud computing	76
Cyber security	95
Digital Strategies	120
Digital Transformation	123
Marketing Strategies	203

Option Valuation

Possible models

Black-Scholes-Merton – standard model based on formula which looks at volatity and other factors

Binomial Lattice – probability based model which looks at different alternative outcomes

Monte Carlo simulation – based on running thousands of scenarios to determine likely outcome

Exam tip – you are not expected to include detailed information here so no need to go beyond the points identified here

Model inputs

Underlying price of the instrument (e.g. share price)

Exercise price – high value for a call option if the exercise price is well below today's price (much larger chance of making a profit on exercise)

Time to exercise – longer time period adds more value as more chance for things to move favourably for the option holder

Volatility – more volatility adds to option value as more chance of a favourable move

Interest rates – rise in interest rates increases the value of a call option (the alternative to an option would be to buy the instrument right now but then the entity will have an opportunity cost of lost interest on that cash whereas using an option it can generate interest whilst "waiting" to buy the instrument)

Income generated from the instrument (e.g. dividends)

Assurance aspects

Is the model designed for the purpose it is applied?

Review of all inputs for reasonableness

Consult with expert in valuations?

The main 2 assurance issues/risks relate to

The fair value of any options issued

Estimate of the number of options that will be exercisable based on the vesting conditions and conditions at the reporting date

Option Valuation

Requirement to check

Share price	easy if a listed company but not if unlisted
Exercise price	should be specified in the option contract
Time to expiry	should be specified in the option contract
Volatility of the underlying share	easy if a listed company but not if unlisted
Interest rates	information easily available
Dividend yields	should be possible to check based on the accounts

Vesting conditions check

Check what the conditions are
Check how many options may be exercised under any given circumstances
Check the likelihood of those conditions being satisfied given the current circumstances

See also   Investment Appraisal Methods topics
                    Real Options   236
                    Valuation topics

Organic Growth

Reasons for

May be cheaper than an acquisition

Much more control than in an acquisition – able to continue existing trends and initiatives

Make use of existing resources fully (employees, supply chain)

Less disruptive for staff and customers

Considerations

Management structure

Overseas issues

Information strategies

Quality maintenance

Company legislation

Tax position

Methods

Investment in marketing

Could be expensive with limited impact

May be more urgent or significant issues to address

Investment in product development

Need to keep up with competitors

Product diversification

Reduces risks but can be expensive

Could increase the level of profits achieved

If penetration to date is limited then it may make sense to focus on developing existing products

Focuses on existing core competencies in the same activity

Ansoff Matrix Ideas

Market development – same product in a different market sector

Uses existing resources and increases their utilisation ("making the assets sweat")

Operational side of the business is identical to the existing business – near complete overlap with existing core competencies in operational activities

Limitations of a market development strategy

Loss of sales in the existing market if too much effort in the new market

Reputational risk

Investment and reorganisation costs likely to be largely sunk if the venture fails

Cash inflows in early years likely to be low and so payback slow if market conditions change

Need reliable market research when entering a less well known market

Related diversification – both the product and market have changed but in neither case is the change substantial

Accesses a new market where there is currently no presence

Margins may be greater

No loss of sales to existing customers

Limitations of related diversification

No current market knowledge

Product is slightly different from the existing product so some departures from existing core competencies

May be significant initial costs which are likely to be sunk costs

Level of synergy may be questionable

See also	Change – Definition & Models	73
	Change – Management & Implementation	75
	Overseas Operations topics	

Outsourcing

General considerations

- Fees
- Cost of the business doing the task itself
- Redundancies
- Time and cost in arranging and monitoring agreement
- Previous experience with outsourcing

Requirements for successful outsourcing

- Ability to specify with precision what is supplied
- Ability to measure what is actually supplied
- Ability to make adjustments elsewhere if specification is not achieved

Deciding what to outsource

- Strategic importance of the system – does outsourcer company have the required information? Can it be provided without creating risks?
- Functions with limited interfaces are most easily outsourced
- Can we manage the arrangement easily?
- Do we know enough about our own systems to make a sensible decision?
- Will our needs change? Can the outsourcer company adapt?

Possible benefits

- Access to cheaper inputs including labour
- Improves competitive advantage
- Reduces fixed costs and operating gearing
- Reduces risk exposure
- Allows the business to concentrate on its core competence
- Allows specialist to do the work
- Outsourcer business may be better able to deal with high demand
- Legal recourse including compensation if something goes wrong
- Positive impact on other divisions

Possible negative impact

- Redundancies and closure costs
- Data protection issues
- Co-ordination with rest of supply chain
- Time, effort and expense of monitoring
- Harder to guarantee and control supply
- Delays
- Quality control
- Hidden costs such as disruption or unexpected charges

Outsourcing

[Useful points from SBM November 2017 Mock 2 Q1]

Selecting an outsourcing partner

This will be a very important decision as the partner could be a **key element** of operations – problems could cause **significant disruption** to the business – factors to consider include:

- **capability and capacity** – experience and ability to meet service requirements – capacity will also be important to provide the opportunity to expand the volume of business

- **cultural compatibility** – a good working relationship is essential – this will be easier to achieve with an organisation that shares a similar culture and values because this will help **communication**, particularly when dealing with **problems** – consideration of the customer base could be relevant here: if one partner works with small organisations but the other works with larger multinationals then there may be **different assumptions** and **working styles**

- **location** – this could be very important to manufacturing operations but also to service organisations – costs of transportation/travel could be very **significant** and **outweigh** costs saved in other respects

- **financial considerations** – using the **cheapest** option may not necessarily be best (skills and capabilities also matter) but costs are obviously important – **a comparison with the costs of performing the work internally should be made** to determine if outsourcing is worthwhile

Managing the outsourced relationship

Managing the relationship **once operations have started** is just as important as **choosing** the right partner in the first place

If performance is not as expected this could affect the company's **sales** and **reputation**

The company should consider a **Service Level Agreement** (SLA) with its outsourcing partner to identify the standards expected by both parties

The company must then ensure that the **terms of the SLA are being adhered to** – if not, this should be **discussed** and **corrective action** should be taken to improve performance

The company must ensure it is not **transferring across overall responsibility** that the work is performed well – in other words, the outsourcing partner must be **monitored** and **held accountable** for any problems which occur

Outsourcing

Issues to include in a Service Level Agreement with an outsourcer company

- Service level — minimum standards required and penalties
- Exit route — arrangements to exit or transfer to another supplier
- Timescale
- Ownership of tangible and intangible assets
- Dependencies
- Employment issues

Types of outsourcing arrangement (example of IT services)

Features	Arrangement Timeshare	Service	Facilities Management (FM)
What is it?	Time-based access to external processing system	Focus on specific function	Outside agency manages organisation's IS/IT facilities. Client retains equipment but all services provided by the FM company
Management responsibility	Mostly retained	Some retained	Very little retained
Focus	Operational	A function	Strategic
Timescale	Short-term	Medium-term	Long-term
Justification	Cost savings	More efficient	Access to expertise, better service, management can focus on core business activities

Overseas Operations – Exporting

Considerations

- Tax
- Exchange risk
- Political risk
- Business risk
- Pre-export financing – period in which export is produced and prepared for delivery
- Post-export financing – period in which export has been sent and payment is being awaited

Pre-export financing sources

- Bank lending – structured lending where the bank funds the exporter but funding is tied to production and export activities
- Export credit agencies – government departments – provide insurance against political and commercial risks and UK Export Credits Guarantees Department (ECGD)

Invoicing in the buyer's currency

Competitive advantage – means that purchasers do not need to concern themselves with the administrative necessity of buying sterling and do not have risks from adverse exchange rate movements

Disadvantage for the seller – exposed to risks of adverse exchange rate movements – may require hedging if there is a long enough period between invoicing and receipt and if the amounts are material

Working Capital Management for Exporters

Factoring – passing debts to an external party who will take on the responsibility for collecting the money due: the factor advances a proportion of the money it is due to collect so the exporter now has funds to pay suppliers and finance growth

If the factoring is "non-recourse" then the factor will not have any claim on the exporter even if the end customer does not pay – this removes the risk for the exporter but at a cost

Documentary credits or letter of credit – fixed assurance from the customer's bank in the customer's own country which states that payment will be made provided that the exporter complies with all terms and conditions – given this assurance, the exporter's own bank may advance some credit before the goods are shipped

Forfaiting – for larger projects and involving a bank purchasing 100% of the value of the invoice at a discount – this allows the exporter to in turn offer financing to the customer, making products and services more attractive. The bank deal will include a discount rate, a number of grace days added to the period to allow for transactions to go through and a commitment fee.

Credit insurance – assigns credit-insured invoices to bank who will offer up to 100% of the insured debt as a loan. These instruments may carry a guarantee from the government of the customer's home country

| **See also** | Finance – Sources for SMEs | 131 |
| | Other Overseas Operations topics | |

Overseas Operations – Financing

Background considerations

- Local finance costs and subsidies
- Taxation
- Restrictions on dividend remittances
- Possibility of flexibility in repayments
- Access to capital – may be easier in local markets to optimise gearing

Methods and considerations

Takeover/merger – quick, can choose established/experienced partner, access to information, market share and distribution channels, disadvantage: premium may have to be paid

Overseas subsidiary – must remit profit back in order for parent to have access, choices over equity share, subsidiary's borrowings and currency

Branches – better than losing withholding tax on dividends from a subsidiary, lower level of formalities, greater profile for sales and marketing

Additional agency costs in setting up, running and monitoring the local subsidiaries

Using local sources of finance – issues

- Local finance costs
- Availability of subsidies
- Tax systems
- Tax structuring
- Restrictions on dividend remittances
- Possibility of flexibility in repayments from parent-sub relationship
- Different covenants and options – subsidiary may be able to gear more than parent

See also   Finance – Sources for SMEs   131
              Other Overseas Operations topics

Overseas Operations – Operational Aspects

- Management structure – could become more complex
- Choice whether to recruit local management or whether senior management will move abroad
- Decision on the amount of autonomy to give the subsidiary management – determine how much central management should be involved in determining strategy
- Determines performance targets and how much emphasis is placed on achieving financial targets

Overseas operations and human resources

Key questions

Use expatriate staff to control local operations or employ local managers with more knowledge but risking loss of control?

Are expatriate staff skilled and comfortable with local culture?

Exporting – considerations

- Often requires financing – pre-export financing and post-export working capital
- Length of time to receive payment
- Costs
- Risks

Exporting – risks

- Loss or damage in transit – use insurance, risk assessment, transfer obligations to delivery agent
- Faults with products
- Non-payment by customers – use references or credit scoring, use export credit insurance, consider stage payments
- Liquidity
- Exchange rate movements – impact on forecasts/NPV
- Discount factor used should be higher due to additional risks
- Inflation
- Higher delivery costs – sensitivity analysis, sourcing low cost transport, breaking large deliveries up
- Price risk – confidentiality, link to order size

Mitigation export risks

- Hedging
- Due diligence on customer and contract terms
- Insurance against default
- Sensitivity analysis

Calculating the breakeven exchange rate (sensitivity analysis)

We need to find how much the present value of a particular flow can change before the project realises an NPV of 0.

Example

PV of revenues	$100,000
NPV of project	$7,000
Current exchange rate	$2:£1
Breakeven exchange rate	100,000/(100,000 – 7,000) x 2 = 2.15

Provided that the dollar does not depreciate to $2.15:£1 then the project will continue to break even. This would be a change in the rate of 0.15/2 or 7.5%

See the model answer to the July 2015 past paper Q1 for further explanation.

Foreign currency transactions

IAS 21 considerations – transactions will be denominated in a currency other than the functional currency of the entity – the entity must translate these items into its own functional currency according to the rules in IAS 21 in its individual company financial statements – sales made in the overseas country and any receivables outstanding will need to be translated at the closing rate, as these are monetary items – these may then need to be translated again into the group presentation currency (if different)

See also	Change – Definition & Models	73
	Change – Management & Implementation	75
	Globalisation	145
	Other Overseas Operations topics	

Overseas Operations – Risks

- Currency risks*
- Physical risks – risk of goods being lost or stolen in transit or documents being lost
- Credit risks – risk that the customer will default
- Trade risks – risk that customer will cancel or refuse to accept the goods
- Liquidity risks – risk that company cannot finance the credit terms given to customers

*Note – do not focus on currency risks too much unless specifically asked to do so

Institutions which can help to reduce risks of overseas operations

- Banks
- Insurance companies
- Credit reference agencies
- Government agencies – UK Export Credits Guarantee Department (ECGD)
- Transfer risks via contractual rules (e.g. courier shares part or all of the losses)

Transactions in a foreign currency – risks

Revenue risks – fixed contract price, credit/default risk, order cancellation

Cost side risks – commodity price volatility, movement in exchange rate

Opportunity cost – if at full capacity and decide to undertake a transaction in a foreign currency which does not materialise then wasted an opportunity to earn income

Liquidity risk – delays in receipt

Note – revenue risks and cost side risks can become benefits if the exchange rate moves favourably

Exchange controls

Note: exchange controls are controls on transfers of funds – the related risks are different to risks relating to movements in exchange rates

Impact is to ration the supply of foreign currency and restrict certain types of transaction

Strategies: transfer pricing, royalty payments, loans, management charges

Legal risks

- Export and import controls for political, environmental or health and safety reasons
- Favourable trade status for some countries
- International trademark, copyright and patent conventions (some countries do not recognise these)
- Restrictions on promotional message and methods

Mitigation of legal risks

- Keep up to date with changes
- Good citizenship – compliance with best practice and going beyond the minimum required
- Ensure staff are fully informed of changes
- Local versus central management

Reputational risks

- Bad press in host and domestic country
- Companies with high standards may be accused of hypocrisy if practices are not as good elsewhere
- May be low quality standards due to need to save costs

Due diligence and auditing of overseas financial risk

- Has management taken legal, taxation and accounting advice
- Has hedging been used?
- Has management considered the cultural and political implications of an overseas investment?
- Other discussions with management – other issues that have arisen
- Examine terms of loan capital
- Examine contractual liabilities
- Check remittance records to bank and cash records
- Review movement of exchange and interest rates
- Obtain details of hedging if used
- Examine financial statements for accurate disclosure of accounting policy and treatment
- Have directors satisfied themselves as to going concern?

See also
Change – Definition & Models	73
Change – Management & Implementation	75
Globalisation	145
Other Overseas Operations topics	

Overseas Operations – Strategic Considerations

Reasons to develop overseas operations

- Earn contribution
- Establish a reputation abroad
- Diversification to reduce risks
- Extend scale of operations – economies of scale, meet targets
- Government incentives
- May be less competition than in mature/home markets
- Changes in tastes
- Changes in regulations
- First mover advantage – be the first into a market
- Follow competitors if not first into a market
- Product life cycle
- Home market image may be a selling point (e.g. fashionable US brands)
- Defeat seasonality – having sales in the other hemisphere can be helpful (e.g. summer clothing)
- Growth rates in foreign market
- Vent for surplus – sell excess production/capacity
- Low cost production

International investment appraisal – further considerations

- Interest rates
- Tax rates and incentives – Corporation Tax in the foreign country, investment allowances in the foreign country, withholding taxes, double tax relief in home country
- Inflation
- Exchange rates – if sterling falls in value, NPV in sterling rises because each unit of foreign currency translates back into a higher amount of sterling
- Reduction in exports (as direct production in the foreign country will account for the sales instead)
- Subsidies
- Exchange restrictions
- Transaction costs

Risks to consider

Transaction risk – future transaction in a foreign currency

Translation risk – impact on translation of foreign subsidiary's accounts

Economic risk – longer term exchange rate movements and impact on sales and present value. Economic risk can affect the company even if it does not trade via foreign currency transactions by affecting competitiveness of imports and other costs

Political risk – quotes, tariffs, legal, safety, expropriation

Cultural risk – unfamiliar language, customs and laws – ignorance of how business transactions take place, media

See also Change – Definition & Models 73
Change – Management & Implementation 75
Globalisation 145
Other Overseas Operations topics

Pensions – Strategic Impact, Accounting and Auditing

Strategic Impact

May retain loyalty of staff if based on years served and rewards more highly weighted to employees with a long employment record

Accounting

Impact on financial statements

Acquisition of a company with a defined benefits scheme

In an exam scenario, more likely to be a net liability (deficit) assumed

Business risk – company will need to consider how to fund this deficit – this will affect reported profits

Business risk – uncertainty as to the contributions needed in future (unlike a defined contribution scheme)

Financial risk – value of assets affected by market factors such as share price movements and interest rate changes – higher market interest rates will reduce the value of the bonds held

Need to report under IAS 19 Employee Benefits: report net obligation (asset or liability) and annual cost of the scheme (depending on the contributions of the employer into the fund, changes in asset values and changes in the FV of the present value of future obligations) – this element is not predictable and is likely to vary

Then consider materiality – is the pension issue a big issue?

Auditing

Obtain client permission to liaise with the actuary and review the actuary's professional qualification

Agree the validity and accuracy of the actuarial valuation

Agree that the actuarial valuation method satisfies the accounting objectives of IAS 19

Review the assumptions made by the actuary e.g. on the expected return on assets

Agree the completeness of the actuarial valuation

Identify major events that should have been taken into account

Scrutinise relevant correspondence

Review minutes of board meetings

Agree opening balances to last year's working papers

Reconcile closing balance provision to the opening SFP

Agree contributions to the cash book and to the funding rate recommended by the actuary in the most recent actuarial valuation

Check that disclosures comply with the requirements of IAS 19

Pricing Strategies

Price penetration

Gain **market share** by setting a low price **initially** to enter the market and get the brand name known amongst as many consumers as possible

Can also help gain **economies of scale**

A **temporary** policy – prices need to be **increased** later to generate profit if sales are being made at full cost price – may be **difficult to increase the price** once this lower price has been established

Low initial prices could **damage** the **brand name**

Price skimming

The initial price is set **high** for **new** products launched into a market and a **smaller** market share is normally gained but at a **greater** margin

Company charges **higher prices** when a product is **first** launched – then spends **heavily** on **advertising and sales promotion** to win customers

Company then **lowers** its prices later to attract more **price-elastic** segments of the market – these price **reductions** are **gradual**

Should generate a **higher** sales volume at a **higher** price

Price could be taken as a **signal of quality** and **image** of the product – therefore a **high price** is **not** necessarily a **bad** thing

Choosing a pricing strategy

The **choice** of strategy should be based on **market research** – a **trial** or A/B testing (using one strategy in one location/market and another strategy elsewhere) could also be used

Professional Scepticism

Forecasts are inherently unreliable and may change

Missing variables and information

Seasonality

Are assumptions in line with **trend**?

Query the weak points of the **methodology** (accounting profit-based, NPV, payback)

Forecast period too long or too short

Source of information – just one view, press report, any reason for the information to be **biased**?

Initial discussions only? Nothing confirmed

Capacity – is this **practical** and **possible** for the business?

How has the **cost of capital** been arrived at? **How** has the estimate of **g** been arrived at? Absolutely key variables

Need for **independent assurance on key figures** before making a decision

Ability and **knowledge** of **staff** who prepared forecasts

Unrecognised assets and liabilities

Perpetuity assumption (including assumption of continual growth) is unrealistic

Proposal is **too much of a change** for the company e.g. merging companies in 2 completely different markets

Contract negotiations – a customer may request lower **prices** but promise that this will be compensated for by greater **volumes** – the lower price will be built into the contract (and so will definitely happen) whereas the volume response may be unknown if not built into the contract – the customer may be making unrealistic promises simply to obtain a better price

See also　　　Q1 – Technique Reminders　　　231

Project Management

Aspects to monitor

1. Targets
2. Timing
3. Cost and keeping within budget
4. Risks and risk management

1. Targets

Should achieve performance targets

Should relate to procedures, systems and outcomes

Design, test and implement operating procedures that achieve certain performance standards

Draw up a list of key targets when the project is initiated

Progress towards each of the targets should be monitored

2. Timing

Complete the project in the planned time

Break down the overall project into activities with estimated times

Critical path chart can be used to monitor progress and ensure that time-critical activities are given the most attention

Consider allocating more resources to critical activities if needed

Identify possible delays in advance

3. Cost and keeping within budget

Break down the budget into time periods, comparing actual costs with budgeted costs

4. Risk and risk management

Consider operational risks with the project work

Create a system to identify and assess risk

Suitable and effective internal controls

Ask internal auditors or an external firm to review the effectiveness of the planned internal controls

See also   Change – Definition & Models   73
                   Change – Management & Implementation 75

Prospective Information (ISAE 3400)

Exam examples

Skeleton Outline of ISAE 3400 Points to Include

The available model answers always include the following points:

Statement that reporting on prospective information is covered by ISAE 3400 *The Examination of Prospective Financial Information*

Statement that ISAE 3400 highlights that prospective information is based on assumptions about the future and is therefore highly subjective – judgement is required in its preparation

Definition of a "forecast" and of a "projection"

Procedures must be used to obtain sufficient appropriate evidence that

> management's best-estimate assumptions are not unreasonable and that any hypothetical assumptions are consistent with the purpose of the information. Then apply these points by referring to the scenario.

> the information has been properly prepared on the basis of the assumptions. Then apply these points by referring to the scenario.

> the information is properly presented and all material assumptions are adequately disclosed, including a clear indication as to whether they are best-estimate assumptions or hypothetical assumptions. Then apply these points by referring to the scenario.

> the information is prepared on a consistent basis with historical financial statements, using appropriate accounting principles. Then apply these points by referring to the scenario.

Statement that as prospective financial information is subjective, it is impossible to give the same level of assurance regarding forecasts as can be provided regarding historical information e.g. may be over a significant future time horizon, which creates uncertainty

Procedures are used to support limited assurance in the form of a negatively expressed opinion in relation to whether

> the assumptions provide a reasonable basis for the prospective financial information

> the information is properly prepared on the basis of the assumptions and relevant reporting framework

Appropriate caveats should be given as to the achievability of any forecasts, together with examples from the scenario as to why they may not be achieved.

Prospective Information (ISAE 3400)

General notes

A **forecast** is prospective financial information based on assumptions as to future events which management expects to take place and the actions which management expects to take: it is a best-estimate

A **projection** is based on hypothetical assumptions and scenarios, rather than events which management necessarily expects to happen

ISAE 3400 governs the reporting of prospective financial information. Under this standard, there should be agreement with the directors regarding the intended use of the information, whether the information will be distributed generally, the types of assumptions used, the elements to be included in the information and the period covered by the information

The opinion expressed should be in the form of a **negative and limited assurance opinion** that nothing has come to the practitioner's attention to doubt the assumptions and proper preparation of the information – caveats should be indicated – assurance given is not to the same standard as for historical statements – as with any forecast, it is important to recognise that assumptions may subsequently prove incorrect even if they were completely reasonable at the time of formulation

The practitioner/auditor must have sufficient knowledge of the business. The assurance provided is **limited** and **negative** in nature.

The options of a **qualified**, **adverse** or **disclaimer of opinion** are available

The procedures for reporting on prospective information noted in the Corporate Reporting Study Manual can be split into 2 types: general and specific

General procedures involve obtaining sufficient appropriate evidence regarding whether management's best-estimate assumptions are not unreasonable and consistent with the purpose of the information. It should also be determined whether the prospective financial information is properly prepared and presented and whether the information is consistent with the historical financial statements

Specific procedures are provided for the areas of profits, capital expenditure and cash flows.

Review of profit forecasts: procedures

- verify projected income figures to suitable evidence, including comparison of the basis of projected income to similar existing projects in the firm

- reviewing competitor prices for the relevant product or service to determine whether projected information is reasonable

- verify projected expenditure figures to suitable evidence, such as quotations or estimates, current bills, interest rate assumptions or costs such as depreciation

- check assumptions about annual revenues based on market prices and estimates of costs and how these have been divided into fixed and variable elements

Prospective Information (ISAE 3400)

Review of capital expenditure forecasts: procedures

- check capital expenditure for reasonableness by ensuring that all relevant costs are included and that costs estimated are reasonable

- verify projected costs to estimates and quotations

- review projections for reasonableness by examining the prevailing market rates

- verify that there is evidence that the required capital assets can be located and purchased

Review of cashflow forecasts: procedures

- review cash forecasts to determine whether the timings involved are reasonable

- check the cash forecast for consistency with profit forecasts, looking at both the expenditure and income side or undertake some other method of verification if there is no relevant or comparable profit forecast

Testing of Prospective Information (past paper review from *Smashing SBM™*)

- is there a **lack of information from the client** on exactly what level of detail will be published (and therefore on the subject matter of the assurance engagement) – scepticism and risk issue

- the **terms of the engagement should be agreed in advance** – the terms would probably involve an arrangement to test the assumptions that management has used in making the forecasts

- **ISAE 3400 provides the guidelines** for this sort of assurance engagement

- **forecasts will be based on assumptions**, generally including historical information

- the practitioner needs to satisfy itself about the **reliability of any historical information** that has been used as the basis of the forecasts

- the practitioner should consider the **reasonableness of the assumptions** that have been used to prepare the forecast **and that the forecast has in fact been prepared on the basis of those assumptions** (and correctly so)

- the **assumptions must be stated as part of the published forecast**

- **predicting the future is a speculative matter** and can lead to errors if events turn out differently

- therefore the assurance provider's task cannot be to say whether the results will be "correct" or turn out as planned – rather **the practitioner's role is instead to consider whether the assumptions are free from any material misstatement or weakness**

Prospective Information (ISAE 3400)

- if the **assumptions appear to be unrealistic**, then the assurance provider **should not accept or continue with the assurance engagement**

- if historical information has been used as the basis for making the forecast then it would be necessary to **check whether the information has been audited** or to obtain other evidence of its reliability

- the report provided at the end of the engagement should include a **statement of negative assurance** as to whether the assumptions used provide a reasonable basis for making the forecast

- the report should **contain an opinion as to whether the forecast has been properly prepared** based on these assumptions

- **caveats should be included regarding the prospective nature of the results** and therefore the fact that the figures included may not necessarily be achievable

See also Professional Scepticism 224

Provisions and Reorganisations

IAS 37 conditions:

Legal or constructive obligation as a result of a past event, and

Probable that an outflow of economic benefits will occur

Exam tip

Look carefully at the dates involved and exactly what the Board has done or (not done) to communicate reorganisation plans to stakeholders

Note that it is possible for there to be some uncertainty as to whether a provision exists – this may need to be discussed

| **See also** | Liquidation | 198 |

Q1 – Technique Reminders

Since we know that Q1 will always be at least 60% of the marks available, this is a very important question so we provide some specific reminders here*

In Q1 DO:

Use a table of data at the start of the answer

Use the scenario-specific indicators/performance measures thoroughly – do not just look at standard points such as gross profit margin or revenue growth

Calculate additional scenario-specific metrics

Look for cause and effect relationships and describe these

Try to separate out different divisions/revenue streams and find something different to say on each one

Look for interconnections between parts of the business

Use appropriate headings – consider a separate section for each set of affected stakeholders

Provide a reasonable and clear discussion of the actions to be taken

Exercise professional scepticism over figures, especially forecasts

Separately and clearly identify your answer to each Task and sub-Task

Start each Task on a new page with a clear heading

Use the estimated mark allocation in Q1 to inform your estimate in Q2 – the marks will balance across the standard allocation*, being

Topic	Standard weighting
Strategy	35-45%
Finance, valuations & investment appraisal	30-40%
Financial reporting[8]	15-20%
Assurance	10%
Ethics	5-10%

In Q1 DO NOT:

Forget to use the data thoroughly – everything needs to be driven by the data given

---

[8] The examiners generally use the term "corporate reporting" to refer to this angle or perspective but because we think this may lead to confusion with the separate Corporate Reporting ACA paper, we have adopted the term "financial reporting" to refer to this perspective. By "financial reporting" we do **not** just mean the lessons that you learned in the Financial Accounting and Reporting paper but also the new IFRS corporate reporting rules that you learn at the Advanced Level.

Q1 – Technique Reminders

Forget to explain why things have changed

Waste time on trivial issues – look at the important issues and changes

Start copying out lists of standard points (including from this book!) – ensure you are **applying** everything to the question set – to ensure that you are applying the point, try to quote the data (numbers, narrative, people, products) back to the examiner in your sentences to show that you have read and used the data

Mix your calculations randomly into the discussion – have a separate table of figures at the start

Forget to look out for the examiner "twists" – can you just list out the standard points on hedging or is there a twist here? Is it a net asset valuation where fair value has already been taken into account (defeating this standard point)?

Forget to look for all Tasks – these are not necessarily just listed at the end of the section (e.g. November 2014 examination)

* See our book *Smashing SBM*™ for further explanation of our strategy to Q1 and for justification of our statement that Q2 will provide a "balancing" of the marks across the SBM topic areas within the table of syllabus weightings indicated above

See also	Financial Performance Review in SBM – Some Advice	132
	Ratios – Calculations	233

Ratios – Calculations

Important notice: we are including these for reference only – do not spend too long on the numbers – **choose only the most relevant ratios** – at the same time, in SBM do not expect the question wording to remind you to use ratios.

Always start by first using the scenario-specific indicators given in the question (e.g. the client's own internal performance metrics) and only move onto these more "generic" analysis points after the scenario-specific indicators have been thoroughly used.

Performance

$$gross\ profit\ margin = \frac{gross\ profit}{revenue} \times 100\%$$

Replace gross profit with **operarting profit to get operating profit margin**. This allows you to see whether cost of sales (gross profit) or admin costs (net profit) are more significant as a constraint on returns

$$return\ on\ capital\ employed\ [ROCE] = \frac{PBIT + associate's\ post\ tax\ earnings}{equity + net\ debt}$$

Net debt = interest-bearing debt (current and non-current) less cash and cash equivalents

Equity = exclude redeemable preference shares, in line with general treatment as a loan, not equity

$$return\ on\ equity\ [ROE] = \frac{profit\ before\ tax}{equity\ or\ net\ assets} \times 100\%$$

Note that ROE is quicker to calculate than ROCE and with less chance of error – ROE was used in the model answer to the November 2015 past paper

$$return\ on\ shareholders'\ funds\ [ROSF] = \frac{profit\ attributable\ to\ owners\ of\ parent}{equity\ less\ NCI}$$

Profit attributable to owners of parent will usually be profit after tax

Note the difference: ROCE uses profit *before* tax; ROSF uses profit *after* tax

You can remember this by thinking of ROSF as measure of what the shareholders get i.e. after tax, whereas ROCE is more of a measure of the capacity of the business to generate a return, and tax is then a subsequent cost to be considered later

Exam tip ROSF is usually quicker and easier to calculate; you can then comment that ROSF only looks at equity as a source of resources

Ratios – Calculations

Liquidity

$$current\ ratio = \frac{current\ assets}{current\ liabilities}$$

Usually expressed as a multiple e.g. 3x (equivalent to 6/2)

$$quick\ ratio = \frac{current\ assets\ less\ inventories}{current\ liabilities}$$

Basically, the current ratio adjusted for inventories as these cannot be turned into cash very **quickly**.

Long-term solvency

$$gearing = \frac{net\ debt\ as\ per\ ROCE}{equity\ as\ per\ ROCE} \times 100\%$$

$$interest\ cover = \frac{PBIT\ plus\ investment\ income}{interest\ payable}$$

Efficiency

$$net\ asset\ turnover = \frac{revenue}{capital\ employed}$$

$$receivables\ period = \frac{trade\ receivables}{revenue} \times 365\ days$$

$$payables\ period = \frac{trade\ payables}{cost\ of\ sales} \times 365\ days$$

Strictly, use credit purchases but usually you will have to use cost of sales

Investor ratios

$$dividend\ cover = \frac{earnings\ per\ share}{dividend\ per\ share}$$

$$price\ earnings\ ratio = \frac{market\ price\ per\ share}{earnings\ per\ share}$$

Other ratios

$$CAPEX\ to\ depreciation = \frac{capital\ expenditure\ (CAPEX)}{depreciation}$$

Measures whether new expenditure compensates for depreciation.

Ratios – Calculations

$$non-current\ asset\ ageing = \frac{accumulated\ depreciation}{non-current\ assets\ at\ cost}$$

Allows an estimate of how far non-current assets are through their working lives. e.g. if depreciation is £2m and the assets cost £4m, then we are 2/4 = 50% through its working life.

Note: the above two ratios require data on depreciation. Hence they are subject to the depreciation method/charge decided upon by management (i.e. subjective).

$$dividend\ yield = \frac{dividend\ per\ share}{current\ market\ price\ per\ share} \times 100\%$$

Cash flow ratios

Least likely to be possible to calculate in SBM but included for completeness

Note: the concept of "cash return" is important here and is used in several ratios

cash return = cash generated from ops + interest received + dividends received

$$cash\ ROCE = \frac{cash\ return}{capital\ employed} \times 100\%$$

$$cash\ from\ operations\ as\ \%\ of\ profit\ from\ operations = \frac{cash\ return}{profit\ from\ operations} \times 100\%$$

$$cash\ interest\ cover = \frac{cash\ return}{interest\ paid}$$

$$cash\ flow\ per\ share = \frac{cash\ return - int\ paid - tax\ paid}{number\ of\ ordinary\ shares}$$

$$cash\ dividend\ cover = \frac{cash\ return - int\ paid - tax\ paid}{equity\ dividends\ paid}$$

Only look at equity dividends.

The result of (cash return – int paid – tax paid) is also known as "cash flow for ordinary shareholders".

See also	Financial Performance Review in SBM – Some Advice	132
	Q1 – Technique Reminders	231

Real Options

These options are traditionally not considered with traditional investment appraisal analysis but they are important

Option to delay

Option to expand

Option to abandon

Option to redeploy

Product options (patents, copyrights and natural resource ownership)

See also   Investment Appraisal Methods topics
Valuation topics

Recommendations – Keeping It Practical

Follow the 8 areas applied in the ACA Case Study:*

1. Pricing
2. Cost reduction
3. Timing
4. Impact on staff
5. Capacity
6. Further information
7. Discuss and negotiate
8. Consider alternatives

* See our book *Smashing SBM*™ for further explanation of the connections between Case Study and SBM.

Remuneration Strategies

Retention of talent – policy needs to ensure sufficient incentives for talented managers and staff to remain at the company

Rolling nature – a rolling set of incentives (with increases and new incentives issued each year) should help as a staff member may lose options or opportunities if he or she leaves the company

Goal congruence – the package should ensure that there is alignment of the interests of managers and shareholders so that what benefits the manager will also benefit the company

Value of share options – must be set in such a way that the exercise price should be below the market price at the end of the vesting period: otherwise there is no benefit to the employee

Controllability – the employee/manager must have some control over the variable which is the basis of the incentive or the employee/manager will not have a reason to improve performance

Cash savings – some incentives such as share options or bonuses payable in several years' time will preserve cash in the short run whilst still improving performance and therefore generating cash

Impact on EPS – this will need to be considered – for example, share options need to be included in the calculation of diluted EPS

Elements

Basic pay

Performance-related bonuses

Shares

Share options – align stakeholder and employee interests

Benefits in kind

Pensions

Behavioural Objectives

Support recruitment and retention

Motivate employees to high levels of performance

Should promote compliance with business rules and strategy

Always consider the impact on motivation and commitment of employees

See also	Bonuses – Audit Procedures	59
	Change – Definition & Models	73
	Change – Management & Implementation	75

Reporting on Information Contained in a Prospectus

Regulated by ISAE 3420, a project undertaken in the context of the increasing globalisation of capital markets which makes it important for financial information to be understandable across borders and for related assurance to be provided

"Pro forma financial information" is defined as financial information shown together with adjustments to illustrate the impact of an event or transaction on unadjusted financial information

The practitioner's sole responsibility is to report on whether the pro forma financial information has been compiled in all material respects by the responsible party on the basis of applicable criteria – the practitioner has no responsibility to compile pro forma information

The practitioner must perform procedures to assess when the applicable criteria used in the compilation of the pro forma information provide a reasonable basis for presenting the significant effects directly attributable to the potential event or transaction – this work must also involve an evaluation of the overall presentation of the pro forma financial information

Under ISAE 3420 the following opinion wording is permitted (2 alternatives are allowed):

"The pro forma financial information has been compiled, in all material respects, on the basis of the (applicable criteria)"

"The pro forma financial information has been properly compiled on the basis stated"

The FRC has also issued guidance in this area in Standard for Investment Reporting (SIR) 1000 *Investment Reporting Standards Applicable to Engagements in Connection with an Investment Circular*

An investment circular is defined as any document issued by an entity pursuant to statutory or regulatory requirements relating to securities on which it is intended that the third party should make an investment decision, including a prospectus, listing particulars, a circular to shareholders or similar document

The approach which the practitioner is required to take under SIR 1000 is similar to that of a statutory audit:

> agree the terms
>
> comply with ethical requirements and quality control standards
>
> plan the work and consider materiality
>
> obtain sufficient appropriate evidence
>
> document significant matters

Reporting on Information Contained in a Prospectus

adopt an attitude of professional skepticism

express an opinion (modified if required)

Revenue accounting (IFRIC 13, IAS 11, IFRS 15)

IFRIC 13 – customer loyalty programmes

A criticism of IAS 18 is that it lacks **detailed guidance** about how to account for customer loyalty programmes – therefore entities have adopted **varying approaches**

Some entities measure their obligation based on the **value of the loyalty award credits to the customer** (loyalty points) – others measure their obligation as the **cost to the entity** of supplying the free or discounted goods or service **when a customer redeems their points**

IFRIC 13 is based on the view that customers are **implicitly paying for points** when they buy other goods or services – therefore **some of that revenue should be allocated to the points**

IFRIC 13 requires companies to **estimate the value of the points** to the customer and **defer** that amount of revenue as a **liability** until the entity has fulfilled its obligation to supply free or discounted goods or other rewards

IAS 11 – construction contracts

In some industries, assets take a **substantial amount of time** to complete e.g. aeroplanes

Therefore, it may be necessary to **recognise profits across several** accounting periods

IAS 11 requires revenue, costs and therefore profit to be recognised as contract activity progresses – this will require **significant professional judgement**

The timing of the recognition of claims, variations and penalties under the contract can also affect revenue and profit significantly

IFRS 15 – replacing IAS 18

Important note – for **exam purposes**, as IAS 18 is still in force you should only refer to IFRS 15 **if you are asked to do so specifically in the question** (for example, as a current issue with regard to how future accounting periods may be affected)

Weaknesses of IAS 18 and IAS 11 include:

- **timing of revenue recognition** – there is a lack of clear guidance in the current standards particularly regarding combined packages of goods and services because goods are sold at a point in time whereas services may be provided over time
- **distinguishing between goods and services** – IFRS accounting does not clearly distinguish between goods and services so some companies may not be sure whether to apply IAS 18 or IAS 11 but these standards are very different
- **multielement arrangements** – these transactions involve the delivery of more than 1 good or service – IFRS does not give sufficient guidance on dealing with such transactions

IFRS 15 will therefore **replace** IAS 18, IAS 11 and IFRIC 13

Revenue accounting (IFRIC 13, IAS 11, IFRS 15)

The IFRS 15 five step model

1. identify the **contract** with the customer
2. identify the **separate performance obligations** in the contract
3. determine the **transaction price** – this is the amount to which the entity expects to be "entitled" – for variable consideration, the probability weighted expected amount is used – the effect of any credit losses is shown as a separate line item (just below revenue)
4. **allocate** the transaction price to the **separate performance obligations** in the contract
5. **recognise revenue** when (or as) the entity **satisfies a performance obligation** – this is when the entity transfers a promised good or service to a customer – the good or service is only considered to be transferred when the customer obtains control of it

Example of IFRS 15 recognition of a combined contract

A company offers a software package to customers.

The company can supply and install the software for £2,000 and offers a separate 2-year technical support service for £1,000. The company offers a combined contract which includes both of these elements for £2,400. Payment for the combined contract is due 1 month after the installation.

When a combined contract is sold, revenue in respect of the supply and installation should be recognised at the time of installation. Revenue for the technical support should be recognised over 2 years. This is because the performance obligation for the installation is satisfied when the package is supplied but the performance obligation for the support service is satisfied over time.

The company should recognise £1,600 at the time of installation, calculated based on the proportion of value relating to the installation within the total package, applying the normal stand-alone pricing. In this case, the installation is worth a proportion of 2,000/(2,000+1,000) or 2/3 of the normal stand-alone pricing: 2/3 of £2,400 (the price of the combined contract) is £1,600.

Impact of the IFRS approach

By far the most significant change is to the **pattern** of revenue reporting – even if the total revenue reported does not change, the **timing will change** in many cases

Separate performance obligations will be recognised for distinct goods or services – this will mean some revenue being attributed to goods or services that are currently considered incidental to the contract.

For example, under IFRS 15 revenue may be allocated to mobile phones that are provided free of charge with airtime contracts and to some post delivery services such as maintenance and installation

The transaction price will be allocated in proportion to the stand-alone selling price – this will affect some practices, particularly in the software sector, that currently result in the deferral of revenue if a company does not have objective evidence of the selling price of the good or service to be provided

Review Engagements (ISRE 2400)

Gives a reduced degree of assurance based on a **negative assurance** statement that **nothing has come to the attention of the auditor which causes the auditor to believe that the statements have not been prepared in accordance with the relevant financial reporting framework**.

Often relates to review of **interim financial information**

ISRE 2400 provides the rules and relevant guidance for this type of review. Note that this standard has not been adopted in the UK.

Materiality should be applied in the same way as for a statutory audit.

Specific inquiries could include:

- how management makes significant accounting estimates
- identification of related parties and related party transactions
- consideration of significant, unusual or complex transactions
- actual or suspected fraud
- whether management has identified and addressed events after the reporting period
- the basis of management's assessment of going concern
- material commitments, contractual obligations or contingencies
- material non-monetary transactions or transactions for no consideration in the reporting period

Analytical procedures should be used to help the practitioner to:

- obtain or update an understanding of the entity and its environment
- identify inconsistencies or variances from expected trends, values or norms
- provide corroborative evidence in relation to inquiry or other analytical procedures
- serve as additional procedures when the practitioner becomes aware of matters that indicate that the financial statements may be materially misstated

The practitioner should also determine whether the data available is adequate for the above purposes.

A typical practitioner's review report should contain the following headings/report sections:

Review Engagements (ISRE 2400)

- **report on the financial statements** – statement regarding which set of statements has been reviewed

- **management's responsibility for the financial statements**

- **practitioner's responsibility**

- **conclusion**

The conclusion can be **qualified**, **adverse** or a **disclaimer** of a conclusion based on the usual rules applicable to a statutory audit and considering whether the matter is pervasive or not.

Suspected non-compliance with laws and regulations

Under ISRE 2400, the practitioner should follow 5 steps if there is a suspicion of non-compliance with laws and regulations:

Communicate the matter to the appropriate level of management/those charged with governance

Request management's assessment of the effects, if any, on the financial statements

Consider the implications for the practitioner's report

Determine whether law, regulation or ethical requirements require that the matter should be reported to a third party outside the entity

Determine whether law, regulation or ethical requirements establish responsibilities under which reporting to an authority outside the entity may be appropriate

The practitioner should always consult internally, obtain legal advice and consult with the regulator or professional body in order to understand the implications of different courses of action

Review of interim financial information (common focus of a review engagement) – procedures

- reading last year's audit file and considering any significant risks identified

- reading the most recent and comparable interim financial information

- considering materiality

- considering the nature of any corrected or uncorrected misstatements in last year's financial statements

- considering significant financial accounting and reporting matters of ongoing importance
- considering the results of any interim audit work for this year's audit
- considering the work of internal audit
- reading management accounts and commentaries for the period
- considering any findings from prior periods
- asking management what their assessment of the risk of fraud in the interim financial statements may be
- asking management whether there have been any significant changes in internal controls or business activity
- reading the minutes of meetings of shareholders, those charged with governance or other appropriate committees
- considering the effect of matters giving rise to a modification of the audit or review report and accounting adjustments
- communicating with other auditors that audit different components of the business
- performing analytical procedures designed to identify relationships and unusual items that may reflect a material misstatement
- reading the interim financial information and considering whether anything has come to the auditors' attention indicating that it has not been prepared in accordance with the applicable financial reporting framework
- agreeing the interim financial information to the underlying accounting records
- reviewing consolidation adjustments for consistency and reviewing relevant correspondence with regulators
- inquire with the members of management responsible for financial and accounting matters regarding issues such as the applicable reporting framework, changes in accounting policies, significant misstatements, fair value assumptions, compliance with debt covenants and fraud issues, amongst others

Comparative information should be considered to determine whether this is consistent with that presented in the interim financial statements.

Written representations should be obtained from management in which management recognises its responsibility for the design and implementation of internal controls and that significant facts

Review Engagements (ISRE 2400)

relating to frauds or non-compliance with law and regulations have been disclosed to the auditor and that all significant subsequent events have been disclosed to the auditor.

The format of the report should be very similar to the above noted format for review engagements: relevant sections to include in the report would be:

- Introduction
- Directors' Responsibilities
- Practitioner's Responsibilities
- Scope of the Review
- Conclusion

See also   Cash Flow Forecasts – Evaluation   72

Risks – Governance

Aspects to consider

The governance structure must be reviewed as the business grows and changes

Governance structures between a single person or entrepreneurial structure and a larger corporate structure are very different

Consider implications of listing, if appropriate – UK corporate governance code may be applicable although there is an exemption for AIM-listed companies and more limited exemptions for non-FTSE 350 companies

Consider the size of the board and the skills

Are there any independent directors who are not shareholders?

Are there any NEDs (Non-Executive Directors)? A complete lack of NEDs would be unusual for a large company

Is there any remuneration committee, and nomination committee or an audit committee, if the company is a large? These committees give shareholders more control and insights into the actions of the directors

Is the remuneration policy transparent, certain and one that ensures **goal congruence** between different stakeholders? (are directors rewarded more if shareholder wealth is promoted, for example?)

Are there any rotation periods? Do these appear reasonable?

Are powers and voting rights clear and transparent?

Is there any risk of a split board and therefore an inability to get anything done?

If the question relates to an acquisition, always consider shareholdings and voting percentages before and after the business change?

See also	Risks topics	
	FRC Risk Guidance	143

Risks – Horizontal Acquisition

Strategic

Overpayment if synergies do not emerge

Significantly different market

May be little or no common customer base

Customers may not continue to be loyal to the new organisation – continuance of relationships is not guaranteed

Contract renewal risk if major suppliers change their views?

Relatively low risk of understanding the market and processes as similar?

Operational

Post-acquisition integration may not deliver the synergies and operational activity that was planned – this could mean a real risk of overpayment

May be unforeseen merging costs such as compatibility of process, employee resistance, skills gaps

May be unforeseen problems in merging information systems and support processes such as accounting, HRM, IT, internal controls, supply chain management, deliveries and marketing

Sale of surplus assets may be uncertain

May be hidden contractual or other legal obligations

Hidden financial liabilities such as tax

If debt financed, then adds to the financial gearing of the group

Management skills and available time may not be as appropriate for the new group

May be issues with covenants and providers of finance with a change of use or disposal of assets

See also   Risks topics

Risks – Types and Examples

Background considerations

- Risk appetite
- Culture
- Response
- Reporting
- Monitoring

Levels of risks

- Strategic
- Operating
- Financing risks

Exam tip – the above represents a very useful framework that you may wish to use

Strategic risks

- Becoming involved in an unfamiliar market
- Overpaying for an acquisition
- Failing to understand demand and supply
- Reliance on others for knowledge and skills
- Lack of strategic fit or direction
- Reputational damage
- Focusing on the wrong product/service with poor margin
- Failing to consider the opportunity cost of a project

Operating risks

- Post-integration problems in an acquisition
- Synergies failing to emerge
- Administrative integration
- Problems in integrating cultures, accounting, HRM, IT, internal controls, supply chain management, deliveries and marketing
- Hidden contractual and other legal obligations (assuming that there are no indemnities)
- Hidden financial liabilities (assuming that there are no indemnities)
- Financing methods such as debt
- Dependence on key suppliers or individuals
- Limited amount of assets against which to raise future debts
- Uncertain sales of surplus assets
- Overuse of fixed assets, causing damage due to a lack of downtime for repairs

Risks – Types and Examples

Key general risks

- Customers
- Currency – revenue, raw material
- Economic/Market
- Transportation
- Financial
- Liquidity
- Operating

Revenue risks

Note – in SBM, may well interact with currency risks

Risk of a fall in revenue

Currency risks

Note that these risks may have offsetting effects (if revenue falls due to a high value of the domestic currency then costs of imports will fall)

Note that there is also **upside** risk – the exchange rate may move in a **more favourable** direction

Currency revenue risks

- Fixed prices but changing exchange rates
- Credit or default risk – the purchaser may fail to pay
- Order cancellation risk – can the materials/WIP be used on another project?

Currency raw material risks

- Some raw materials have very volatile and fluctuating market prices
- Changes in currency value can change import costs

Cultural risks

- Cultures and practices of customers and consumers to individual markets
- Media and distribution systems in overseas markets
- Different ways of doing business in overseas markets
- National cultural differences

Governance risks

- Structure – weak? Control methods?
- Style – entrepreneurial v corporate
- Individual management style
- Listed company – Corporate Governance Code may apply (AIM exempt; non-FTSE 350 limited exemptions)
- Size of company
- Non-Executive Directors (NEDs) – independent? quality?

- Committees for remuneration, nomination and audit – exist? transparency?
- Correct balance between performance and pay
- Rotation of control/power (but not so often that lose skills)
- Changes in voting rights and power

Information technology risks

Strategic IT risks

- Loss of competitive advantage by not staying up to date
- Dependence on IT – breakdown could threaten the business
- Cost of updates etc

Operational IT risks

- Theft of information/hacking
- Penalties for non-compliance with laws e.g. Data Protection Act
- Loss of information – human error, virus

Political risks

- Government stability
- Economic stability
- Inflation
- Degree of international indebtedness
- Financial infrastructure
- Level of import restrictions
- Remittance restrictions
- Evidence of expropriation
- Special taxes or investment incentives

Dealing with political risks

- Negotiations with the host government
- Insurance such as export credit guarantees
- Production strategies such as outsourcing or producing locally
- Management structure – consider JVs, giving control to local investors to keep government happy

Operating risks

- Capacity – hitting full capacity has an opportunity cost: will have to reject new orders – also may have impact on costs and staff morale/working hours
- Transportation risks

Liquidity risks

- Timing – difference between outlays on a contract and the cash returns generated – may leave the entity short of liquid cash resources at just the wrong time

Supply chain risks

- Short-term disruption to supply
- Inadequate quality of goods
- Increases in purchase costs
- Reputation risk
- Delays in delivery
- Lack of capacity to cater for demand

See also   Risks topics
                   IT Due Diligence   186

Risks – Risk Reviews

Considerations in creating a risk review

Objective setting	consider the objectives of the business, in the light of risks faced
Risk appetite	consider how much risk is acceptable
Risk culture	consider attitudes and examples of senior management, documentation, training and emphasis placed on risk in performance appraisal
Risk consolidation	consider systems in place for identifying and assessing risk
Risk response	consider how risks are managed and the priorities for action
Risk reporting	consider if risks are reported frequently enough and to the right level of management and that external reporting is appropriate
Risk monitoring	consider whether risk management is considered at all board meetings and whether any applicable governance codes are being followed

See also   Risks topics

Sale and Operating Leaseback

Financial reporting

The difference between **fair value and carrying amount** can be recognised immediately as a profit (if FV > CA) – we are saying that the asset is worth more than the amount shown in the accounts and so should be updated

The **excess proceeds above fair value** are unusual and so are deferred and recognised over the lease period on a straight line basis

The **lease rentals paid** are charged to the IS

Segmental Reporting (IFRS 8)

Applies to entities with equity and/or debt which is listed on a public market (so check that the question relates to a listed entity) – **if so, any business change could potentially affect this aspect**

Examples could include a large diversification into a new geographical area or product

An operating segment is a component of an entity:

- That engages in business activities from which it may earn revenues and incur expenses (including revenues and expenses relating to transactions with other components of the same entity)

- Whose operating results are regularly reviewed by the entity's Chief Operating Decision Maker to make decisions about resources to be allocated to the segment and assess its performance

- For which discrete financial information is available

Consider whether discrete financial information about different revenue streams is provided and whether this is reported to the Chief Operation Decision Maker to assess performance and/or allocate resources

Consider whether different activities/products are similar enough to be aggregated (similarity of products, similar production processes, customers, regulation and distribution methods)

If represents 10% of revenue, profits or assets then needs to be disclosed as a separate segment

Must also meet the 75% external revenue test – if insufficient segments have been added then need to keep disclosing segments until 75% of external revenue has been analysed

Information which must be given includes information regarding the determination of the operating segments, the products and services they provide, profit or loss, significant income and expense items and segment assets and liabilities

See also   Acquisitions topics
Change topics
Organic topics

Sensitivity Analysis

Assesses how responsive the project's NPV is to changes in the variables used to calculate the NPV

Could vary depending on changes in selling price, sales volume, cost of capital, initial cost, operating costs, benefits, cost savings and residual value

Sensitivity = NPV / PV of project variable %

Weaknesses of a sensitivity analysis

Requires variables to be changed one at a time which is not realistic

Looks at factors in isolation which is not realistic as variables are interdependent

Sensitivity does not examine the probability that any particular variation in costs or revenues might occur

The critical factors may not be under the control of managers

Does not provide a decision rule itself – managers must still interpret the results to reach a decision

See also   Investment Appraisal Methods topics

Share Options – Strategic Impact, Accounting and Auditing

Strategic Impact

Incentivise strong performance from Directors and managers – ensure goal congruence with other stakeholders such as shareholders

No **immediate cash flow outflow** – no cash outflow on maturity either if equity settled (but will be cash outflow if cash settled) – therefore can boost cash flows immediately at limited short term risk

Fair value scheme has **constant** impact on earnings but **cash settled** scheme is more **variable** as the expense is based on amounts **remeasured** at each year end

Volatility introduced into the financial statements due to staff leaving and joining each year

Cash settled schemes can lead to perverse outcomes – a **rising share price** will increase the FV used to determine the P&L expense and therefore depress **profits/earnings**

Accounting (IFRS 2)

See also your Corporate Reporting notes

Equity settled

Find FV at inception and then leave this alone over time – constant yearly charge

(However, if the share price is rising and there are new issues of options then the yearly charge will be higher in later years as the FV at inception will be higher)

Cash settled

Use the latest available FV when determining the expense for the year – in other words, introduce a variable P&L charge as FV fluctuates

As the share price increases, then the P&L expense will increase – possible tension for the Directors and shareholders?

Market-based vesting condition – connected to the share price in some way

Non-marked-based vesting condition – all other conditions

Modifications – continue to recognise the original FV of the instrument in the normal way, recognise any increase in FV at the date of modification spread over the period between modification date and vesting date (if the modification occurs after the vesting date then recognise the additional expense immediately unless there is an additional service period, in which case spread the increase)

Cancellations and settlements – immediately charge any remaining FV (accelerate the charge rather than avoiding it) and recognise any amount paid to the employees on settlement as a buy back, treated as a deduction from equity (if this amount exceeds FV then recognise the excess immediately in the IS)

Auditing

Number of employees/leavers – examine HR records for historic and forecast patterns, check whether new joiners are eligible, examiner HR budgets and plans, consider whether level of recruitment is sensible in the light of the stated aim to expand the business

Note: dependence on future forecasts does not matter for audit purposes because these will be confirmed in future years (and these would be irrelevant to an equity-settled scheme anyway as the FV already reflects the probability of settlement)

See also	Option Valuation	207
	Remuneration Strategies	238

Shareholding Percentages – Narrative Comments

Why acquire less than 100%?

Cost reasons
Existing shareholders may be unwilling to sell their shares
A controlling shareholding of 50% may be considered enough

Shareholding of 75%+

75% is enough to give full control – Articles of Association can be altered

Shareholding of 50%-74%

Should have a control premium attached and therefore a value above a simple pro-rata valuation

Articles of Association

Worth checking these to see if there are any special rules e.g. on acquisitions or appointment of directors – there may also be specific rules on valuation principles e.g. if a founding shareholder is leaving the business – there may be restrictions on the percentage shareholding which can be required for control or specific decisions and sometimes control is even possible with less than 50%

Largest single holding but below 50%

Gives power but look at the other shareholdings: if these are concentrated amongst a few groups/individuals, those other groups/individuals may have effective control

Discount Rules of Thumb

Always explain that these are suggested discounts, not precise figures, and an element of judgement is involved

To gain extra credit, mention 1-2 judgemental areas briefly

Other Factors to Consider Regarding Discounts

Where the shareholders are likely to vote together to obtain a 50% or 75% vote – for example, are there any related parties such as brothers and sisters or very close friends who are likely to work together?

Will dividends be paid in future?

Consider the concentration of other shareholdings – are there other groups that are likely to work together to have a high percentage of votes?

Shareholding Percentages – Narrative Comments

75% share – with this share of votes or more, the Articles of Association can be changed so any protections within those articles would not be applicable

What role will the shareholder have, if any – will he or she be a director, for example? This would give them additional power

See also Valuations topics

Stakeholders and Stakeholder Management

Very important SBM topic – always look for different stakeholders and even consider using them as headings in your answer

Managers and employees

Shareholders

Lenders

Suppliers

Customers

Government and regulatory agencies

Environmental and social bodies and other non-governmental organisations

Industry associations and trade unions

Local communities

Focus of the stakeholders can be **economic or social**, **local or national**

Mendelow's Matrix

	Level of interest Low	Level of interest High
Power Low	Not significant "Minimal effort"	Passive, but may change "Keep satisfied"
Power High	Could influence others "keep informed"	Key players "make strategy acceptable to them"

Strategic Analysis Tools & Models

Note: use your judgement but in SBM you are very unlikely to be rewarded just for drawing out any of the following models – what matters is the **application of the concepts within the models**, which may be rewarded in your narrative analysis (e.g. reference to a "cash cow" or using PESTEL to create your report headings)

PESTEL

- Political
- Economic
- Socio-cultural
- Technological
- Environmental protections
- Legal

Porter's Five Forces

- Threat of new entrants
- Threat of substitute products or services
- Bargaining power of customers
- Bargaining power of suppliers
- Rivalry amongst current competitors in the industry

Product life cycle

- Introduction
- Development and growth
- Maturity
- Decline

Boston matrix

		Market share	
		High	*Low*
% rate of market growth	*High*	Star	Problem child/ Question mark
	Low	Cash cow	Dog

Strategic Analysis Tools & Models

SWOT analysis

Strengths
Weaknesses
Opportunities
Threats

(Hopefully you did not need reminding of these elements but just in case ...)

Market positioning

			Cowboy brands		Premium brands	
Price	High					
	Low		Economy brands		Bargain brands	
		Very poor	Poor	Reasonable	Good	Very good
				Perceived quality		

Porter's 2 generic competitive strategies

Low cost
Differentiation

Ansoff matrix

		Product Existing	Product New
Market	Existing	Market penetration	Product development
	New	Market development	Diversification

Resource audit

Identify the resources available to an organisation:

- Financial
- Human
- Intangible
- Physical

Value chain analysis

Activities of the organisation that add value to purchased inputs

Used to identify critical success factors and opportunities to use information strategically

Primary activities   those involved in the production of goods and services
Support activities   provide necessary assistance
Linkages activities   relationships between activities

Benchmarking

Internal – versus company's own historical performance, or perhaps against branches
Competitive – compare against other firms in the same industry or sector*
Activity/best in class – best practice in any industry
Generic benchmarking – conceptually similar procedure

* problem here is that whole sector might be performing badly, hence the third or "activity/best in class" alternative

GE Business Screen

		Weak	Average	Unattractive
Business strength	**Strong**	Invest for growth	Invest selectively for growth	Develop for income
	Average	Invest selectively and build	Develop selectively for income	Harvest or divest
	Weak	Develop selectively Build on strengths	Harvest	Divest

Market attractiveness

Business process analysis

Helps organisation to improve how it conducts functions and activities

Reduce costs
Improve efficient use of resources
Better support for customers

Balanced scorecard

- Customer
- Internal business
- Innovation and learning
- Financial

Industry analysis

- Degree of rivalry – growth rate, number and relative size of firms, product differentiation, scale economies, degree of operating leverage, capital specificity
- Barriers to entrance – minimum size of operation, early entry advantage, distribution channels, regulation and legal constraints
- Product substitutability
- Price elasticity
- Structure of input markets

See also

	Balanced Scorecard	48
	Key Performance Indicators	194

Strategic Case Study – Tips from the Study Manual

Based on the SBM Study Manual, here are some key questions to consider:

Company's main line of business

Current strategy and long-term objectives

Conflicts in objectives

External issues and stakeholders

Financial performance

Areas for obvious improvement

Particular company strengths it could exploit

Limitations on resources

What are competitors doing?

Is the company generating value for its shareholders?

Ruth Bender's 4 Factors (Impact on Shareholder Value)

Product

Business – activity

Company – management of that activity

Investment

See also	Financial Performance Review in SBM – Some Advice	132
	Q1 – Technique Reminders	231

Supply Chain Improvements

Supply chain management – definition

The planning and management of all activities involved in sourcing and procurement, conversion, and all associated logistics and distribution activities.

Activities include procurement, inventory management, production, warehousing, transportation, customer service, order management, logistics and distribution.

Try to distinguish between goods and services as these will require different types of supply chain management.

Principles of effective supply chain management

For services, the process should be "pull" driven – for goods, the process should be "push" driven

Services – "pull" approach responding to demands

Ensure that all activities are undertaken with the needs of customers in mind

Be aware of the needs of customers and keep in communication

Use flexible manufacturing systems to commence manufacture as soon as possible in the case of bespoke orders

Implement effective transportation methods

Ensure a local presence with associated expertise in the case of supply of maintenance services

Goods – "push" approach with the entity taking action in advance

Hold inventories in response to uncertainty in customer orders -- should reduce lead time and improve customer service

Produce goods according to schedules based on historical sales patterns – may be hard in a new market

Ensure all staff employed are appropriately skilled

Improvements possible

Economies of scale leading to increased margins

Reducing the number of suppliers to reduce administrative time and ensure economies of scale

Reduce pressure on logistics

Supply Chain Improvements

Consider using generic inputs rather than specialised to create purchasing economies of scale and reduce wastage

Reduce the range of products offered whilst maintaining choice and quality

Establish clear and effective criteria for selecting suppliers – develop these in advance and apply them carefully

Ensure reliability by offering incentives and discussing with suppliers at all times

Revising the terms of supply chain contracts – considerations

Will take time whilst a period of notice is given or the contract is fulfilled until its natural end date (e.g. a time limited contract)

Otherwise there may be breach of contract resulting in significant legal costs

Use a suitably qualified member of the legal team before finalising any changes

Consider the time frame of the new contract and any minimum order guarantees

Carefully consider bonuses and incentives – could these lead to unethical behaviour?

Consider the new balance of power between the different companies

See also   Risks – Types and Examples   249
                     Working Capital   305

Sustainability Reporting and Social Reporting

Examination example points

For a good example, see **SBM July 2016 past paper** (model answer pages 24 and 25) (worth **7 marks**)

Sustainability is about ensuring that development meets the needs of the present without compromising the ability of future generations to meet their own needs.

Recycling is an aspect of sustainability as an organisation should only use resources at a rate that allows them to be replenished. However, sustainability is about much more than simply just recycling. Wider social, environmental and economic issues also need to be addressed to demonstrate genuine corporate responsibility.

Sustainability reporting is considered in the ICA EW publication *Outside Insights: Beyond Accounting* which indicates that sustainability policy in an annual report should include information such as:

- who the report is for
- links to corporate/business strategy
- materiality of issues reported
- validity of indicators
- reliability of indicators
- objectivity of reporting
- transparency of information
- comparability of information
- balance of information
- understandability of the report
- audit/assurance of the report and corporate performance
- external stakeholder engagement
- integration with financial reporting
- addressing true sustainability

(The model answer states that only some of the examples from this list would need to be mentioned by candidates to score the marks relating to the type of disclosures needed for sustainability reporting.)

Integrated report should explain how the organisation creates value, using both quantitative and qualitative information.

Natural capital includes the impact of the company's activities on air, land, water, minerals and forests – recycling could be one element of addressing this area.

The benefit of sustainability disclosures for the company is that such disclosures communicate the company's attempts to demonstrate corporate responsibility by explaining what the proposed sustainability policy is.

Including environmental issues within integrated reporting makes environmental assurance more feasible as it provides a statement of policies which have been implemented – the effectiveness of implementation can then be confirmed as part of the assurance purpose.

Why apply assurance to social responsibility reports?

Entities are increasingly supplying more information of this type to stakeholders so stakeholders need reassurance that the information is correct – however, the information is not part of the financial statements and so will not be audited as part of a statutory audit engagement

An independent, external party can verify the data and information – this will increase credibility – the stakeholders can have more confidence the information is drawn from reliable sources and that it has been calculated accurately using a consistent methodology over time

The assurance engagement should provide assurance as to compliance with certain fundamental standards promised but also more detailed assurance as to whether performance indicators are accurately and consistently recorded

Difficulties

Often performance will relate mainly to non-financial indicators – these may not be part of standardised information flows and may involve judgement – it is also not possible to apply certain types of assurance procedures to information which is not financial e.g. analytical procedures, ratio analysis or computer analytics

Sometimes questionnaires are issued to the entity or its staff or interviews are conducted – a problem here is knowing whether the information is truthful

The Triple Bottom Line

According to the Study Manual, the triple bottom line in reporting should be to consider the **economic**, **environmental** and **social** impacts of the operations of an entity. You may therefore wish to use this framework in your answer.

Reporting Frameworks

There is currently no single consensus framework on social and environmental reporting so you need to be aware of the following frameworks:

Global Reporting Initiative (GRI)

Designed to promote transparency, accountability, reporting and sustainable development.

Revised in May 2013 – new "universal standards" subsequently launched in October 2016

Based on the following principles:

- stakeholder inclusiveness
- sustainability context
- materiality

- completeness
- balance
- comparability
- accuracy
- timeliness
- clarity
- reliability

New Sustainability Reporting Standards replace the previous G4 Guidelines but the new Standards are based on the previous Guidelines – the new "universal standards" should be used by every organisation that prepares a sustainability report under GRI – the "universal standards" are:

GRI 101: Foundation – this sets out the Reporting Principles

GRI 102: General Disclosures – contextual information about an organisation and its sustainability reporting practices, including information about an organisation's profile, strategy, ethics and integrity, governance stakeholder engagement practices and reporting processes

GRI 103: Management approach – information about how an organisation manages a material topic

Companies Act 2006

Requires the business review in the Directors' Report for quoted companies to include information on environmental, social and community issues. The information should include both financial and non-financial key performance indicators.

From 1 October 2013, Companies Act 2006 requires all UK quoted companies to report on their greenhouse gas emissions within the annual Directors' Report. Other companies are encouraged to report this information but it remains a voluntary process for unquoted companies.

DEFRA Guidelines

Originally published in 2006 and updated in June 2013

The guidelines help companies to understand what to report in various situations such as when preparing a Business Review, making mandatory greenhouse gas emissions statements and for SMEs who are part of a larger supply chain and who need suppliers to behave responsibly

Accounting for Sustainability Connected Reporting Framework

Aims to help ensure that sustainability is embedded in the DNA of an organisation – 3 core aims of A4S:

> To inspire finance leaders to adopt sustainable and resilient business models

> To transform financial decision-making to enable an integrated approach, reflective of the opportunities and risks posed by environmental and social issues

> To scale up actions across the global finance and accounting community

Requires sustainability to be clearly linked to the organisation's overall strategy and requires consistency in presentation to aid comparability between years and organisations

Contains 5 key elements:

- explanation of how sustainability is connected to the overall operational strategy of an organisation

- five key environmental indicators to be considered in all reporting: greenhouse gas emissions, energy usage, water use, waste and significant use of other finite resources

- other key sustainability information should be given where the business or operation has material impacts

- use of industry benchmark key performance indicators when available

- upstream and downstream impact of the organisation's products and services

Advantages of sustainability reporting

- employee satisfaction with working for a company that behaves appropriately

- improved stakeholder satisfaction

- investors may want to see a company adopt sustainable practices

- abuses of social and environmental issues can damage reputation

- using resources effectively can save money

Disadvantages of sustainability reporting

- moves focus away from financial returns which could be argued to be the main point of the business

- shareholder value may be reduced if profits are lost
- costs incurred to become more green

Impact of environmental and social issues on statutory audit

- impairment of assets after introduction of new laws and regulations
- accruals for remediation, compensation or legal costs
- constructive obligations
- contingent liabilities and provisions
- development cost expenditure for new products
- going concern issues
- impact on understanding the entity and assessing risks
- need for the auditor to ask environmental questions such as what laws and regulations are applicable or any history of legal penalties or proceedings

Social Audits

A social audit involves:

- establishing whether the entity has a reason for engaging in social activities
- identifying that all current environmental programmes are congruent with the mission of the company
- assessing the objectives and priorities related to these programmes
- evaluating company involvement in such programmes past, present and future

See also   Integrated Reporting   165

Treasury Operations

Role of the Treasury team

Corporate financial objectives – policies, aims and strategies and systems

Liquidity management

Funding management – managing investments, policies and rates

Currency management

Corporate finance – raising share capital, dividend policies and obtaining a stock exchange listing

Advantages of having a separate treasury department

Centralised liquidity management avoids mixing cash surpluses and overdrafts

Bulk cash flows allow lower bank charges to be negotiated

Larger volumes of cash can be invested, giving better short-term investment opportunities

Borrowing can be agreed in bulk, probably at lower interest rates than smaller borrowings

Better currency risk management

Specialist department can employ staff with a greater level of expertise than would be possible in a local, more broadly based finance department

Company will be able to benefit from the use of specialised cash management software

Access to treasury expertise should improve the quality of strategic planning and decision-making

Hedging

Consider time scale needed for the hedge: are the instruments dated too far into the future?

Treasury department's task involves measuring as accurately as possible the company's net exposures in each currency and its exposure to cost and revenue changes

Complete accuracy is not possible and 100% hedging accuracy is not possible

Treasury department should have some discretion as to whether it should hedge or not, based on the amounts involved and its estimation of the probability that spot prices will move in a particular way

Not hedging is a valid choice in many situations

United Nations Sustainable Development Goals

The United Nations 2030 Agenda for Sustainable Development is a 15-year plan, adopted by the UN in September 2015, which includes 17 global goals:

1. No poverty
2. Zero hunger
3. Good health and well-being
4. Quality education
5. Gender equality
6. Clean water and sanitation
7. Affordable and clean energy
8. Decent work and economic growth
9. Industry, innovation and infrastructure
10. Reduced inequality
11. Sustainable cities and communities
12. Responsible consumption and production
13. Climate action
14. Life below water
15. Life on land
16. Peace, justice and strong institutions
17. Partnerships for the goals

These overall goals are supported by a range of associated targets (169 in total)

ICAEW and the UN Sustainable Development Goals

ICAEW has championed the relevance of the UN's goals to business and to the accounting profession

The **actions** that **businesses** will take will be **critical to translating the UN's vision into reality** – businesses have a duty to act in the **public interest** and the UN Sustainable Development goals provide a **definition** of what "public interest" means

The accounting profession will have a **major role** in **aligning measurement systems** across countries to **help monitor progress** in achieving the Sustainable Development Goals

There is a **role** for the **accountancy profession** in providing **high quality reporting**, **audit** and **assurance** of organisations' performance – **timely**, **reliable** and **relevant** information will be central

SDG Compass

The **SDG Compass** has been developed by various organisations to provide companies with guidance about how to align their strategies towards realisation of the Sustainable Development Goals

The **Compass** identifies 5 steps for companies to take:

1. **Understanding the SDGs** – companies need to familiarise themselves with the SDGs

2. **Defining priorities** – companies should define priorities based on an assessment of their impact (positive and negative) on the SDGs across their value chain – companies should consider both current and potential future impact

3. **Setting goals** – setting goals will help to foster shared priorities and better performance across the organisation – by aligning company goals with the SDGs, leadership can demonstrate its commitment to sustainable development

4. **Integrating** – the integration of sustainability into the core business and governance is key

5. **Reporting and communicating** – the SDGs enable companies to report information on sustainable development performance using **common indicators** and shared sets of priorities – the SDG Compass encourages companies to incorporate the SDGs into their communication and reporting with stakeholders

Benefits of the SDGs

Identifying future business opportunities – the SDGs aim to redirect public and private investment flows towards the **challenges** highlighted in the goals – the SDGs therefore **define markets** that could grow in future for companies that can deliver innovative solutions and transformative change

Enhancing the value of corporate sustainability – the SDGs could strengthen **economic incentives** for companies to use resources **more efficiently** as sustainability indicators are increasingly **quantified** and **measured**

Strengthening stakeholder relations – by aligning their priorities with the SDGs, companies can strengthen **engagement** with their customers, employees and other stakeholders – companies whose **strategies** are **not aligned** with the SDGs could be exposed to **growing legal and reputational risks**

Stabilising societies and markets – the SDGs look to support and develop the infrastructure necessary for business success including transparent financial systems and non-corrupt and well-governed institutions

Using a common language and shared purpose – the SDGs define a common **framework** of action that will help companies **communicate more consistently and effectively with stakeholders** about their impact on performance

Encourages businesses to think about the wider, longer term implications of business decisions rather than focusing on just internal, financial ones

As an example of the last benefit, 2 of the indicators raised in relation to Global Goal 8 (promoting decent work and sustainable economic growth) involve consideration of (1) whether the company's buying practices impact the price volatility of key commodities, materials, crops and/or inputs that suppliers rely on in local or national markets and (2) what type of business model the company plans to invest in, a matter which will help to assess security of income for suppliers and workers in the longer term

Valuations – Standard Points

The biggest risk in a valuation is **overpaying** for the target

Exercise professional scepticism over the figures given (including distortions caused by accounting principles)

Always consider the **percentage shareholding** on offer – always marks on this

    75% shareholding gives almost complete control (can amend Articles of Association)

    50% shareholding gives substantial power over ordinary resolutions

Valuations are subjective and only a starting point for negotiations – **final value to a specific purchaser** determined by:

    Cost of acquiring a similar company

    Cost of purchasing assets and setting up a similar company

    Value of the brand name

    Future earnings potential

    Value of key personnel

    Strategic fit

    Nature of the consideration required

    Bargaining power

    Results of a risk analysis

Valuations based on accounting figures may be subject to distortion due to accounting principles (not cash-based)

Is there a perpetuity calculation involved? If so, then this is obviously a simplification

Is the assumed growth rate (if any) reasonable?

Query the discount rate and query any synergistic savings

In an acquisition we should also always consider

    Synergies

    Risk

    Real options

    Financing

Valuations – Standard Points

Opening Bid

If the valuation is for a first suggested opening bid to buy a target, it makes sense to estimate everything very conservatively

Of course, if we are the seller facing an opening bid then we want the opposite to occur!

Exceptionals and adjustments to revenue and costs

Particularly for cash flow and earnings based models, it is important to know whether there are any exceptional one-off items which have distorted (decreased or increased) profits and whether these are anticipated

Lost revenue opportunities as a result of the acquisition should be allowed for (e.g. a customer may not be willing to continue to deal with the merged entity or the acquirer may have to give up a revenue stream to preserve the cash needed for the acquisition)

Changes in the cost basis as a result of the acquisition should be allowed for (e.g. will more or fewer Directors be needed in the new business? Will we now have to allow for salaries of a management team for a smaller company which was previously owner-managed?)

IFRS 13 Levels for discussion

Level 1 inputs – quoted prices in an active market – not normally relevant as a brand is unique

Level 2 inputs – other observable prices e.g. in non-active markets such as a recent bid

Level 3 inputs – unobservable inputs, including internal company data

Methods set out in IFRS 13:

Market basis – market price and other market transactions – difficult if intangible is unique

Income basis – present value of **incremental** income generated by the intangible, considering value including any possible price premium effect and additional sales

Cost basis – current replacement cost of the intangible, which might be estimated as the present value of the expenditure needed to set up an equivalent intangible, including an allowance for risk and how expenditure could replicate the intangible in varying market conditions (this requires a large amount of judgement and estimation, hence apply **professional scepticism**)

Valuation of synergies

State first that this is a subjective area and synergies may often not occur as expected – likewise there may be other possible synergies not considered (try to give some specific examples)

Consider a quick perpetuity valuation of the synergies – you may have to assume a cost of capital to do this (give a reason for your assumption, based on the scenario) – simply divide the annual synergy value by the cost of capital to gain some quick skills marks for the value of the synergies

Valuations – Standard Points

e.g. synergies will contribute £5m per year for the foreseeable future and estimated cost of capital is 10% so value of the synergies is £5m/0.1 = £50m – this amount should be added to the valuation but with various caveats on the subjective and uncertain nature of the estimate

Discounts to apply

Discount the valuation if the company is a private limited company (less marketable, higher risk, smaller size, lower expectations of a cash return from dividends)

Discount if the shareholding is small (below 25% of the shares)

Discount if another single party holds a substantial amount such as 50% – easy for that party to assert itself

Note that it may be necessary to **apply 2 discounts** if the company is a limited company – one discount for the fact that its shares are not as easily marketable and another for the specific shareholding being discussed

Discounts Rules of Thumb

Discounts for shareholding %

Shareholding	Discount
75%+	0-5%
50% to 74%	10-15%
50%	20-30%

Discounts for the status of the company

Status	Discount
Plc	Nil
AIM	20-30%
Limited company	40-50%

See also	IFRS 13 and Valuation of Intangibles	160
	Shareholding Percentages – Narrative Comments	259
	Valuation topics	

Valuations – Asset-Based Model

Often used for companies whose value can be accurately reflected by the value of assets held

Examples: property development companies, companies which invest in capital assets with long lives

For other companies, likely to be an undervalue (see below) so used to establish a minimum value or lower floor

Can be considered to show a measure of the security of the share value (i.e. asset backing for the shares)

May also be used in a merger or business combination – if one company has a low asset backing compared to the other company then the shareholders of the company with the higher asset backing may want some compensation for the risk they are taking on

Criticisms

For many companies, there are sources of value which are not reflected in the SFP such as brands and staff expertise so this method would result in a significant **undervaluation** (common exam position)

A business with lots of future opportunities to generate cash flows might have an approximate **balance of assets and liabilities** simply from normal trading but this would give an incorrectly low valuation

Update to fair value (see also IFRS 13 notes)

The examiners seem to like the point **that carrying value (book value) is not necessarily an indication of market value (and is not intended to be)** – mention this as a theory point but then apply to the scenario

Look out for any indications that fair value may vary from book value and suggest adjustments

Establishing FV can be difficult, costly or time-consuming – FV may fluctuate between the valuation date and the acquisition date

FV is subjective and could lead to disagreement

Determining FV requires an active market and a large number of similar items but in practice many assets are unique

Add brand value and unrecognised assets/liabilities

In addition to updating recognised assets/liabilities to fair value (see above), look out for any assets or liabilities which cannot be recognised for accounting purpose but which affect the practical business value/cash flows of the target

Additions

Brands

Staff quality

Technologies

Unrealised gains on financial instruments and/or pension schemes

Deductions

Legal or tax disputes

Deduct goodwill shown on the SFP

Goodwill already on the SFP indicates goodwill from a previous purchase by the target company.

This simply records a previous transaction and does not mean that the same amount still remains (since under IFRS goodwill is an historic balance and is not adjusted for any increases in value (but may have been reduced for impairment))

Therefore deduct goodwill from the net asset value used

Preference shares: possible discussion point

If preference shares are presented on the SFP within liabilities rather than equity, these shares are a type of loan and should be excluded from the equity value of the company.

See also	IFRS 13 and Valuation of Intangibles	160
	Valuation topics	

Valuations – Administration Scenario

Key questions

What is the company worth to the potential acquirer?

What will the administrator be willing to sell the company for?

Company cannot remain in administration indefinitely as the Enterprise Act 2002 puts a one year time limit on administration

Methods of acquisition

Acquire share capital – this would mean acquiring the liabilities

Acquire business assets, leaving the liabilities in the insolvent company

Acquire assets on an individual or piecemeal basis

Position of the administrator

Must save the company as a going concern as the first priority

Must act in the best interests of the creditors

Company cannot remain in administration indefinitely as the Enterprise Act 2002 puts a one year time limit on administration

Probably should not break up the business if possible as the return will then be lower – the Enterprise Act 2002 requires the administrator to attempt to save the business as a going concern

Establishing asset values – possible methods

Historic costs

Historic replacement costs

Current replacement costs

Net realisable values

Value in use

Assets to consider

Goodwill, PPE, Inventories, Receivables

Brand value may be an off-SFP asset to be valued – could have been damaged by going into administration

Liabilities to consider

Under the Transfer of Undertakings (Protection of Employment) Regulations 2006, even if the acquirer only purchases business assets, then that acquirer assumes obligations with respect to employees and potentially also some subcontractors – however, there will be no obligations regarding directors' service contracts unless shares were being acquired

Other off balance sheet contractual rights

Rights or charges over assets held by third parties – this could reduce their value or prevent individual sale

There may be a discount for sale of business assets – the cost of liquidating assets individually on a piecemeal basis may be greater than selling all the assets in one transaction so the administrator may offer a discount for the latter

Need for re-evaluation

In this scenario, things will change quickly over time so there may need to be another valuation at the date of acquisition rather than based on historic reporting date figures

Enterprise Act 2002

Permits the administrator to continue to trade for a while if he or she cannot sell the company as a going concern immediately – this is to give time to enable a sale on a going concern basis in the near future if possible

If the company is making losses there is greater urgency for disposal in order to prevent losses accruing to the creditors

Exit risks

If the acquisition of a struggling company does not result in the realisation of strategic and financial benefits then exit may be necessary

If the acquirer only pays the fair value of the assets, then the exit routes should not result in a significant loss and could even be a gain

Issues relating to obligations and penalties under contracts insofar as these relate to disengagement

Obligations to employees which will incur costs

Errors or uncertainties in the fair value estimates e.g. the cash flows and discount rate used

Closure costs

Delays in closing down the trading may alter the commercial viability of the company – the longer the time period, the more risk there is of a fall in the fair value of assets

Issues relating to inventories unsold – these will increase over time

See also   IFRS 13 and Valuation of Intangibles   160
Valuation topics

Valuations – Dividend Valuation Model (DVM)

Value of a share estimated as the present value of all future expected dividends on the shares, discounted at the shareholders' cost of capital

Dividend Valuation Model – no growth assumed

Apply the formula **D_0 / discount rate**

where

D_0 = most recent dividend

Dividend Valuation Model – growth assumed

Apply the formula **D_0 (1 + g) / (discount rate - g)**

where

D_0 = most recent dividend

g = expected growth rate

Estimating g

Use a compound growth formula

(end value / start value)$^{1/n}$) -1

where n is the number of growth periods

For example, with 3 growth periods use the third root of the bracketed value

Remember to look at the **number of growth periods** possible – **this is always one less than the number of years analysed**:

2008	2009	2010	2011
50	75	98	110

There are **4** years of figures but only **3** years of growth as the 2008 figure is the end of 2008.

Therefore growth can occur in 2008 to 2009, 2009 to 2010 and 2010 to 2011 so therefore calculation would be

$[(110 / 50)^{1/3}] - 1$

As an alternative, we can use the Gordon growth formula where **g = rb** and r is the rate of return on capital employed and b is the proportion of earnings (after tax profits) that are retained in the business r can also be calculated as profits/equity

DVM Criticisms

Assumed that investors have perfect information and are motived by dividends – may not be correct

Assumes that figure used for D_0 is not divergent from trend and so is a reasonable indication (rather than an exceptional figure)

Cost of capital (discount rate) may be hard to establish with confidence – **the acquisition process may change the risk profile and make this rate out of date**

Assumes a constant growth rate, which is unlikely to be the case in practice

There are many other factors that will influence share price such as acquisitions, analyst estimates, earnings performance and these are not considered in DVM

Dividends may not be a fair reflection of the strength of the company

DVM and Professional Scepticism

Always review all variables for reasonableness – D_o, g and the cost of capital are all very important variables and slight changes

If g is greater than the discount rate, then the model does not work as the bottom of the fraction is negative

Dividend growth cannot exceed the growth in earnings forever or there will be no earnings available to pay those dividends

If you feel you have time, perhaps re-estimate the outcome with slightly changed g and/or cost of capital and comment on the sensitivity – you should find major changes in the valuation with minor changes in the variables because you are estimating flows into perpetuity so a very long time for changes to have an impact on the outcomes!

Due diligence involving DVM should therefore definitely undertake a lot of work on these variables

We may need information on the entity's cash position to evaluate if a dividend is even possible

Dividend yield

As well as being used to calculate the value of the company, the dividend yield % shows the income that can be generated from holding the shares of the target – this provides a useful income stream

See also	IFRS 13 and Valuation of Intangibles	160
	Valuation topics	

Valuations – Earnings-Based

Start with maintainable earnings but should also consider forecasts if reasonable and company is clearly growing

Apply a multiple – this choice of multiple is very important

Examiners seem to like the point that this method should only be used if a cash flow based model is not possible

Apply a net assets-based model as well as a lower benchmark

Possible equation – perpetuity flows with growth

earnings x (1 + g) / (discount rate – g)

Fixed costs

May need to deduct the present value of fixed costs

Tax

Difficult to estimate – depends on profit flows and tax rule changes in the future – unpredictable

May need to allow for capital allowances as well

Appropriateness of using earnings/accounting profit as an indicator of value

Problems

Not appropriate for a loss-making business

Accounting profits are a financial reporting-based measure so may not reflect the cash flows of the operation

Does not consider the incremental, relevant cash flows of the operation or any savings made

Does not weight results based on the level of risk involved

No allowance made for the costs of financing the expansion

Might only consider a limited number of years of results rather than future possibilities (assuming that the appraisal does not look into perpetuity – if it does look at a perpetuity, use the criticism of a perpetuity that it is a simplification and flows cannot continue forever: similarly growth cannot continue at the same rate forever)

Might not take account of improvements over time

Valuations – Earnings-Based

Include interest in sustainable earnings?

Arguably interest should not be included for these purposes as there is no guarantee that it will be received in perpetuity

Possible adjustments

Consider all incremental costs and revenues that may result

Will Director salaries and remuneration change if the Board of Directors is changed?

Eliminate one off items

Adjustments for inflation and other similar changes?

Deduct earnings from opportunities now foregone?

See also	IFRS 13 and Valuation of Intangibles	160
	Investment Appraisal Methods – APV	180
	Valuations topics	

Valuations – EBITDA Model

EBITDA = approximation to operating cash flows (earnings before interest and taxation and also before non-cash flows such as depreciation and amortisation)

Earnings before interest, tax, depreciation and amortisation

Commonly used figure which is considered to be a good (although not perfect) proxy for operating cash flows

Strips out depreciation, amortisation and usually any separately disclosed items such as exceptionals

Concerns with EBITDA as a valuation method

Does not exclude all subjective accounting practices such as revenue recognition

There may be unusual accounting aspects which are not disclosed separately and therefore not added back or deducted to arrive at a cash position

The presentation of items as exceptional can be subjective

EBITDA is not a sustainable figure as there is no charge for capital replacement such as depreciation or CAPEX

Does not create a separate valuation for equity only – this is because it does not represent the flow of earnings to equity holders only as interest is not taken into account – the method values debt and equity jointly at the same time as both shareholders and debt holders need to be paid from the EBITDA figure

Excludes taxation which may be a significant, relevant cost

Usually based on a current year only – ignores growth and the current year may be exceptionally high or low

Sometimes based on an estimate of the current year which is a forecast and unaudited – the actual figure may be different

EBITDA – Professional Scepticism

Like the PE Model, the choice of multiple is absolutely fundamental to the EBITDA calculation

Always query the multiple!

Model is very sensitive to what is put into the IS – for every £1 change there will be a multiplied effect

Look for any disputed figures

Look for exceptionals

Ignores importance of CAPEX

Ignores expectations of future growth (although sometimes based on a prospective multiple: check what data you are using)

Valuations – EBITDA Model

Remember to discount a listed company/industry multiple if this is used as a benchmark

Look out for any inappropriate accounting adjustments or policies – unlike the Free Cash Flow approach, accounting adjustments/policies will continue to affect EBITDA

You may wish to suggest some adjustments before applying the multiple

Using a Multiple to Estimate the Cost of Capital

Assume a multiple of 5 and no growth – value of a company with EBITDA of £1m is £5m. This is the same thing as 1/0.20, so **cost of capital is 1/multiple** (since 1/5 = 0.20 or 20% as needed)

Assuming a multiple of 5 and growth of 2% – we can use the following formula based on the dividend valuation model and replacing the future dividend D_1 with future earnings E_1 (which is today's earnings x 1.02 to represent growth to earnings in 1 year):

$$\text{cost of capital} = (E_1 / P_0) + g$$

We know that for every £1 of earnings then the valuation or price (P_0) must be 5 times that figure. Therefore applying the formula:

$$\text{cost of capital} = [(1 \times 1.02) / 5] + 0.02 = 22.4\%$$

See also　　IFRS 13 and Valuation of Intangibles　　160
　　　　　　　　Valuations topics

Valuations – Economic Value Added (EVA®)

Find the extent to which earnings exceed the minimum rate of return that shareholders require

In other words, how much better are we doing than the minimum to keep shareholders happy and invested into our company?

Assume that the WACC represents the minimum that the shareholders require.

EVA® works using NOPAT (net operating profit after tax)

Advantages of EVA®

Emphasises the importance of the cost of capital to managers and sets them a target to beat the minimum acceptable return – takes into account the **financing** aspect of a project/valuation

Disadvantages of EVA®

Based on historical figures which could be distorted by accounting conventions (a disadvantage shared with other techniques of course)

Method

1. Find the Return on Invested Capital (ROIC)

Divide **this year's** NOPAT by **last year's** invested capital

This generates a percentage figure, representing the return on last year's invested capital (ROIC).

2. Compare ROIC to the WACC to find EVA® percentage

Perform the calculation EVA® = ROIC – WACC

This will indicate the extent to which our returns exceed the minimum required by the shareholders/debtholders.

(Note that it is possible for EVA® to be negative if the WACC exceeds ROIC)

This again generates a percentage figure, representing an EVA® percentage.

3. Apply EVA® percentage to last year's capital invested

This will find the absolute EVA® for that particular year

4. Discount absolute EVA® figures at the WACC

Apply discounting as normal to the absolute EVA® figures and then total these as normal to find the present value of the EVA®

Note – nothing really needs to be completed in the Year 0 column for NOPAT, ROIC etc.

Valuations – Economic Value Added (EVA®)

EVA® – Worked Example

Assumes a WACC of 10%

		Year 0	Year 1	Year 2
	Invested capital	2,000	1,600	800
	NOPAT		88	400
Step 1	ROIC (NOPAT/PY invested capital)	-	4.4%	25%
Step 2	EVA® % = ROIC less WACC assumed of 10%	-	(5.6%)	15%
Step 3	Apply EVA® % to PY investment capital		(112)	240
Step 4	Discount factors	n/a	0.91	0.83
	Discounted EVA	n/a	(102)	199

Then complete as per an NPV calculation but do not apply any discounting to the Invested capital – EVA® simply evaluates the flows that occur from year 1 onwards and does not treat the initial capital investment as an outflow – the EVA® only occurs once we compare ROIC to the WACC to analyse flows in subsequent years. Therefore the figures of 2,000, 1,600 and 800 are used to calculate the ROIC but are not themselves discounted.

See also   IFRS 13 and Valuation of Intangibles   160
Valuations topics

Valuations – Free Cash Flow Model

Exam tip – do not forget to **knock off the value of debt** at the final stage of the calculation to obtain the **equity value of shares only** (students always seem to forget to do this!).

Advantages of the FCF approach

Start with PBT

Model is flexible to allow for specific data and details, including a period of temporary growth followed by a perpetuity (with or without growth)

Depreciation and CAPEX

Add back depreciation and deduct CAPEX

If no data given, perhaps the best you can do is assume that these are approximately equal but make sure you state this and then criticise this assumption (as it is not realistic)

Perpetuity cash flows – the correct discount factor

Example: exam paper gives detailed specific cash flows for years 1 to 4 followed by a perpetuity from year 5 onwards

Remember that the correct discount factor to apply to the perpetuity is the **year 4** value (not the year 5 value) – this is because the perpetuity formula provides the present value of flows starting with **1 year of delay** – so applying the formula to the flows from **year 5** onwards gives the present value in **year 4** and therefore needs to be discounted by the **year 4 discount factor**

Professional scepticism points

Perpetuity assumption may be simplistic and unsustainable – requires forecasts to be reliable and the discount rate to be correct – future cash flows are just estimates

Query whether there is enough information on capital cash flows, CAPEX outlays and taxation

Determine whether depreciation assumptions/add backs are reasonable

Query validity of the discount rate (risk, changes in business, size, nature of business (private?))

Possible adjustments

Consider all incremental costs and revenues that may result

Will director salaries and remuneration change if the Board of Directors is changed?

Eliminate one off items

Adjustments for inflation and other similar changes?

Deduct earnings from opportunities now foregone?

CAPEX

See also	IFRS 13 and Valuation of Intangibles	160
	Valuations topics	

Valuations – High Growth Startup

Challenges in valuing a high growth startup company (often undervalued)

No track record so hard to estimate

Might have historical losses but bright prospects

Few revenue streams and products/services are untested

Unknown level of market acceptance and demand

Unknown levels of competition

Unknown cost structures

High development or infrastructure costs

Inexperienced management

Which valuation method to use?

Free Cash Flow model is probably the most sensible …

Net assets method – not appropriate because probably has low amount of tangible assets (value of the startup is from its people, marketing and intellectual property)

PE method and EBITDA multiple method – difficulty of finding a quoted comparator in the same stage of development – lack of disclosed information

EVA® method – very short investment period so not enough years to consider and may not have an established WACC

Consider whether there have been acquisitions by the company (goodwill on SFP) – can indicate improved earnings and may be possible to value the acquisitions based on historic information (assuming that the targets have existed longer than the company)

Entry cost valuation – consider the cost that would be involved in entering the market and establishing a new business of the same type: costs of raising finance, costs of assets acquired, cost of product development, cost of recruiting and training employees and costs of building up the customer base

First Chicago method – produce best case, worst case and base case scenario and discount these figures – use an expected value approach by weighting each calculation by the probability of each type

Limitations with using the Free Cash Flow model

Very sensitive to small changes in variables such as the growth rate

May not adequately reflect growth potential and flexibilities of a company in an early stage of development

May not adequately reflect the options to expand, delay, abandon or switch investments at various decision points

See also IFRS 13 and Valuation of Intangibles 160
Valuations topics

Valuations – PE Model

Value of a company is given by

PE ratio x maintainable earnings x discount for shareholding % (x discount for not being a plc)

Used to value the shares of a quoted company where it is recognised that the offer price for the shares must be higher than the current market price in order to gain acceptance of the offer from the target company's shareholders

Shares of an unquoted company where the PE ratio is derived from the PE for similar quoted companies

Discounts Rules of Thumb

Discounts for the shareholding % acquired

Shareholding	Discount
75%+	0-5%
50% to 74%	10-15%
50%	20-30%

Note – the discount may need to consider the position of the other shareholders: is there another single shareholder with a 50%+ holding (powerful) or is the shareholding dispersed over many shareholders (less powerful as will need united co-ordination to achieve 50%+)

Narrative points

Discuss the difference between a 75% and 50% shareholding (special versus ordinary resolutions)

Discounts for the status of the company

Status	Discount
Plc	Nil
AIM	20-30%
Limited company	40-50%

Professional scepticism

All 3 elements (PE ratio, maintainable earnings and the discount percentage) are uncertain and so can be queried

It can be difficult to find comparable companies as every company is different in some way

Should be based on future maintainable earnings – how do we know what is maintainable (we need to adjust for exceptionals but this requires judgement) and how to we estimate future possibilities?

Valuations – PE Model

What Might a High PE Ratio Reflect?

Optimistic expectations – if future growth is expected, a high price will be paid now

Security of earnings – a well-established, low-risk company may be worth more than a new startup

Status – quoted companies should not have any discount applied

Low level of earnings without a reduction in share price – note that a high PE is achieved if earnings drop but the share price stays the same or falls by a proportionately smaller amount – hence a high PE ratio is not always a good thing

Calculating an Implied PE Ratio from the Cost of Equity

See the July 2015 past paper Q2 for an example calculation and related discussion.

If the cost of equity is known, the implied PE Ratio can be calculated as **1/cost of equity**.

For example, if the cost of equity is 10% then the implied PE Ratio is 10.

This is because if earnings are £2m valued on a perpetuity basis then the value of the company using the cost of equity will be £2m/0.10 or £20m. This is the same thing as applying a PE Ratio of 10 to the earnings as £2m x 10 is £20m.

Note that the standard scepticism points regarding use of perpetuities would also apply here i.e. a perpetuity approach assumes that earnings/cash flow will be earned for ever and that the relevant growth rate (if used) is constant.

See also	IFRS 13 and Valuation of Intangibles	160
	Valuations topics	

Valuations – Shareholder Value Analysis (SVA)

Based on the idea that shareholder value comes from 7 main sources

Sales growth

Operating profit margin

Tax rate

Changes in working capital

Fixed capital investment

Cost of capital

Competitive advantage period

Steps in the SVA Approach

1. Calculate the present value of the estimated future annual free cash flows

2. Add the value of non-operational assets held by the business, such as short-term investments and cash

3. Subtract the value of the company's debt to obtain a valuation of the company's equity

See also	IFRS 13 and Valuation of Intangibles	160
	Valuations topics	

Value-Based Management

A management process which links strategy, management and operational processes with the aim of creating shareholder value

Elements

Strategic planning

Capital allocation

Operating budgets

Performance measurements

Management remuneration

Internal communication

External communication

See also   Key Performance Indicators   194

Withdrawal from a Business

General methods

- Flotation of the company onto a stock market
- Sale of shares to a private investor or institution (followed by flotation)
- Sale of the business to a competitor or customer
- Sale of shares to fellow directors or employees
- Maintaining existing shareholders but obtaining a cash withdrawal from the company (methods: bonus, dividend, share buyback)

Flotation – advantages

- May obtain a better price because shares are more easily marketable than as a private limited company
- Increased access to third party capital
- Increased marketability of shares
- Increased public profile, resulting in greater shareholder confidence
- Possibility of future share for share exchange if company wishes to expand in future

Flotation – disadvantages

- Costs of obtaining a flotation
- Management time involved
- Increased regulation by the stock exchange (possible need for interim financial statements)
- UK Corporate Governance Code may now apply, reducing the powers of directors
- If selling individual retains control, this may reduce the sales price – others will have less power

Sale of shares to a third party – advantages

- May increase value of shares since more easily realisable into cash
- Sale of at least 50% of shares could attract a control premium

Sale of shares to a third party – disadvantages

- Discount may need to apply for lack of marketability

Sale of the business to a competitor or customer – advantages

- Diversifies risk for both parties if share for share exchange
- Increase liquidity and marketability
- Avoids costs of a flotation
- Possibility of horizontal/vertical integration

Sale of shares to fellow directors and/or employees – advantages

- Likely to obtain a fair price as worked together for some time
- Could be a way to reward staff and fellow directors for their loyalty

Sale of shares to fellow directors and/or employees – disadvantages

- Relies on fellow directors having the cash available to purchase the shares
- May not generate as much cash as the other options

How to withdraw cash from the business

Bonus

- If a controlling shareholder then could elect to pay a large bonus (but could be considered to breach fiduciary duties if excessive: could lead to an action for unfair prejudice against the non-controlling (minority) shareholders)
- Corporation tax for the company but taxable as earnings for the directors/shareholder

Dividend payment

- Not deductible for corporation tax and taxable as earnings for the director

Share buy-back

- Governed by Companies Act – permanent capital of the company must be maintained
- Any premium on repayment would need to be covered by distributable reserves
- May be necessary to transfer amounts to a non-distributable capital redemption reserve to cover the reduction in share capital (exam tip: can you quantify this amount?)
- Company's Articles of Association must provide for this method
- Likely that off-market purchase of shares would need approval by Special Resolution

Sell to a competitor or customer

- Could be done by share for share exchange to maintain some control/influence and for tax reasons
- Vertical/horizontal integration possibilities for purchaser
- May offer diversification for seller and purchaser

Stock market flotation

Advantages
- Makes shares marketable – easier to withdraw fully or partially later
- Increased access to capital
- Increased public profile and public confidence for company
- Future share for share exchanges easier

Disadvantages
- High costs
- Uses management time
- High level of regulation e.g. London Stock Exchange listing rules
- UK Corporate Governance Code procedures required
- May have to offer a discount on shares if maintaining control via retained shares

Cash withdrawal

Advantages
- Dividends – may be tax efficient if structured correctly
- Bonuses – tax deductible for the company (dividends are not)
- Appropriate use of cash if no better investment alternatives

Disadvantages
- Impact on cash available for working capital
- Limits ability to replace assets
- Limits ability to have later acquisitions

Share buy back
- May be beneficial tax effects
- Impact on reserves – do Articles allow action to take place?

Sale of shares to Directors
- Simple solution
- Should be a fair price for everyone – all parties have knowledge
- Does the company have enough cash available?

Partial withdrawal/sale/disposal by existing owners

Is the offer attractive and suitable? Considerations

Control retained?

Cash received up front – amount and will this help the business (e.g. unable to obtain otherwise)?

Non-cash advantages such as technology received?

Exam tip – always consider the percentage shareholdings involved and then consider any agreement on director appointments

Note that if the shareholding is below 50% but close to that figure (e.g. 48% or 49%) then you could argue that if this is held by a single company/individual then it is a very powerful position particularly if the other 51% is spread across a large number of shareholders (since these may not all agree and work together)

Note that with a 49% shareholding but an ability to appoint several directors, it can be argued that the shareholder has considerable power

Withdrawal from a Business – Director Considerations

This topic considers some matters that Directors leaving a business may want to consider when negotiating the best deal for their future

Control

Will the Directors retain shares and therefore some element of control?

How many Directors are leaving and therefore how will control be shared?

Is the entire Board being replaced or just a few Directors? What will be the impact on management quality in future?

Can the Directors act together if they are retaining shares?

Financial Impact

Consider how the departure will be financed – termination payment? Bonus? Receiving or giving up share options?

Will new shares be issued as part of the departure and how will this affect the control aspects?

Shares versus Termination Payment

Will the Directors receive shares? Are these marketable (quoted) or not?

Sale of shares could offer a convenient exit route and may allow for tax-planning

Can the shares be sold easily or will the Directors have such a large amount that they have to "drip-feed" into the market?

Current value of a shareholding – affected by:

Role within the company – does the director earn a return through a salary? This may be above market rates due to the control connected with ownership of shares (but if it is below market rates it could actually be considered a cost to the director of holding the shares and being involved)

Dividends received

Whether a forced sale is required to realise cash urgently

Considerations for new shareholders

Dividends

Price paid

Percentage acquired and percentage of voting rights – ordinary resolution, special resolution and so on

Control

Withdrawal from a Business – Director Considerations

Ability to earn a salary if appointed as a director

Requirement to borrow personally?

Change in level of diversification, depending on the shareholders' other holdings

Consider any bonuses or share options and future potential benefit

Working Capital

Working capital is the excess of current assets over current liabilities – it represents the resources required to run the daily operations of a business

Why does effective working capital management matter?

Source of competitive advantage and therefore corporate and shareholder value – ensures that the right inventory is on hand when needed

Key element of the value chain – management of inventories, supplier relationships and customer relationships are important for operations, the supply chain and logistics management

Significant source of customer satisfaction

Concepts to consider

Working capital ratios (trade, payables and inventory days)

Cash operating cycle

Overtrading

Methods of managing inventory

Economic Order Quantity (EOQ) model – see below

Using trade credit

Credit control finance and management

Cash management

Cash budgets

Strategic Management of Working Capital

The 2 main objectives of working capital management are (1) to ensure that a company has sufficient liquid resources to meet its short and long-term requirements and (2) to increase its profitability.

This involves achieving a balance between the requirement to minimise the risk of insolvency (liquidity) and the requirement to maximise the return on assets (profitability).

The differences between businesses regarding working capital characteristics are generally of 3 main types:

> inventory holding period
>
> time taken to pay suppliers and other accounts payable
>
> time allowed to customers to make payments

Generally, a service business will have a low requirement for working capital whereas a manufacturing business will have a high requirement for working capital. This is because many service businesses do not require large inventories.

Organisations such as supermarkets and retailers will receive much of their sales in cash, via credit card or debit card – however, they will buy from their suppliers on credit so they have the advantage of significant cash holdings, which they could invest.

At the other end of the scale, a company that supplies other companies is likely to be selling and buying mainly on credit – coordinating the flow of cash can then be a problem – such a company may make use of short-term borrowing such as an overdraft to manage its cash but smaller companies with a limited trading record may face particular problems, such as difficulties in getting credit from suppliers – at the same time, the customers of a small company are likely to expect to receive the length of credit that is normal for that particular business activity and they will not allow any alternative terms just because the business is smaller.

The effective management of inventory, customer accounts, cash resources and supplier accounts can therefore be a source of competitive advantage.

Effective working capital management can also comprise a key element of the value chain. The management of inventories, supplier relationships and customer relationships are closely related to operations, supply chain and logistics management.

The working capital requirement

Determining the working capital requirement is a matter of calculating the value of current assets less current liabilities, perhaps by taking averages over a one-year period.

Over-capitalisation

Indicators of over-capitalisation (investing in excessive inventories and having a large amount of accounts receivable and cash) include:

- sales/working capital ratio reduced compared with previous years, or less than in similar companies
- high level of liquidity, indicated by a high current ratio of more than 2 and a high quick ratio of more than 1
- long turnover periods for inventory and accounts receivable

Conservative approach

Financing net current assets with medium-term loans – only an occasional need for short term financing when net current assets exceed the amount of medium-term borrowing

Net current assets fluctuate in amount but using a medium-term loan (which has a longer time period than the fluctuations) means that the loan is financing not just permanent net current assets but also temporary net current assets too

Often leads to surplus cash – interest earned on this is likely to be less than the interest paid on borrowings – so having surplus cash has a net cost from over-borrowing

Aggressive approach

Financing net current assets entirely with short-term finance such as a bank overdraft

Cost of this is likely to be lower than a medium term loan because overdraft interest accrues only when the overdraft is being used (rather than all the time under a loan) and the interest rate on an overdraft may be lower

But risky as overdraft can be called in at any time

Influences on working capital style

Industry norms – especially for receivables: will be hard to match shorter payment periods

Products – length of the production cycle will differ in different industries

Management issues – quality of management and degree of control and monitoring

Managing the Operating Cycle

Companies that are **more efficient at generating cash** are **better able to implement strategic plans** so effective management of the operating cycle can be a source of **competitive advantage**

Good control over **inventory** can be important in ensuring that there are items **on hand** when customers want them and that items are in **good condition**

Good management of **supplier accounts** enhances **supply chain management** and ensures that **costs** and **delivery times are minimised**

A **significant** part of working capital management affects the **interaction** with **customers** and can be a significant source of customer **satisfaction** (or **dissatisfaction**) – customers have grown accustomed to the time between order and delivery being **very short** so companies which **focus upon shortening** the **period** between order and invoice (and related eventual collection of cash) are **better placed to meet customer expectations**

Short-term actions to improve cash generation include delaying payments to suppliers or reducing inventory – however, this will **not create sustained competitive advantage** which instead requires a **longer-term** approach and engagement from departments across the business involved in procurement, sales, inventory management and finance

Effective working capital management can also comprise a **key element of the value chain** – enterprise resource planning (ERP) systems can integrate an entity's systems and facilitate the flow of information between all business functions within an organisation and can also be used to manage connections to outside stakeholders such as suppliers

Integration of the operating cycle could include:

- initial recording of the sales order
- procurement of necessary parts or components
- production planning and resource utilisation
- work-flow automation
- real-time order status updates including delivery and billing information
- electronic invoicing
- electronic payment interfaces with customers and suppliers
- credit management

Management of inventory

Modern systems of **inventory** management such as just-in-time techniques aim to **minimise** the level of inventory held

However, one of the **concerns** with **reducing** inventory to **minimal** levels is the potential **impact** on **customers** and their orders – if there are **problems**, it could lead to cancelled **orders** and lower sales

Developing **relationships** with **customers** to better **understand the likely demand levels** will improve service, ensuring that **sufficient** inventory is available whilst at the same time making sure that inventory levels are **not excessive**

Management of accounts receivable

Offering credit **incurs an interest cost** charged on an overdraft to fund the period of credit or the interest lost on the cash not received and deposited in the bank – it is also likely to lead to an **increase in bad debts**

If offering credit generates **extra sales**, then those extra sales will have **additional repercussions** on the amount of **inventory** maintained in the warehouse, to ensure that the extra demand can be satisfied – the amount of money the company owes to its **accounts payable** will also be affected as it will be increasing its supply of raw materials

Early settlement discounts may be employed to shorten average credit periods and reduce investment in accounts receivable and therefore interest costs – the **benefits and interest costs saved should exceed the cost of the discounts allowed**

Businesses can enter into arrangements with a **factor** or **invoice discounter** to improve cash flow and shorten the cash cycle

Management of accounts payable

Taking credit from suppliers is a **normal** feature of business and **paying suppliers as late as possible** is a **common working capital management technique** – **trade credit** is usually a **cheap** source of finance as **suppliers rarely charge interest** – this form of financing is **particularly important to small and fast-growing firms**

Working Capital

However, it is **important** that such a technique is **managed** in a way that **does not damage relationships** with the supplier – **doing so** could **adversely affect the smooth functioning** of the **supply chain**

If a supplier offers a discount for the early payment of debt, a company must consider whether the benefits of accepting the discount outweigh the finance costs of having to pay earlier (as the company may now require a greater overdraft or, alternatively, will have lost the opportunity

Economic Order Quantity Model (EOQ)

$EOQ = \sqrt{2cd/h}$

where

c = cost of placing one order

d = estimated usage of the inventory item over a particular period

h = cost of holding one unit of inventory for that period

Limitations of the EOQ Model

Not simple to apply

Unjustified assumptions about usage and constant purchase price that may be unjustified

Ignores the potential benefit of taking advantage of bulk discounts

Can be very difficult in practice to estimate holding costs and the cost of placing each order

See also	Supply Chain Improvements	267

© ACA Simplified 2018. No copying or reproduction permitted.

Printed in Great Britain
by Amazon